Bloom's Modern Critical Interpretations

Bloom's Modern Critical Interpretations

Bloom's Modern Critical Interpretations

Harper Lee's
To Kill a Mockingbird
Updated Edition

Edited and with an introduction by
Harold Bloom
Sterling Professor of the Humanities
Yale University

CHELSEA HOUSE
P U B L I S H E R S
An imprint of Infobase Publishing

Bloom's Modern Critical Interpretations: To Kill a Mockingbird, Updated Edition

© 2007 by Infobase Publishing
Introduction © 2007 by Harold Bloom

Chelsea House
An imprint of Infobase Publishing
132 West 31st Street
New York NY 10001

ISBN-10: 0-7910-9308-5
ISBN-13: 978-0-7910-9308-5

Library of Congress Cataloging-in-Publication Data
Harper Lee's To kill a mockingbird / Harold Bloom, editor. — Updated ed.
    p. cm. — (Bloom's modern critical interpretations)
    Includes bibliographical references and index.
    ISBN 0-7910-9308-5 (hardcover)
    1. Lee, Harper. To kill a mockingbird. 2. Fathers and daughters
in literature. 3. Race relations in literature. 4. Lawyers in
literature. 5. Racism in literature. 6. Girls in literature.
I. Bloom, Harold. II. Title: To kill a mockingbird. III. Series.

    PS3562.E353T6337 2006
    813'.54—dc22   2006020212

Chelsea House books are available at special discounts when purchased in bulk quantities for businesses, associations, institutions, or sales promotions. Please call our Special Sales Department in New York at (212) 967-8800 or (800) 322-8755.

You can find Chelsea House on the World Wide Web at http://www.chelseahouse.com

Contributing Editor: Amy Sickels
Cover designed by Ben Peterson
Cover photo © Universal/Photofest

Printed in the United States of America
IBT EJB 10 9 8 7 6 5 4 3

This book is printed on acid-free paper.

All links and web addresses were checked and verified to be correct at the time of publication. Because of the dynamic nature of the web, some addresses and links may have changed since publication and may no longer be valid.

Contents

Editor's Note

My introduction centers upon Scout Finch as the fictive person who prevents *To Kill a Mockingbird* from dwindling into one more Period Piece.

Claudia Durst Johnson traces the history of early censorship of the novel, after which Fred Erisman emphasizes the more hopeful mode of Southern Romanticism he attributes to Harper Lee.

R. A. Dave, from an Anglo-Indian perspective, inflates the book's status to tragedy, and oddly compares it to Jane Austen, while William T. Going contrasts *Mockingbird* to another Alabama novel, T. S. Stribling's *The Store*.

Colin Nicholson compares the film version of the novel to Harper Lee's story and finds it somewhat inadequate, which would not be my own judgment.

Eric J. Sundquist severely criticizes Harper Lee for over-idealizing Atticus, and thus falsifying the actual desegregation of the South.

The film and novel again are contrasted by Dean Shackelford, who emphasizes Scout's augmenting feminism, after which Patrick Chura centers on the historical relationship between the novel and the Emmett Till case.

Christopher Metress traces the gradual decline of Atticus Finch in critical esteem, while Gary Richards examines the subtle intimations of Truman Capote's homosexuality in Dill, for whom Capote served as model, and in Scout Finch's perpetual boyishness.

HAROLD BLOOM

Introduction

I find that rereading *To Kill a Mockingbird* (wonderful title!) is, for me, a somewhat ambivalent experience. Scout Finch charms me, as she has so many millions of people, and yet she seems to me better than her book, which has dated into a period piece, while she herself remains remarkably vital and refreshing. Since Scout is her book, I find my own reaction an enigma, and hope to enlighten at least myself in this introduction. No one could expect Scout to rival Huck Finn (from whom she serenely derives), and yet her sensibility, intelligence, and decency strongly recall aspects of Huck. This, I think, is all to the good: a younger, female Huckleberry Finn fills a void in American fiction. The aesthetic problem is not Scout Finch, but her father, Atticus, and the entire range of major and minor characters in the story. Atticus and all the others are ideograms rather than people, while Harper Lee's portrait of the artist as a young girl has the individuality, of consciousness and of speech, that allows the representation of a person to be much more than a name on a page.

Harper Lee cannot sustain comparison with Eudora Welty and Flannery O'Connor, or even with Carson McCullers. It would be wrong to make such a contrast, except that to see the limits of *To Kill a Mockingbird* is also to perceive better the novel's relative success in portraying Scout Finch. It is very difficult to represent any healthy consciousness in literature, whether we are being shown an eight-year-old girl or a fully mature woman.

1

Shakespeare, most prodigious of all writers ever, has an astonishing triumph in the Rosalind of *As You Like It*, a heroine who is not only a superb wit, like Falstaff and Hamlet, but who manifests an absolutely normative consciousness, free of all neuroses and darknesses. As an audience, we cannot achieve any perspectives upon Rosalind in which she has not preceded us. She sees all around, as it were, and has a largeness that inspired Jane Austen to emulation. A wholesome sensibility attracts us in life, yet rarely confronts us in literature. One cannot expect Scout Finch to grow up into Rosalind; Scout is perceptive and quick, but her mind is essentially conventional. And yet her spirit is free, in a kind of proto-feminist variation upon Huck Finn's.

The story that Scout tells is circumscribed by time and by region, and also by an America before the Fall, in our final Age of Innocence, the Fifties. Harper Lee and her book emerged from a country yet to experience the Vietnam War, and the subsequent advent of the Counterculture. The United States is a nation desperately losing faith in all authority, whether governmental or familial. *To Kill a Mockingbird*, in its societal aspects, is already a period piece, and its faith in essential human nature can seem very naive. The book's continued popularity, still extraordinary, partly suggests that we find in it a study of the nostalgias. Yet nostalgia itself dates; the reader becomes alienated from it, when nothing restores a sense of its relevance. There remains the portrait of Scout Finch. Her voice, for now, retains immediacy, and speaks for and to many among us. Whether she will survive the aspects of her story that time has staled, I cannot prophesy.

CLAUDIA DURST JOHNSON

The Issue of Censorship

*T*o *Kill a Mockingbird* is one of the most widely read novels of all time. Ever since its publication in 1960, it has also been one of the books most frequently challenged by would-be censors. Objections have been raised to its presence on library shelves and to its use as required reading in schools.

A careful look reveals that most of the elements would-be censors object to can be found in *To Kill a Mockingbird*: (1) references to the sex act, (2) slang and ungrammatical speech, (3) curse words and obscene words, (4) racial slurs, (5) descriptions of rebelliousness or challenges to authority, (6) unfavorable portrayals of the establishment, including organized religion and the government, (7) questioning of absolutes, and (8) the imposition of values. Author Julian Thompson, in categorizing the most frequent objections to literature, cites three main categories that are all pertinent to Harper Lee's novel: (1) vulgar language, (2) references to sexual activity, and (3) expression of anti-establishment attitudes.[1] *To Kill a Mockingbird* has raised objections on all counts.

As students approach the record of controversy over *To Kill a Mockingbird* in Hanover County, Virginia (see the documents that follow), they should be reminded that the impulse to have certain books removed from school reading lists and library shelves is very strong indeed. To grasp

From *Understanding To Kill a Mockingbird: A Student Casebook to Issues, Sources, and Historic Documents.* © 1994 by Claudia Durst Johnson.

the issue clearly, one must consider the arguments that provoke efforts to censor books.

What is the other side of the censorship issue? Who challenges books? Why do these individuals argue that certain materials should not be available in school libraries and classrooms? Studies indicate that the single largest group of censors are parents, but that teachers, school administrators, and other citizens who are not necessarily speaking as parents also challenge books. In addition, there are a number of so-called watchdog organizations that scrutinize school library shelves and textbooks and raise objections to materials. These organizations have on several occasions gone to court in attempts to have materials removed from schools. The "classics" most frequently challenged on moral grounds are *The Scarlet Letter*, *The Catcher in the Rye*, *Lord of the Flies*, *Snow White*, *The Wizard of Oz*, *The Grapes of Wrath*, and *Slaughterhouse Five*. *To Kill a Mockingbird* has also been challenged frequently.

Those who are interested in removing certain books from shelves or classrooms believe students are harmed by reading these materials, that particular books lead students in inappropriate directions. In writing about why parents want to protect their children from reading material they consider offensive or dangerous, R. C. Small, Jr., says that teachers have been telling their students for decades that books are powerful and have the capacity to change lives. Why should anyone be surprised, he writes, when some parents take seriously what they have been taught about the power of books and decide that some books can have the power to harm?

> We have led parents—our former students, after all—to believe that great works contain great truths and that masterpieces are such because of their power to influence. Why should it now be so surprising that parents, discovering curse words, scenes of sexual relations, arguments against the current American social order, questions about the existence of God, believe that we are now pushing ideas as we formerly pushed the ideas in *Silas Marner* and *Julius Caesar*?[2]

One big difference between those who challenge books and those who support the freedom to read (e.g., members of the American Library Association) is that the former see adolescents as somewhat "passive," as Frances Beck McDonald has written.[3] Would-be censors tend to believe that adolescents are easily influenced and led by what they read, that they are not capable of making independent judgments. The latter assume that adolescents can make judgments and that the more information they receive, the better they will be able to cope with reality.

Judging from hearings in the state of Texas, where parents were permitted to speak out on particular textbooks before they were approved for adoption, the most frequent challenges were made to materials that were "depressing," that revealed people "at their worst," and that showed rebelliousness or lawlessness, which "is not good enough for impressionable young minds!"[4] One powerful group in Texas asked that horror stories be removed from reading lists because they are "conducive to causing emotional instability in young minds."[5] Many books, the group argued, especially those "(1) stressing *change*, (2) *questioning* just about everything, and (3) [making] *no* acknowledgment of anything fixed or *absolute* must, as steady dripping water, gradually indoctrinate students away from traditional, basic, biblical, exact values."[6]

In 1974 a community group in Kanawha County, West Virginia, engaged in a long and violent battle to remove certain textbooks from the classroom and then set out guidelines to be followed in approving books for school use. Only those books would be approved that (1) acknowledged the sanctity of the home as the backbone of American society, (2) did not ask personal questions about the students' feelings or their families, (3) did not contain profanity, (4) did not demean anyone's ethnicity, race, or religion, (5) did not provoke racial hatred, (6) did encourage national loyalty, (7) did not show any other form of government as being better than our own, (8) did not criticize the nation's founders, and (9) did stress conventional English grammar.[7]

Often parents' objections to certain books are met by providing alternative readings for their children. But in a few cases the schools and courts have decided that such children must meet the same requirements demanded of other children, and thus must use the same books even if their parents object. In any case, the substitution of alternative texts is also controversial. Schools sometimes argue that providing alternative materials can mean that some children are being exposed to information very selectively and therefore are not being adequately educated. Parents of such children have argued that schools should accommodate those whose religious beliefs are violated by required readings.

Unfortunately, there is little documented evidence on the objections to *To Kill a Mockingbird*. Objections are usually raised orally in public meetings, which are not widely reported in the press. From records accumulated by the American Library Association, we know that most of the objections to Harper Lee's novel fall into three categories: objections to foul language, to the theme of rape, and to racial slurs. The history of censorship of *To Kill a*

Mockingbird is complex; it has been summarized by Jill P. May in an article entitled "Censors as Critics: *To Kill a Mockingbird* as a Case Study" and is continually updated in the American Library Association's *Newsletter on Intellectual Freedom*.[8]

Objections to the use of *To Kill a Mockingbird* in the classroom or its presence on library shelves were made chiefly in the South in the years just after its publication. The most highly publicized case occurred in 1966 in Hanover County, Virginia, where the school board initially decided that the novel would not be on the list of books approved for school use. The chief reason given was that it was immoral. Challenges to the book spread to other parts of the country during the 1970s and 1980s. The reference to rape and the use of obscene and curse words continued to be cited as objections. In Eden Valley, Minnesota, in 1977 the novel was removed from schools because of the use of "damn" and "whore lady," and in the Vernon-Verona-Sherill, New York, school district in 1980 on the grounds that it was a "filthy, trashy novel." In a school in Pennsylvania the novel was removed from shelves on the complaint of a teacher that it contained the word "piss." In Alabama it was challenged by a parent who objected to the word "damn." Language in the novel has also provoked objections in Wisconsin, Washington, West Virginia, and Illinois.

Although all the black characters are sympathetic and the novel exposes racism as abhorrent and white racists as ludicrous and hypocritical, *To Kill a Mockingbird*, like *The Adventures of Huckleberry Finn*, has frequently been challenged by African-American parents chiefly because it contains racial slurs. The American Library Association provides us with a partial list of challenges on these grounds. In Warren, Indiana, in 1981 several citizens found the novel to "represent institutionalized racism under the guise of 'good literature.'" The book was not banned, but three African-American members of a race relations advisory board resigned in protest. In 1984 in Waukegan, Illinois, objections were raised to the novel's use of the word "nigger." In 1985 the novel was challenged in Kansas City and Park Hill, Missouri, and in Casa Grande, Arizona, because it included profanity and racial slurs.

To Kill a Mockingbird does indeed contain racial slurs, spoken from the mouths of some of its characters. But those who would censor it on these grounds should consider the alternative: Would we want a novel about race relations in the South of the 1930s to ignore the language used at the time? to "pretty up" the language of racists? in short, to distort reality and to portray racists as less objectionable than they are?

NOTES

1. "Defending YA Literature against the Pharisees and Censors: Is It Worth the Trouble?" *ALAN Review* 18, no. 2 (1991): 2–5.
2. "Censorship and English: Some Things We Don't Seem to Think about Very Often (But Should)," *Focus* 3 (1978): 18–24.
3. "Appendix B. Freedom to Read: A Professional Responsibility," in Richard Beach and James Marshall, eds., *Teaching Literature in the Secondary School* (New York: Harcourt Brace Jovanovich, 1991).
4. James C. Hefley, *Are Textbooks Harming Your Children?* (Milford, MI: Mott Media, 1979), p. 85.
5. Ibid., p. 85.
6. Ibid., p. 103.
7. Ibid., p. 172.
8. Jill P. May, "Censors as Critics: *To Kill a Mockingbird* as a Case Study," in *Cross-Culturalism in Children's Literature* (New York: Pace University, 1988). *The Newsletter on Intellectual Freedom* is printed bi-monthly in Chicago, Illinois.

A CENSORSHIP ATTEMPT IN HANOVER, VIRGINIA, 1966

This group of documents reflects the history of one very public instance in which *To Kill a Mockingbird* was challenged. The incident began when a prominent physician, W. C. Bosher, the father of a Hanover County student, took a look at the novel his son had brought home to read and decided it was immoral. Dr. Bosher, who was a County Board of Education trustee, was disturbed that his son was reading a book about rape and reported to the school board that the book was "improper for our children to read." On the strength of his motion, the board voted to remove *To Kill a Mockingbird* from the shelves of the Hanover County school libraries.

In the flurry of reportage and exchange of opinions that followed, the board blamed the state, arguing that the County Board had had the novel removed because *To Kill a Mockingbird* had never been on the *state's* list of books approved for state subsidy. When the State Board of Education was challenged about banning the novel, it pointed its finger at the county, saying that the county was free to keep the book on county shelves. The State Board of Education members argued that Harper Lee's novel was not on the approved list solely because no publisher had ever presented *To Kill a Mockingbird* to them for state subsidy. However, it was eventually discovered that thousands of books presented by publishers for places on the approved list had been rejected by the state's censoring board. As in most cases, except for Dr. Bosher's statements to the press, no reason for rejection by county or state was ever given to the public.

The controversy over *To Kill a Mockingbird* is documented in the pages of the Richmond press. Included are news stories reporting the action of the board, editorials, letters to the editor on both sides of the question, and a response from the author, Harper Lee herself. Eventually, the Board backed away from its original decision to take the book out of the library.

MR. BUMBLE AND THE MOCKINGBIRD

The Hanover County School Board last night ordered all copies of Harper Lee's novel, *To Kill a Mockingbird*, removed from the county's school library shelves. In the dim vision of the Hanover board, the novel is "immoral literature." It is "improper for our children to read." And so, by unanimous vote, out it goes—and all other books not on the State Board of Education's approved list are to be taken out of circulation also.

As grown-ups who have been out of Hanover County doubtless are aware, *To Kill a Mockingbird* has become a contemporary classic. It is the tender and moving story of a rape trial in Alabama, and of a white lawyer's effort to obtain justice for a Negro client. A more moral novel scarcely could be imagined. The book was a best-seller; it was made into a notable motion picture; it won the Pulitzer Prize for fiction in 1961; it is read by high school students everywhere else in America but in Hanover County, Virginia.

Fortunately, there exists a remedy for this asinine performance by the Hanover board. Let us now turn to the Beadle Bumble Fund. For some years, we have maintained the fund (named for the famous character in *Oliver Twist*, also an immoral novel) with the sole object of redressing the stupidities of public officials.

Mr. Bumble will gladly purchase and mail a paperbacked copy of *To Kill a Mockingbird* to the first 50 students of Lee-Davis High School who write in. The address is Mr. Bumble, The *News-Leader* Forum, 333 East Grace Street, Richmond.

Editorial Page, *Richmond News-Leader*, Wednesday, January 5, 1966, p. 12.

SOME NOVELS' FATE REMAINS UNCERTAIN

HANOVER SCHOOL BOARD TO USE STATE LIST AS GUIDE

"To Kill a Mockingbird" is dead in Hanover County schools, as far as county school officials are concerned, but the fate of such books as "1984," "Catcher in the Rye," and "Grapes of Wrath" remains in doubt.

The Pulitzer Prize-winning book by Harper Lee will not be used in Hanover County schools because in 1960 it was submitted for inclusion on the state aid book list and rejected, said School Board Chairman B. W. Sadler yesterday.

Under a resolution passed by the county school board Tuesday night, all books taken off the state-approved list must be removed from Hanover schools. The resolution also excludes from county schools books that have been rejected for inclusion on the state list, Sadler said.

The three other widely acclaimed novels also were attacked by W. C. Bosher, the Cold Harbor district school board member who initiated the board's action against "immoral literature."

Son Was Reading

He said the use of "To Kill a Mockingbird" at Lee-Davis High School had come to his attention when he discovered his son, a junior there, reading the book.

"To Kill a Mockingbird," the story of a rape trial in Alabama and of a white lawyer's attempt to obtain justice for a Negro client, is used as supplemental reading by the English department at Lee-Davis, according to the school's principal, B. V. Aylor.

Bosher labeled George Orwell's "1984," depicting the despotism of a regimented society, a "very seductive and suggestive piece of literature."

The books "1984," "Catcher in the Rye," and "Grapes of Wrath" have never been submitted by publishers for inclusion on the state list. J. D. Salinger's "Catcher in the Rye" is about a prep-school youth. John Steinbeck's "Grapes of Wrath" concerns the poverty of Oklahomans in the 1930s. Steinbeck's book was published in the 1930s; "Catcher in the Rye" and "1984" are post–World War II.

All books not appearing on the state aid list, the school board's resolution says, must be approved by a school faculty committee of not fewer than three members including the principal and librarian, if any, before they may be used at a county school.

"We are not censoring any books," declared Sadler. "We are saying in this instance that since the State Department of Education does have a library committee to review those books that are submitted to them, we would make a mockery of the committee, if we disregard their disapproval of books," he said.

Sadler said the school board's resolution was a general policy statement on the selection of books for county schools and would be turned over to school authorities for execution.

A spokesman for the State Department of Education explained that the list compiled by the state does not necessarily attempt to approve or disapprove of books from a moralistic standpoint.

The list is compiled to advise local school boards of books that the state will subsidize the purchase of, the spokesman said. Last year, 4,521 books were submitted by publishers and 3,361 were placed on the approved list.

Aylor, Lee-Davis principal, said he had received no official notification of the school board's action and that he has not attempted to stop the use of "To Kill a Mockingbird" at the school.

English teachers at the school declined comment on the controversy yesterday, as did Bosher.

At no point in the Tuesday meeting did the board consider a general ban of books not on the state-approved list. But Bosher appeared to express the sentiment of the board when he said "there should be a lot of screening" of the books used in our schools.

Richmond Times-Dispatch, Thursday, January 6, 1966, p. 2.

COLLEGE STUDENT DEFENDS MORALITY OF BANNED BOOK

Editor, *News-Leader*:

It is with deep regret that I must announce my ineligibility to request a copy of Harper Lee's immoral novel from Mr. Bumble. Unfortunately, I am now a college student and never resided in Hanover County. That is not to say I have not read the book, nor will consider re-reading it at some future date.

As a matter of fact, I can't think of any book I've ever been afraid of.

I recall my high school days very clearly (a very short time ago, critical elders). They were rich with new literary discoveries—many brought to me by a strongly book-minded mother. From the variety of philosophy consistently handed me, I don't believe she ever attempted to do anything more than make me read.

Ah, but parents so often err—for one day she brought me Harper Lee's story (perhaps she didn't realize that it contained the evil word "rape").

What did it do to me? This horrid piece of trash made me laugh and cry a little inside, forced me to live a life that wasn't mine for some hours, actually had the nerve to make me think of problems I had not yet faced.

It was traumatic.

I'm sure it was even immoral ... if the good people of Hanover say it is.

Only one thing bothers me—why, if the book were so immoral, didn't I ever commit some criminal act as presented in the indecent tale?

People of the northern county, please learn that your brand of conservatism disgusts those of us with minds.

I tell ya, Mr. Bumble, I don't mind some of the citizens of Hanover County, but I sure wouldn't want my sister to marry one.

Alan Markow

"Forum," *Richmond News-Leader*, January 7, 1966, p. 12.

HIDING "SEAMY SIDE" IS FALSE PROTECTION

Members of the Hanover County School Board are absolutely wrong to ban "To Kill a Mockingbird."

"To Kill a Mockingbird," Mr. Salinger's "Catcher in the Rye," and George Orwell's "1984" are sensitive, frightening, awakening, truthful presentations of what could happen and is happening in our life today. Why hide truth from our young people? We need to teach them right from wrong.

We say "Don't," but fail to explain "Why," which is important whenever anyone is corrected or disciplined. We reinforce learning, even in the smallest toddler, as we correct, then accompany it with simple explanations.

Teach them, show them, but let them make choices whenever possible. Values are formed when one confronts and wrestles with truth. Hiding the "seamy" side of life is false protection. Sound instruction based on free choice of reading material is one way to develop character. We seem to be sadly lacking both at home and school in such instruction.

(Mrs.) Mary Lisle King
Mother of Four

"Voice of the People," *Richmond Times-Dispatch*, January 9, 1966, p. 14-B.

TWO BOOKS BANNED—NO DOUBT

The only thing not open to debate in Hanover County's book-banning battle today was that "To Kill a Mockingbird" and "1984" no longer were on the bookshelves of county schools.

Hanover's top school officials bluntly blamed the State Board of Education for the county school board action banishing the two modern classics from public school libraries.

The state dodged and weaved and disclaimed responsibility. It said even though the books aren't on its approved list, the decision to ban or not to ban is entirely up to local school boards.

"If we cannot depend on the competence of the state library committee, who can be depended on for guidance as to what books should be in our schools?" asked Hanover's school board chairman, B. W. Sadler.

"The school board or the superintendent of schools doesn't have the time, nor are we competent, to judge the books," Sadler said. "We are simply trying to set standards for books in the county system."

POLICY CHANGE?

"We might change this policy if the state board tells us that their disapproval of any books is not meaningful."

Other books missing from the list, including John Steinbeck's "The Grapes of Wrath" and J. D. Salinger's "The Catcher in the Rye," also will be affected by the school board ruling, Sadler confirmed.

"Voice of the People," *Richmond News-Leader*, January 10, 1966, p. 9.

WHO KILLED THE MOCKINGBIRD?

All of today's Forum is given to the beautiful controversy that has blown up since the Hanover County School Board voted unanimously last Tuesday night to ban Harper Lee's Pulitzer Prize-winning novel, *To Kill a Mockingbird*. While the local board's action has a couple of defenders, the overwhelming bulk of the mail reaching us is critical of the decision.

Yet it has become evident that the criticism is missing its mark—or more accurately, is hitting only one of two appropriate targets. The Hanover School Board exhibited the kind of small-bore stupidity that deserves to be roundly condemned; but the Hanover board was merely following the larger stupidity of the State Board of Education.

News stories have made it clear how the incredible system works. Book publishers submit copies of their books to a committee of the State Board of Education. The committee then recommends that some books be approved and some disapproved. Last year, 3,361 titles won approval; 1,160 were rejected. Because the State extends grant-in-aid funds to local school boards only for purchase of books on its approved list, the effect is to discourage purchase of books not on the approved list.

Miss Lee's novel, widely acclaimed as a contemporary classic, was submitted for approval in 1960, but rejected. George Orwell's great work, *1984*, was approved by the State in 1952, and then removed from the list a year later.

It occurs to us that the fire in this absurd business ought to be shifted from the local board members of Hanover County to the selection committee of the State Board of Education. Who are these dimwitted censors who would deny their sanction to *1984* and *To Kill a Mockingbird*? What credentials, if any, could support such astoundingly bad judgment? Do such broad-gauged men as Lewis Powell and Colgate Darden, members of the State Board of Education, condone this nonsense?

Off and on in recent years, we have detected encouraging signs that Virginia was emerging from the peckerwood provincialism and ingrown "morality" that H. L. Mencken, in a famous phrase, attributed to this Sahara of the Bozart. But if this dimwitted committee of the State Board of Education is fairly representative of the wisdom that prevails in high levels of State education policy, Mencken's old indictment stands reconfirmed today. If Messrs. Powell and Darden would like to start the New Year with a signal public service, perhaps they would take the lead in firing this committee and abolishing the State's Index of Approved Books altogether.

Editorial Page, *Richmond News-Leader*, January 10, 1966, p. 10.

LETTERS AND EDITOR'S COMMENTS FROM
"Forum," *Richmond News-Leader*

Editor, *News-Leader*:

Your editorial comments on the action of the Hanover County School Board were very disappointing, to say the least. As a citizen of Hanover and parent of a Lee-Davis student, I am pleased with the action of the Board. Our School Board members and school administrators are interested and concerned with the educational policy for the promotion of the welfare of the children of this county. To establish a reading list of the caliber that would exclude books such as "To Kill a Mockingbird" is an important phase of their welfare. I cannot conceive of this being interpreted as "dim vision," as you termed it.

The book in question is considered as immoral literature and, therefore, is certainly not proper reading for our students. Books on suggested and approved reading lists for high school students should, in my estimation, contribute something or be of some value to a person's education—or why require them to be read? People will always read this type of book, but it certainly should never be on a required reading list of a student using his or her time to the best advantage in getting an education for the future. In your defense of the book, you stated it was a best-seller and had been made into a notable movie. This does not give it a stamp of approval. Needless to say, it is read by people everywhere—even Hanover—and more so, now that curiosity has been aroused by publicity. This again does not make it acceptable.

However, this is not the direct cause of my response to your editorial. My reason is to congratulate the Superintendent of Schools, the School Board members, principals and teachers of Hanover County for their efforts and decision in guiding the moral development of our boys and girls. We, as parents, have a tremendous responsibility in the development of our children's moral and spiritual character, as they develop physically. The action taken by our school administrators will have great influence on their moral development. I thank God for them and their vision.

As to your "remedy" of giving 50 copies free to the students of Lee-Davis: I challenge those taking you up on this offer, to write a "Letter to the Editor" and inform us honestly of exactly what the book contributed to their education.

Mrs. L. L. Hollins

BOARD ACTED WISELY IN BANNING OF NOVEL

Editor, *News-Leader*:

Our radios and TV screens and newspapers of today are constantly overflowing with news of people who are against one thing or the other, but in Wednesday's paper, on the front page was something almost unheard of! Somebody actually had the courage to dare to say that something was immoral.

That in itself made a newsworthy story, and was correctly placed on the front page. On every hand we are told that indecent pictures are not really indecent—they are actually art in its finest form—and if you don't see it that way—then it is because of your nasty little dirty mind. And so most of us are so brainwashed that we say hesitantly, "Well, maybe we are being too harsh," and fall back into a comfortable listlessness.

Such a stand in favor of morality and possibly the reason for our mass spinelessness, is flustrated [sic] by the news that a school board group stood for something smacking of morality, and the paper's editor gives them "what for" on the editorial page. Dare to stand for something and you're publicly ridiculed! And, of course, plain John Q. Citizen doesn't have a widely circulated newspaper with which to withstand such criticism! It's a bit like slapping the face of a man who has his hands tied behind him, isn't it? The offer to mail the books to students from the Beadle Bumble Fund was so generous that I would like to offer you, absolutely free, a membership in the "Mind Your Own Business Club," established and maintained by a Hanover citizen. Your generosity to us makes me wonder—when the Catholic Church denounces a book or movie, doesn't the Beadle Bumble Fund get frightfully low in cash?

Mrs. Claude E. Tuck

IMMORAL ACTORS SIDE WITH STUDENTS

Editor, *News-Leader*:

How heartening to know that Harper Lee's novel, "To Kill a Mockingbird," has been removed from school library shelves in Hanover County. It's been a nagging worry to realize that our young people were being exposed to a philosophy which says that innocence must be defended; that legal procedures are preferable to mob violence; that in small, southern communities there are heroic people to whom truth and respect for all men are the cornerstones of character. After all, it's a big, cruel world out there, and what youngster has developed sufficient bigotry to withstand the idea that to hurt a less fortunate fellow is as senseless and sad as killing a mockingbird.

We're also reassured to see that our Hanover officials still move without haste when making such a crucial decision, so that the book's offensiveness became obvious only after five years of availability on these same shelves. Do you suppose there's some sort of memory-erasing machine that could remove injurious impressions from those who have already read it?

There may, of course, be some recalcitrant teen-agers who will insist upon taking Miss Lee's book out behind the fence to read. Since theater people have, through the ages, been notoriously immoral, we offer to these few not only our copy, but the fence as well.

The *News-Leader*, too, is certainly subject to censure for making the Beadle Bumble Fund available to Lee-Davis truants who wish to own paperback editions of the book. But let us not add discrimination to immorality. What about the students at Hanover's second high school, Patrick Henry?

Muriel McAuley, David and Nancy Kilgore
Barksdale Theatre, Hanover C. H.

Thanks to generous contributions, the Beadle Bumble Fund has been able to extend its benefactions to Patrick Henry High School also. A number of Patrick Henry students already have written for their free copies; and while the supply lasts, all requests from Hanover high school students will be filled.   —Editor

ZEALOTS SHIELD STUDENTS FROM GOOD LITERATURE

Editor, News-Leader:
Unfortunately, performances such as the Hanover County Board's banning of "To Kill a Mockingbird" are repeated far too often by those overzealous, self-appointed protectors of our morals.

Such was the case a short time ago when the dramatics department of Thomas Jefferson was almost prevented from using the words "sex-starved cobra" in their production of "The Man Who Came to Dinner."

When are these zealots going to realize that the only thing they are "shielding" the students from is good literature?

I am confident that most students are mature enough to read about the shadier side of life without being permanently perverted.

Michael K. Tobias
N.C. State University

"MOCKINGBIRD" NOT ALONE ON LIST OF BANNED BOOKS

Editor, News-Leader:
I enthusiastically applaud and concur with your comments concerning the removal of "To Kill a Mockingbird" from Hanover County school libraries. I have long held that the only Mockingbird which deserves to be killed is the one which screeches outside my window at some ungodly hour every morning, but the board's move came as no great surprise. Nor would it have surprised anyone who generally reads bulletins posted in Virginia public libraries.

These official guardians of literary morality enshrined on the State Library Board (or whatever it is) have, I am sure, produced some ethical gems in the past. Now they have turned again upon children and really outdone themselves. Among the latest batch ordered removed from circulation in public libraries one will find the Tom Swift series, the Hardy Boys' series, the Uncle Wiggly series, the "Wizard of Oz" (shame on Judy Garland), and, no kidding, "The Bobbsey Twins."

We are informed that these books, among others named, constitute cheap sensationalism. God, what a twisted kid I must have been! I actually enjoyed them! And I still can't even rationalize how they contributed significantly to my complete degeneration. My sympathy to Dick and Jane.

Bruce S. Campbell
Virginia Beach

Richmond News-Leader, January 10, 1966, p. 10.

LETTERS FROM "Forum," *Richmond News-Leader*

SUGGESTS OTHER BOOKS FOR POSSIBLE BANNING

Editor, *News-Leader*:
Regarding the removal of "To Kill a Mockingbird" from the library shelves of the Hanover schools, I suggest the Hanover County School Board check closely into "Rebecca of Sunny Brook Farm." Also, I thought that several passages in "Five Little Peppers and How They Grew" were pretty gamey.

Howard Taylor

IMMORAL LITERATURE IS SIGN OF MORAL DECAY

Editor, *News-Leader*:
I am surprised, shocked, and dismayed to learn that you are not supporting the efforts of our police, school boards, and churches to prevent immoral literature from corrupting our young people. Did not Senator Goldwater warn us in 1964 that its spread is another sign of moral decay in our country?

I would suppose your personal influence and that of your paper would be directed against it, and that you would be among the last to adopt the liberal line of "Anything goes in a work of art."

W. H. Buck
Junction City, Kansas

Richmond News-Leader, January 12, 1966, p. 8.

LETTERS AND COMMENTS FROM *Richmond News-Leader*

BOOK BAN IN HANOVER GETS MORE ATTENTION

Still more reaction has cropped up to the Hanover County school board's banning of two highly praised novels from the county's schools.

In developments reported yesterday:

• The county's executive secretary, Rosewell Page, Jr., a former school board member, attacked the board's action and called on members to rescind it.

• The Ashland Ministers Association resolved to ask the General Assembly to clarify the functions of the state library committee's book list. Further, the ministers called for expressed authority to be given to local school boards to select books not on the approved list. (Legally, local boards may do this. But the Hanover board, in ordering removal of "To Kill a Mockingbird" and "1984," based its action on the fact that the former was rejected by the state and the latter removed from the list.)

• Faculties at Lee-Davis and Patrick Henry high schools, the county's two predominantly white secondary schools, declared that they should have been consulted before such a book selection policy was adopted.

Page said it is impossible to rear a child to choose good and evil "if his experience, gained through the reading of books, is to be hampered in such a manner."

The State Department of Education and the Hanover school board "in their wisdom" might consider banning parts of the Old and New Testaments and numerous literary classics, Page said.

(A spokesman for the State Department of Education, in response to a reporter's query, confirmed that the Bible is on the approved state list).

RAPS SCHOOL OFFICIALS FOR BANNING BOOK

Chairman B. W. Sadler of the Hanover School Board has finally said something close to the heart of the issue in this book-banning fiasco. "The school board or the superintendent of schools has not the time, nor are we competent to judge the books" (*Times-Dispatch*, January 10).

Since both "1984" and "To Kill a Mockingbird" are short and easy to read, it takes little time to read them—probably less time than it takes to defend having banned them. And it is appalling to realize that the men who banned these books refuse to invest that little time that might give them some idea of what they have done.

More appalling, however, and more relevant to the issue, is that, as Sadler says, the School Board is not competent to judge the books. Yet these are two fairly clear and simple works of fiction. If the board members are incompetent to judge the books, can they be competent to set educational policies for the public schools of an entire county? I think not. Most fiction, including "1984" and "To Kill a Mockingbird," is written for general consumption, not for specialized scholars. Anyone who can read can read it; anyone who can reason can judge it. Sadler's statement implies that the Hanover School Board and school superintendent can neither read nor reason. If this is true, steps should be taken to remedy the situation.

(Mrs.) Christina H. Halsted

REASSURED BY BOARD'S DECISION TO BAN BOOK

The Hanover County School Board has taken a firm stand against "slummy" books. When "new English" is accepted as a part of the curriculum along with "new math," "To Kill a Mockingbird" will hardly find a place in any school library. The main characteristic of "new English" is the use of literature from the first grade through high school. Fictionalized court records and case studies in sociology do not meet the established standards for high school fiction, regardless of the fine craftsmanship they illustrate or the prizes they have won.

Literature is used in school to help students develop the right attitude toward life, as well as to improve reading comprehension, build vocabularies, and to supply new ideas. It is doubtful that a judge in a Virginia court would try a case like the one in "To Kill a Mockingbird" with young people in the audience. And, no parent who cares about the character of his son would send him out with the hero of "Catcher in the Rye" to learn the ways of the world. It is true that many of the novels which have stood the test of time and are regarded as classics depict unfavorable scenes and bad characters. But they are plainly labeled as bad and show the disadvantages of unacceptable social behavior. The current books under discussion fail to do this.

[...]

Our selection committee prevents the stocking of library shelves with books purchased with taxpayers' money to discredit the American way of life and the principles of good taste.... If this is censorship, I am for it.

(Mrs.) Noral Miller Turman
Parksley School Librarian

Richmond News-Leader, January 14, 1966, p. 6.

LETTER FROM "Voice of the People," *Richmond Times-Dispatch*

NOT ALL "CLASSICS" ARE FIT FOR JUVENILES

As a writer of sixteen published books, including two for children, I heartily support the State Department of Education's policy in withholding state funds from local school authorities for the purchase of books not on the department's approved list. This does not ban the book, since local school boards may acquire any volume they want, provided they use local funds.

The policy, therefore, is not an exercise of censorship, but one of guidance sorely needed in a time when pruriency—occasionally admittedly accompanied by some literary merit—floods the bookstores.

A certain maturity of mind is required for appreciation of genuine literary worth. None at all is needed to produce adolescent snickers or a potentially harmful excitement at the discovery of a phrase or a passage on page so-and-so. Such books, after being awhile in any library, tend to fall open at such well-thumbed pages.

It should be obvious to all Virginians that a measure of restraint or control—call it "guidance" again—must be exercised toward public school library selections. If no line at all were drawn, the titles might conceivably include a new edition of Henry Miller, or "The Memoirs of a Lady of Pleasure," (better known, but not favorably, as "Fanny Hill.")

The fact that a book has become a "classic" does not necessarily make it fit for juvenile reading; the fact that it is on the best-seller list, or has been awarded literary prizes, or made into a motion picture, is even less reason to make it so.

It is true that cheap trash is available to the young, in cheap paperbacks, at too many newsstands and corner drugstores. This problem is out of the hands of all the school authorities, state and local. Here the guidance must come from the parents and the homes.

No one man, in a long lifetime, could possibly read all the good, clean, entertaining and constructive books that have been printed in the five centuries since Gutenberg allegedly invented movable type. Let the parents, then, begin at the ABC stage to inculcate a love for such reading in the minds and hearts of their children. Neither the State Department of Education nor the school librarian can do this.

Allan R. Bosworth
Captain, U.S. Navy (ret.), Roanoke

Richmond Times-Dispatch, January 18, 1966, p. 14.

LETTERS AND EDITOR'S COMMENTS FROM "Forum," *Richmond News-Leader*

AGREES WITH DECISION TO BAN BOOK IN HANOVER

Editor, *News-Leader*:

As a regular reader of your paper I am very disappointed in your recent position regarding a certain book in a Hanover County school. I have not read the book (nor do I intend to do so) but I did see the diabolical movie, which was repulsive enough. No doubt, had I read the book, I should have found a rather detailed and descriptive account of what actually took place in the story.

The decision of our School Board does not deny anyone the right to purchase this controversial book, nor any other book, if he so desires.

In our community, Mr. Bosher is a respected businessman of irreproachable character. Were there more such officials of his caliber in the "driver's seat" of the local, state, and federal government of this nation, the rampant moral decline with which we are currently oppressed might have been avoided.

Someone had the audacity to refer to Mr. Bosher as "ignorant." This term is employed today, often indiscriminately by some folks who attempt to categorize those who disagree with them. All of us are ignorant of various matters.

To put so much emphasis on the fact that the author of "To Kill a Mockingbird" was awarded the Pulitzer Prize does not impress me. Martin Luther King was awarded the Nobel Peace Prize. What irony!

I am thankful that at an early age my parents introduced me to wholesome reading material. Consequently, never having cultivated an appetite for the baser literature (and I use the word "literature" loosely), I have always sought undefiled reading matter.

I don't recall that such a commotion as this came about when an atheist in Maryland carried to the federal courts her protest against the use of prayer in the public schools.

Everyone should be cognizant of the fact that a young mind is a flexible and a vulnerable mind. Therefore, influences such as books, movies, etc. can either elevate or degrade that mind.

It takes a strong back to stand up and be counted. May I say, bravo, Mr. Bosher! Carry on!

Miss Vivian Blake

AUTHOR HARPER LEE COMMENTS ON BOOK-BANNING

Editor, *News-Leader*:
Recently I have received echoes down this way of the Hanover County
School Board's activities, and what I've heard makes me wonder if any of its
members can read.
Surely it is plain to the simplest intelligence that "To Kill a
Mockingbird" spells out in words of seldom more than two syllables a code
of honor and conduct, Christian in its ethic, that is the heritage of all
Southerners. To hear that the novel is "immoral" has made me count the
years between now and 1984, for I have yet to come across a better example
of doublethink.
I feel, however, that the problem is one of illiteracy, not Marxism.
Therefore I enclose a small contribution to the Beadle Bumble Fund that I
hope will be used to enroll the Hanover County School Board in any first
grade of its choice.

Harper Lee
Monroeville, Ala.

*In most controversies, the lady is expected to have the last word. In this par-
ticular discussion, it seems especially fitting that the last word should come from the
lady who wrote "To Kill a Mockingbird." With Miss Lee's letter, we call a halt, at
least temporarily, to the publication of letters commenting on the book-banning in
Hanover County.*

Editor
Richmond News-Leader, January 15, 1966, p. 10.

FRED ERISMAN

The Romantic Regionalism of Harper Lee

When Mark Twain stranded the steamboat *Walter Scott* on a rocky point in Chapter 13 of *Huckleberry Finn*, he rounded out an attack on Southern romanticism begun in *Life on the Mississippi*. There, as every reader knows, he asserted that Sir Walter Scott's novels of knighthood and chivalry had done "measureless harm" by infecting the American South with "the jejune romanticism of an absurd past that is dead." This premise does not stop with Twain. W. J. Cash, writing almost sixty years later, continues the assertion, observing that the South, already nostalgic in the early nineteenth century, "found perhaps the most perfect expression for this part of its spirit in the cardboard medievalism of the Scotch novels." As recently as 1961, W. R. Taylor, in *Cavalier and Yankee*, several times alludes to Scott as he traces the development of the myth of the planter aristocracy.[1]

For these three men, and for many like them, Southern romanticism has been a pernicious, backward-looking belief. It has, they imply, mired the South in a stagnant morass of outdated ideas, from which there is little chance of escape. A more hopeful view, however, appears in Harper Lee's novel of Alabama life, *To Kill a Mockingbird* (1960). Miss Lee is well aware of traditional Southern romanticism and, indeed, agrees that it was and is a pervasive influence in the South; one of the subtlest allusions in the entire novel comes in Chapter 11, as the Finch children read *Ivanhoe* to the dying but

From *The Alabama Review* 26, no. 2. © 1973 by The University of Alabama Press.

indomitable Southern lady, Mrs. Henry Lafayette Dubose. At the same time, she sees in the New South—the South of 1930–1935—the dawning of a newer and more vital form of romanticism. She does not see this newer romanticism as widespread, nor does she venture any sweeping predictions as to its future. Nevertheless, in *To Kill a Mockingbird*, Miss Lee presents an Emersonian view of Southern romanticism, suggesting that the South can move from the archaic, imported romanticism of its past toward the more reasonable, pragmatic, and native romanticism of a Ralph Waldo Emerson. If the movement can come to maturity, she implies, the South will have made a major step toward becoming truly regional in its vision.

As Miss Lee unfolds her account of three years in the lives of Atticus, Jem, and Scout Finch, and in the history of Maycomb, Alabama, she makes clear the persistence of the old beliefs. Maycomb, she says, is "an old town ... a tired old town," even "an ancient town." A part of southern Alabama from the time of the first settlements, and isolated and largely untouched by the Civil War, it was, like the South, turned inward upon itself by Reconstruction. Indeed, its history parallels that of the South in so many ways that it emerges as a microcosm of the South. This quality is graphically suggested by the Maycomb County courthouse, which dominates the town square:

> The Maycomb County courthouse was faintly reminiscent of Arlington in one respect: the concrete pillars supporting its south roof were too heavy for their light burden. The pillars were all that remained standing when the original courthouse burned in 1856. Another courthouse was built around them. It is better to say, built in spite of them. But for the south porch, the Maycomb County courthouse was early Victorian, presenting an unoffensive vista when seen from the north. From the other side, however, Greek revival columns clashed with a big nineteenth-century clock tower housing a rusty unreliable instrument, a view indicating a people determined to preserve every physical scrap of the past.[2]

Miss Lee's courthouse, inoffensive from the north but architecturally appalling from the south, neatly summarizes Maycomb's reluctance to shed the past. It is, like the South, still largely subject to the traditions of the past.

The microcosmic quality of Maycomb suggested by its courthouse appears in other ways, as well. The town's social structure, for example, is characteristically Southern. Beneath its deceptively placid exterior,

Maycomb has a taut, well-developed caste system designed to separate whites from blacks. If Maycomb's caste system is not so openly oppressive as that of John Dollard's "Southern-town" (where "caste has replaced slavery as a means of maintaining the essence of the old status order in the South"[3]), it still serves the same end—to keep the blacks in their place. The operations of this system are obvious. First Purchase African M. E. Church, for example, "the only church in Maycomb with a steeple and bell," is subjected to minor but consistent desecration: "Negroes worshiped in it on Sundays and white men gambled in it on weekdays" (p. 128). The whites, moreover, clearly expect deferential behavior of the blacks. One of the good ladies of the Methodist missionary circle interrupts her paeans to Christian fellowship to remark, "There's nothing more distracting than a sulky darky.... Just ruins your day to have one of 'em in the kitchen" (p. 245). The Finch children, attending church with Calpurnia, their black housekeeper, are confronted with doffed hats and "weekday gestures of respectful attention" (p. 128). And, in the most telling commentary of all upon the pervasive pressures of the caste system, when Calpurnia accompanies Atticus Finch to convey the news of Tom Robinson's death, she must ride in the back seat of the automobile (p. 252).

Even more indicative of Maycomb's characteristically Southern caste system is the power of the sexual taboo, which has been called "the strongest taboo of the system."[4] This is dramatized by the maneuverings during Tom Robinson's trial of allegedly raping Mayella Ewell, a central episode in the novel. Although Tom's infraction of the black man–white woman code is demonstrated to have been false, he is nonetheless condemned. The caste taboo outweighs empirical evidence. As Atticus says later of the jury, "Those are twelve reasonable men in everyday life, Tom's jury, but you saw something come between them and reason.... There's something in our world that makes men lose their heads—they couldn't be fair if they tried" (p. 233). Despite the presence of a more than reasonable doubt as to his guilt, despite the discrediting of the Ewells, the chief witnesses for the prosecution, Tom Robinson is condemned. As Atticus points out, the entire prosecution is based upon "the assumption—the evil assumption—that *all* Negroes lie, that *all* Negroes are basically immoral beings, that *all* Negro men are not to be trusted around our women" (p. 217). Tom's conviction is mute testimony to the strength of that caste-oriented assumption.

Another illustration of Maycomb's archetypal Southernness that is as typical as its caste system is the ubiquitous system of class distinctions among the whites. Miss Lee's characters fall readily into four classes, ranging from the "old aristocracy" represented by Atticus Finch's class-conscious sister,

Alexandra, to the poor white trash represented by Bob Ewell and his brood, who have been "the disgrace of Maycomb for three generations" (p. 37). In presenting the interaction of these classes, she gives a textbook demonstration of the traditional social stratification of the American South.[5]

The upper-class-consciousness so manifest in Aunt Alexandra appears most strongly in her regard for "family", a concern that permeates Part II of *To Kill a Mockingbird*. Like the small-town aristocrats described in Allison Davis's *Deep South*, she has a keen appreciation of the "laterally extended kin group."[6] Although the complex interrelationships of Maycomb society are generally known to the Finch children, it is Aunt Alexandra who drives home their social significance. After a series of social gaffes by Scout, Aunt Alexandra prevails upon Atticus to lecture the children concerning their status. This he does, in his most inflectionless manner:

> 'Your aunt has asked me to try and impress upon you and Jean Louise that you are not from run-of-the-mill people, that you are the product of several generations' gentle breeding ... and that you should try to live up to your name.... She asked me to tell you you must try to behave like the little lady and gentleman that you are. She wants to talk to you about the family and what it's meant to Maycomb County through the years, so you'll have some idea of who you are, so you might be moved to behave accordingly' (pp. 143–44).

In her insistence that family status be preserved, Aunt Alexandra typifies the family-oriented aristocrat of the Old South.

No less well developed is Miss Lee's emphasis upon the subtleties of class distinction. In this, too, she defines Maycomb as a characteristically Southern community.[7] It has its upper class, in Aunt Alexandra, in the members of the Missionary Society, and in the town's professional men—Atticus, Dr. Reynolds, Judge Taylor, and so on. It has its middle class, in the numerous faceless and often nameless individuals who flesh out Miss Lee's story—Braxton Underwood, the owner-editor of *The Maycomb Tribune*, or Mr. Sam Levy, who shamed the Ku Klux Klan in 1920 by proclaiming that "he'd sold 'em the very sheets on their backs" (p. 157). It has its lower class, generically condemned by Aunt Alexandra as "trash," but sympathetically presented in characters like Walter Cunningham, one of the Cunninghams of Old Sarum, a breed of men who "hadn't taken anything from or off of anybody since they migrated to the New World" (p. 235). Finally, it has its dregs, the Ewells, who, though more slovenly than the supposedly slovenliest of the blacks, still possess the redeeming grace of a white skin. These distinctions Aunt Alexandra reveres and protects, as when she remarks, "You can scrub Walter Cunningham till he shines, you can put him in shoes and a new suit, but he'll never be like Jem.... Because—he—is—trash" (p. 237). For Aunt Alexandra, the class gap between the Finches and the Cunninghams is one that can never be bridged.

The existence of a caste system separating black from white, or of a well-developed regard for kin-group relations, or of a system of class stratification is, of course, not unique. But, from the simultaneous existence of these three systems, and from the way in which they dominate Maycomb attitudes, emerges the significance of Maycomb's antiquity. It is a representation of the Old South, still clinging, as in its courthouse, to every scrap of the past. Left alone, it would remain static, moldering away as surely as John Brown's body. So too, Miss Lee suggests, may the South. This decay, however, can be prevented. In her picture of the New South and the New Southerner, Miss Lee suggests how a decadently romantic tradition can be transformed into a functional romanticism, and how, from this change, can come a revitalizing of the South.

The "New South" that Harper Lee advocates is new only by courtesy. In one respect—the degree to which it draws upon the romantic idealism of an Emerson—it is almost as old as the Scottish novels so lacerated by Mark Twain; in another, it is even older, as it at times harks back to the Puritan ideals of the seventeenth century. By the standards of the American South of the first third of the twentieth century, however, it is new, for it flies in the face of much that traditionally characterizes the South. With Emerson, it spurns the past, looking instead to the reality of the present. With him, it places principled action above self-interest, willingly accepting the difficult consequences of a right decision. It recognizes, like both Emerson and the Puritans, the diversity of mankind, yet recognizes also that this diversity is unified by a set of "higher laws" that cannot be ignored. In short, in the several Maycomb townspeople who see through the fog of the past, and who act not from tradition but from principle, Miss Lee presents the possible salvation of the South.

Foremost among these people is Atticus Finch, attorney, the central character of Miss Lee's novel. Though himself a native of Maycomb, a member of one of the oldest families in the area, and "related by blood or marriage to nearly every family in the town," Atticus is not the archetypal Southerner that his sister has become (pp. 9–11). Instead, he is presented as a Southern version of Emersonian man, the individual who vibrates to his own iron string, the one man in the town that the community trusts "to do right," even as they deplore his peculiarities (p. 249). Through him, and through Jem and Scout, the children he is rearing according to his lights, Miss Lee presents her view of the New South.

That Atticus Finch is meant to be an atypical Southerner is plain; Miss Lee establishes this from the beginning, as she reports that Atticus and his brother are the first Finches to leave the family lands and study elsewhere. This atypical quality, however, is developed even further. Like Emerson, Atticus recognizes that his culture is retrospective, groping "among the dry bones of the past ... [and putting] the living generation into masquerade out of its faded wardrobe."[8] He had no hostility toward his past; he is not one of the alienated souls so beloved of Southern Gothicists. He does, though, approach his past and its traditions with a tolerant skepticism. His attitude toward "old family" and "gentle breeding" has already been suggested. A similar skepticism is implied by his repeated observation that "you never really understand a person until you consider things from his point of view ... until you climb into his skin and walk around in it" (p. 36). He understands the difficulties of Tom Robinson, although Tom Robinson is black; he understands the difficulties of a Walter Cunningham, though Cunningham is—to Aunt Alexandra—"trash"; he understands the pressures being brought to bear upon his children because of his own considered actions. In each instance he acts according to his estimate of the merits of the situation, striving to see that each receives justice. He is, in short, as Edwin Bruell has suggested, "no heroic type but any graceful, restrained, simple person like one from Attica."[9] Unfettered by the corpse of the past, he is free to live and work as an individual.

This freedom to act he does not gain easily. Indeed, he, like Emerson's nonconformist, frequently finds himself whipped by the world's displeasure. And yet, like Emerson's ideal man, when faced by this harassment and displeasure, he has "the habit of magnanimity and religion to treat it godlike as a trifle of no concernment."[10] In the development of this habit he is aided by a strong regard for personal principle, even as he recognizes the difficulty that it brings to his life and the lives of his children. This is established early in the novel, with the introduction of the Tom Robinson trial. When the case is brought up by Scout, following a fight at school, Atticus responds, " 'If I didn't [defend Tom Robinson] I couldn't hold up my head in town, I couldn't represent this county in the legislature, I couldn't even tell you or Jem not to do something again.... Scout, simply by the nature of the work, every lawyer gets at least one case in his lifetime that affects him personally. This one's mine, I guess" ' (p. 83). He returns to this theme later, observing that " 'This case ... is something that goes to the essence of a man's conscience—Scout, I

couldn't go to church and worship God if I didn't try to help that man.'"
Scout points out that opinion among the townspeople runs counter to this,
whereupon Atticus replies, "'They're certainly entitled to think that, and
they're entitled to full respect for their opinions ... but before I can live with
other folks I've got to live with myself. The one thing that doesn't abide by
majority rule is a person's conscience'" (pp. 113–14). No careful ear is needed to hear the echoes of Emerson's "Nothing can bring you peace but your-
self. Nothing can bring you peace but the triumph of principles."[11] In his
heeding both principle and conscience, whatever the cost to himself, Atticus
is singularly Emersonian.

The Emersonian quality of Atticus's individualism is emphasized in two
additional ways—through his awareness of the clarity of the childhood vision
(suggesting Emerson's remark that "the sun illuminates only the eye of the
man, but shines into the eye and the heart of the child. The lover of nature
is he ... who has retained the spirit of infancy even into the era of manhood."[12]), and through his belief in the higher laws of life. The first of these
appears at least three times throughout the novel. Early in the Tom
Robinson sequence, an attempted lynching is thwarted by the sudden
appearance of the Finch children, leading Atticus to observe, "'So it took an
eight-year-old child to bring 'em to their senses, didn't it? ... Hmp, maybe we
need a police force of children ... you children last night made Walter
Cunningham stand in my shoes for a minute. That was enough'" (p. 168).
The view is reinforced by the comments of Dolphus Raymond, the town
drunk, who sees in the children's reaction to the trial the unsullied operations
of instinct (p. 213). And, thus suggested, it is made explicit by Atticus himself, as, following Tom Robinson's conviction, he tells Jem: "'If you had been
on that jury, son, and eleven other boys like you, Tom would be a free man....
So far nothing in your life has interfered with your reasoning process'" (p.
233). The point could not be more obvious; in the unsophisticated vision of
the child is a perception of truth that most older, tradition-bound people
have lost. Atticus, like Emerson's lover of nature, has retained it, and can
understand it; it only remains for that vision to be instilled in others.

Linked to this belief is Atticus's recognition of the diversity of man and
his faith in the higher laws—although, significantly, his higher laws are not
the abstruse, cosmic laws of Emerson, but the practical laws of the courts.
Atticus, by his own confession, is no idealist, believing in the absolute goodness of mankind. In his courtroom argument he acknowledges his belief that
"'there is not a person ... who has never told a lie, who has never done an
immoral thing, and there is no man living who has never looked upon a
woman without desire.'" To this he adds his recognition of the randomness

of life: "'Some people are smarter than others, some people have more opportunity because they're born with it, some men make more money than others, some ladies make better cakes than others—some people are born gifted beyond the normal scope of most men.'" At the same time, he also believes that these flawed, diverse people are united by one thing—the law. There is, he says, "'one way in this country in which all men are created equal—there is one human institution that makes a pauper the equal of a Rockefeller, the stupid man the equal of an Einstein, and the ignorant man the equal of any college president. That institution, gentlemen, is a court'" (pp. 217–18). In this, his climactic speech to the jury, Atticus makes clear his commitment. Like the Puritans, he assumes the flawed nature of man, but, like Emerson, he looks to the higher laws—those of the court and of the nation—that enable man to transcend his base diversity and give him the only form of equality possible in a diverse society. Like the Emerson of the "Ode to Charming," he argues:

> Let man serve law for man;
> Live for friendship, live for love;
> For truth's and harmony's behoof;
> The state may follow how it can.[13]

Atticus will, indeed, serve law for man, leaving the state—his contemporaries—to follow how it can. He, at least, has absolved him to himself.

Throughout *To Kill a Mockingbird*, Harper Lee presents a dual view of the American South. On the one hand, she sees the South as still in the grip of the traditions and habits so amply documented by Davis, Dollard, and others—caste division along strictly color lines, hierarchical class stratification within castes, and exaggerated regard for kin-group relations within particular classes, especially the upper and middle classes of the white caste. On the other hand, she argues that the South has within itself the potential for progressive change, stimulated by the incorporation of the New England romanticism of an Emerson, and characterized by the pragmatism, principles, and wisdom of Atticus Finch. If, as she suggests, the South can exchange its old romanticism for the new, it can modify its life to bring justice and humanity to all of its inhabitants, black and white alike.

In suggesting the possibility of a shift from the old romanticism to the new, however, Miss Lee goes even further. If her argument is carried to its logical extension, it becomes apparent that she is suggesting that the South, by assimilating native (though extra-regional) ideals, can transcend the confining sectionalism that has dominated it in the past, and develop the breadth of vision characteristic of the truly regional outlook. This outlook, which Lewis Mumford calls a "soundly bottomed regionalism," is one that "can achieve cosmopolitan breadth without fear of losing its integrity or virtue: it is only a sick and puling regionalism that must continually gaze with enamored eyes upon its own face, praising its warts and pimples as beauty marks. For a genuine regional tradition lives by two principles. One is, *cultivate whatever you have*, no matter how poor it is; *it is at least your own*. The other is, *seek elsewhere for what you do not possess*: absorb whatever is good wherever you may find it; *make it your own*."[14] If the South can relinquish its narcissistic regard for the warts and pimples of its past, it can take its place among the regions of the nation and the world.

Miss Lee sees such a development as a distinct possibility. Maycomb, in the past isolated and insulated, untouched by even the Civil War, is no longer detached from the outside world. It is, as Miss Lee suggests through the Finch brothers' going elsewhere to study, beginning to seek for what it does not possess. (This quest, however, is no panacea, as Miss Lee implies with the character of the pathetically inept Miss Caroline Fisher, the first-grade teacher from North Alabama, who introduces the "Dewey Decimal System" to revolutionize the Maycomb County School System (pp. 22–25).) Moreover, Maycomb is being forced to respond to events touching the nation and the world. The Depression is a real thing, affecting the lives of white and black alike; the merchants of Maycomb are touched by the fall of the National Recovery Act; and Hitler's rise to power and his persecution of the Jews make the power of Nazism apparent even to the comfortable Christians of the town (pp. 11–12, 27, 257–64). Maycomb, in short, like the South it represents, is becoming at last a part of the United States; what affects the nation affects it, and the influence of external events can no longer be ignored.

The organic links of Maycomb with the world at large extend even further, as Miss Lee goes on to point out the relationship between what happens in Maycomb and the entirety of human experience. The novel opens and closes on a significant note—that life in Maycomb, despite its Southern particularity, is an integral part of human history. This broadly regional vision appears in the first paragraphs of the novel, as the narrator, the mature Scout, reflects upon the events leading up to the death of Bob Ewell:

> I maintain that the Ewells started it all, but Jem, who was four years my senior, said it started long before that. He said it began the summer Dill came to us, when Dill first gave us the idea of making Boo Radley come out.

I said if he wanted to take a broad view of the thing, it really
began with Andrew Jackson. If General Jackson hadn't run the
Creeks up the creek, Simon Finch would never have paddled up
the Alabama, and where would we be if he hadn't? We were far
too old to settle an argument with a fist-fight, so we consulted
Atticus. Our father said we were both right. (p. 9)

The theme of this passage—that events of long ago and far away can have
consequences in the present—is echoed at the novel's end. Tom Robinson is
dead, Bob Ewell is dead, Boo Radley has emerged and submerged, and
Scout, aged nine, is returning home. The view from the Radley porch evokes
a flood of memories, which, for the first time, fall into a coherent pattern for
her: the complex interaction of three years of children's play and adult
tragedy is revealed in a single, spontaneous moment of intuitive perception.
"Just standing on the Radley porch was enough," she says. "As I made my
way home, I felt very old ... As I made my way home, I thought what a thing
to tell Jem tomorrow.... As I made my way home, I thought Jem and I would
get grown but there wasn't much else left for us to learn, except possibly
algebra" (p. 294). She has learned, with Emerson, that "to the young mind
every thing is individual.... By and by, it finds how to join two things and see
in them one nature; then three, then three thousand; and so, tyrannized over
by its own unifying instinct, it goes on tying things together ... [discovering]
that these objects are not chaotic, and are not foreign, but have a law which
is also a law of the human mind."[15] When the oneness of the world dawns
upon a person, truly all that remains is algebra.

Miss Lee's convictions could not be more explicit. The South, embodied here in Maycomb and its residents, can no longer stand alone and apart.
It must recognize and accept its place in national and international life, and
it must accept the consequences for doing so. It must recognize and accept
that adjustments must come, that other ways of looking at things are perhaps
better than the traditional ones. Like Emerson's individual, it must be no
longer hindered by the name of goodness, but must explore if it be goodness.
If, to a perceptive and thoughtful observer, the old ways have lost their value,
new ones must be found to supplant them; if, on the other hand, the old ways
stand up to the skeptical eye, they should by all means by preserved. This
Atticus Finch has done, and this he is teaching his children to do. By extension, the South must do the same, cultivating the good that it possesses, but
looking elsewhere for the good that it lacks. Only in this way can it escape
the stifling provincialism that has characterized its past, and take its place as
a functioning region among human regions. If the South can learn this fun-

damental lesson, seeking its unique place in relation to human experience, national experience, and world experience, all that will remain for it, too, will be algebra.

NOTES

1. Mark Twain, *Life on the Mississippi*, Harper's Modern Classics (New York: Harper & Bros. 1950), 375; W. J. Cash, *The Mind of the South* (New York: Alfred A. Knopf, 1941), 62; William R. Taylor, *Cavalier and Yankee* (New York: George Braziller, 1961).

2. Harper Lee, *To Kill a Mockingbird* (Philadelphia: J. B. Lippincott, 1960), 11, 140–41, 173. Further references to this work will be given in the text.

3. John Dollard, *Caste and Class in a Southern Town*, 3rd ed. (1949; rpt. Garden City: Doubleday-Anchor, 1957), 62.

4. Allison Davis, Burleigh B. Gardner and Mary R. Gardner, *Deep South: a Social Anthropological Study of Caste and Class* (Chicago: University of Chicago Press, 1941), 25.

5. Davis, et al, 65.

6. Davis, et al, 87.

7. Davis, et al, 60ff.

8. Ralph Waldo Emerson, *Nature*, in *The Selected Writings of Ralph Waldo Emerson* (ed.), Brooks Atkinson (New York: The Modern Library, 1950), 3. Cited hereafter as *Writings*.

9. Edwin Bruell, "Keen Scalpel on Racial Ills," *English Journal*, 53 (December, 1964), 660.

10. Emerson, "Self-Reliance," in *Writings*, 151.

11. Emerson, "Self-Reliance," in *Writings*, 169.

12. Emerson, *Nature*, in *Writings*, 6.

13. Emerson, "Ode Inscribed to W. H. Channing," in *Writings*, 771.

14. Lewis Mumford, quoted in Howard W. Odum, *Southern Regions of the United States* (Chapel Hill: University of North Carolina Press, 1936), 531.

15. Emerson, "The American Scholar," in *Writings*, 47.

R.A. DAVE

To Kill A Mockingbird:
Harper Lee's Tragic Vision

*T*o *Kill a Mockingbird* is quite an ambiguous title, the infinitive leaving a wide scope for a number of adverbial queries—how, when, where, and, of course, *why*—all leading to intriguing speculation and suspense. One is left guessing whether it is a crime-thriller or a book on bird-hunting. Look at it any way, the title hurts the reader's sensibility and creates an impression that something beautiful is being bruised and broken. It is only after he plunges into the narrative and is swept off into its current that he starts gathering the significance of the title. After buying the gift of an air gun for his little son, Atticus says: 'I would rather you shot at tin cans in the backyard, but I know you will go after birds ... but remember, it's a sin to kill a mockingbird.' And when Scout asks Miss Maudie about it, for that is the only time when she ever heard her father say it is a sin to do something, she replies saying:

> 'Your father is right. Mockingbirds don't do one thing but make music for us to enjoy. They don't eat up people's gardens, don't nest in corncribs, they don't do one thing but sing their hearts out for us. That's why it is a sin to kill a mockingbird.'

And as the words 'it's a sin to kill a mockingbird' keep on echoing into our ears, we are apt to see on their wings the mockingbirds that will sing all day

From *Indian Studies in American Fiction.* © 1974 by Karnatak University, Dharwar and the Macmillan Company of India.

and even at night without seeming to take time to hunt for worms or insects. At once the moral undertones of the story acquire symbolical expression and the myth of the mockingbird is seen right at the thematic centre of the story. The streets of Maycomb were deserted, the doors and windows were instantaneously shut the moment Calpurnia sent round the word about the dog, gone mad in February not in August. The dog 'was advancing at a snail's pace, but he was not playing or sniffing at foliage: he seemed dedicated to one course and motivated by an invisible force that was inching him towards us.' There was hush all over. 'Nothing is more deadly than a deserted waiting street. The trees were silent, the mockingbirds were silent.' During moments of peril, such as these, even the mockingbirds do not sing! That the little girl should see in the dog's march to death some motivation of 'an invisible force' is as significant as her being struck by the silence of the mockingbirds. We have several such moments of eloquent silence in the novel. But what is more disturbing is the behaviour of the neighbours, who open their 'windows one by one' only after the danger was over. Atticus could protect them against a mad dog: he could not protect the innocent victim against their madness! As the Finch children along with their friend Dill waver at the portals of the Radley House on their way to solve the Boo mystery, we again hear the solitary singer:

> High above us in the darkness a solitary mocker poured out his repertoire in blissful unawareness of whose tree he sat in, plunging from the shrill kee, kee of the sunflower bird to the irascible qua-ack of a bluejay, to the sad lament of Poor Will, Poor Will, Poor Will.

And when they shoot Tom Robinson, while lost in his unavailing effort to scale the wall in quest of freedom, Mr Underwood, the editor of *The Montgomery Advertiser*, 'likened Tom's death to the senseless slaughter of songbirds by hunters and children'. As we find the mockingbird fluttering and singing time and again, the whole of Maycomb seems to be turning before our eyes into a wilderness full of senseless slaughter. The mockingbird motif, as effective as it is ubiquitous, and a continual reminder of the thematic crux, comes alive in the novel with all its associations of innocence, joy, and beauty.

The mockingbird myth is there in American literature and folklore. In Walt Whitman's 'Out of the Cradle Endlessly Rocking', we have a tender tale of mockingbirds, the tale of love and longing and loss. The poet, while wandering on the sea-shore, recaptures the childhood memories of the tragic drama of the mockingbirds, 'two feather'd guests from *Alabama*':

> Two together!
> Winds blow south, or winds blow north,
> Day come white, or night come black,
> Home, or rivers and mountains from home,
> Singing all time, minding no time,
> While we two keep together—

'till of a sudden, maybe killed', the she-bird 'did not ever appear again.' The mockingbird myth is most powerfully used by Whitman, who travels back and forth on the waves of childhood memories with a mist of tears through which 'a man, yet by these tears a little boy again', sings a reminiscence. The mockingbird symbol in the novel acquires a profound moral significance. For, unlike the world of tender love and longing of Walt Whitman's Alabama birds, Harper Lee's Alabama presents a bleak picture of a narrow world torn by hatred, injustice, violence and cruelty, and we lament to see 'what man has made of man'. It brings out forcefully the condition of Negro subculture in the white world where a Negro, as dark as a mockingbird, is accepted largely as a servant or at best as an entertainer. But apart from the symbolical identity, *To Kill a Mockingbird* has an astonishing technical kinship with Whitman's 'Out of the Cradle Endlessly Rocking'. Both, Whitman and Harper Lee, recollect childhood memories after many years have gone by. In both, the poem and the novel, we see a parabolic pattern. After years, the narrator goes back into the past, swimming across a flood of memories, and then comes back floating onwards towards the present moment and beyond. The way childhood memories impinge on adult consciousness, turning 'a man, yet by these tears a little boy again', gives a new dimension to the autobiographical mode, and heightens dramatically the reported impressions by the fact that what happens to the artist's consciousness is more important than the actual happening itself. In the novel, Harper Lee installs herself avowedly as the narrator and depicts not only the external world of action, but the internal world of character also. It is certainly not an innovation. Chaucer had done it in his *Canterbury Tales*.

> The characterised 'I' is substituted for the loose general 'I' of the author, the loss of freedom is more than repaid by the more salient effect of the picture ... the use of the first person is no

doubt a source of relief to the novelist in the matter of composition. It composes of its own accord.
(PERCY LUBBOCK *The Craft of Fiction*: London, 1960 p. 127 and
p. 131)

Here is a novel that seems to be composing itself of its own accord.
Harper Lee has a remarkable gift of story-telling. Her art is visual, and with
cinematographic fluidity and subtlety we see a scene melting into another
scene without jolts of transition. Like Browning's poet, Harper Lee is a
'maker-see'. She unfolds the wide panorama of Maycomb life in such a way
that we, the readers, too, get transported in that world within world and
watch helplessly, though not quite hopelessly, the bleak shadows of the adult
world darkening the children's dream world.

To Kill a Mockingbird is autobiographical not merely in its mode of
expression but also in quite a personal sense. If David Copperfield is Charles
Dickens and Stephen Dedalus in *A Portrait of the Artist as a Young Man* is
James Joyce, Jean Louise Finch (Scout) is unmistakably Harper Lee. If we
examine the internal evidence, we can easily infer that in 1935, while Hitler
was persecuting the Jews in Germany and Tom Robinson was being tried in
Maycomb, Jean Finch Scout, the narrator, was 'not yet nine'; perhaps she was
born, like her creator, in 1926. The identification between the narrator and
the novelist is apparent. The novel with its autobiographical mode strikes a
psychological balance between the past, the present, and the future. The
writer projects herself into the story as Scout in the present. What she narrates is the past. And as the past is being unfolded the reader wonders how
the writer's retrospect will lead her on to the future, which is a continual
mystery. This evokes in the novel considerable suspense. We follow the trial
of Tom Robinson and the ostracising of the Finch family, holding our breath.
But unlike David Copperfield who casts a backward glance over a long-trav-
elled road or Stephen Dedalus who grows from childhood to youth and to
manhood seeking aesthetic vision and development in exile, Scout Finch
concentrates on a single phase, a moment of crisis in which childhood innocence was shattered by the terrifying experiences of the adult world.

It is a memory tale told by a little girl, Jean Louise Finch, called Scout
in the novel. She becomes a mirror of experience and we see reflected in her
the Maycomb world. Her memories recollected in imaginative tranquillity
become a dramatised action and the fiction gets an extraordinary gloss of
veracity. A white girl's accusation of her rape by a Negro causes a huge
upheaval that rocks 'the very old and tired town of Maycomb'. It all began
the summer when Scout was six and her brother Jem ten. We find the Finch

family caught in the storm of the white, popular reaction, but braving it all with remarkable steadfastness, courage and fortitude. The two motherless children and their father face the ordeal so heroically that it lifts the story from the probable melodramatic and sentimental doldrums and makes *To Kill a Mockingbird*, which is a winter's tale, a heroic one told in a lyric way. Apart from the mockingbird symbol which is pervasive, we have several other symbols. When it snows in Maycomb, after years and years, the county school declares a holiday, and we see the Finch children trying to make a snow-man. But there is more mud than snow:

> 'Jem, I ain't ever heard of a nigger snowman,' I said.
> 'He won't be black long', he grunted.

And he tries to cover it with some snow-flakes, making it white. But at night Miss Maudie's house is on fire, and Scout watches 'our absolute Morphodite go black and crumble'. The snowman turning alternately white and black suggests how frail and skin-deep is the colour. Besides, Miss Maudie's flowers, too, caught in the flames, symbolise innocence in the grip of fire. And as we see the yellow flames leaping up in a snowy, dark night we have the symbols of the white snow and the coloured flames standing for cold hatred and fiery wrath that might lead to the crack of the world as visualised by Robert Frost in his poem 'Fire and Ice'. Symbolism lends poetic touch to the novel that depicts not only the external world of action but also the internal world of character. For, here the novelist registers the impact of the central action not so much on the protagonist as on the others. Both Boo Radley locked in his own home for fifteen long years for some trifling adolescent pranks so that his father could find the vanity fair of the society congenial, and Tom Robinson sentenced to death for a rape he never committed, are kept as invisible as the crimes they never committed. Two such innocent victimisations paralleled with each other intensify the tragic view of the world and recall the terrifying prognosis: 'So shall the world go on: to good men malignant, to bad men benign.' What happens to the innocent victims, who are largely shut out from us like beasts in a cage, is really not as important as the way it stirs the world around. The novel that opens with the theme of persecution taking us back to the ancestor, Simon Finch, who sailed across the Atlantic to escape religious persecution in England, keeps the victims generally off the stage, invisible while the prolonged tensions between the protagonist minority and the antagonist majority shake the small world of Maycomb with an ever increasing emotional and moral disturbance. In this oblique handling of the central theme we have, what Virginia Woolf describes as 'a luminous halo, a semi-transparent envelope'. It is an effective artistic device. All this is presented through the fascinating, though disturbing, flash-backs, and the continual backthrust intensifies the unforgettableness of the narrator's experience.

Maycomb is a microcosm, and the novelist's creative fecundity has peopled it well. We have a cross-section of humanity: men and women, young and old, good and bad, white and black. *To Kill a Mockingbird* presents a memorable portrait gallery. Generally it is the evil characters that are better portrayed than the good, Satan rather than God. But Harper Lee's emotional and moral bias seems to put her more at ease with good people than bad. The wicked characters tend to be hazy whereas the good characters stand out prominently throbbing with life. Bob Ewell and his allies are just paper-figures. Again, the women in the novel are better delineated than the men, with the probable exception of Atticus. But her highest achievement in characterisation is manifest in children who at once spring to life. If the successful delineation of children characters is a mark of creative genius, Harper Lee has attained a notable success. Unlike her grown-up characters who easily tend to be caricatures seen in concave and convex mirrors, these children are wonderfully true to life. We have some most unforgettable vignettes. Here they are, trying to make Boo come out of the sombre Radley House:

> Jem said, 'Lemme think a minute ... it's a sort of like making a turtle come out...'
> 'How's that?' asked Dill.
> 'Strike a match under him...'
> Dill said striking a match under a turtle was hateful.
> 'Ain't hateful, just persuades him—.' Jem growled.
> 'How do you know a match don't hurt him?'
> 'Turtles can't feel, stupid,' said Jem.
> 'Were you ever a turtle, huh?'
> 'My stars, Dill: Now lemme think ...'

Or think of Dill getting sick of the trial and breaking down. It is Mr Raymond, the man 'who perpetrated fraud against himself by drinking Coca Cola in a whiskey bag' who says:

> 'Let him get a little older and he won't get sick and cry. Maybe things will strike him as being—not quite right, say, but he won't cry, not when he gets a few years on him.'

And we have the sad juxtaposition of the two worlds. We have children—Jem, Scout, Dill and the whole lot of them with an insatiable sense of wonder and curiosity. It is they who are bewildered by the ways of the grown-up world and confronted with the most disturbing problems like 'What exactly is a Nigger-lover Atticus?' 'What is rape, Cal?' When Tom Robinson is adjudged to be guilty, it is their young hearts that we see bleeding:

> I shut my eyes. Judge Taylor was polling the jury: 'Guilty ... guilty ... guilty ... guilty ...' I pecked at Jem: his hands were white from gripping the balcony rail, and his shoulders jerked as if each 'guilty' was a separate stab between them.

And here is Atticus, the defence counsel, the hero of the trial scene, but for whom the trial would have seemed as if out of Kafka's world. At least the phantasmal jury and the accusers all seem to have been people who should not have surprised even Joseph K. The trial was over, but not so the heartquakes of the young, although they knew, as Scout points out, 'in the secret courts of men's hearts Atticus had no case'.

> 'Atticus—' said Jem bleakly.
> He turned the door way. 'What, son?'
> 'How could they do it, how could they?'
> 'I don't know, but they did it. They've done it before and they did it tonight and they'll do it again, and when they do, it seems that only children will weep. Goodnight.'

Atticus is the protagonist, reticent, dignified and distant. When the entire white world seems to have lost its head, it is he who remains sane and firm. He is a wonderful combination of strength and tenderness. He is a stoic and can withstand the ostracism and persecution with almost superhuman courage and fortitude. He is a widower but treats his motherless children with so much affection and understanding that they call him 'Atticus'. They are about his only friends in a world in which he is lonely. It is in the trial scene that we see Atticus at his best, exposing the falsehood and meanness of the white world intent on destroying an innocent Negro. If Jean Scout, the daughter, keeps the wheel of the story turning, Atticus is the axle. He is a man who seems to have been made to approximate to Newman's idea of a gentleman. He never inflicts pain on others, but strives to relieve them of it even at the cost of his own and his children's suffering. It is a highly

idealised character. He stands up like a lighthouse, firm, noble, and mag-
nanimous.

But the children and Atticus, with a few other probable exceptions like
Calpurnia and Sheriff Tate, and the victims are about the only normal fold in
the novel. These Maycomb women are quite funny. They are the comic
characters in a tragic world; they play the chorus in the novel. Here is Aunt
Alexandra, 'analogous to Mount Everest .... she was cold and there', betraying the novelist's eye for the ridiculous:

> She was not fat, but solid, and she chose protective garments that
> drew up her bosom to giddy heights, inched in her waist, flared
> out her rear, and managed to suggest that Aunt Alexandra's was
> once an hour-glass figure. From any angle it was formidable.

We have 'Miss Stephanie Crawford, that English channel of gossip', and
Miss Dubose who was horrible: 'Her face was horrible. Her face was the
color of a dirty pillow-case, and the corners of her mouth glistened.' But
Calpurnia, the nurse, who reminds us of Dilsey in Faulkner's *The Sound and
the Fury*, and Miss Maudie are the only two women who have beneath their
tough exterior abundant humanity. Calpurnia, who leads a double-life, takes
Jem and Scout to the Negro church the way Dilsey takes Benjy to the Easter
service in Faulkner. Here we are in the church; the novelist has almost actually taken us in:

> The warm bitter sweet smell of clean Negro welcomed us as we
> entered the churchyard—Hearts of Love hair-dressing mingled
> with asafoetida, snuff, Hoyt's Cologne, Brown's Mule, pepper-
> mint, and lilac talcum.

But there is a counterpoint. Lula, a Negro, protests against the visit of the
white children; and Calpurnia retorts: 'It's the same God, ain't it?' Calpurnia
has brought up these motherless children. It is the persons like Atticus and
Calpurnia who try to bridge the chasm dividing the whites from the blacks.
But it is in Miss Maudie that we have a most remarkable woman. When her
house is burnt up, she replies to Jem with robust optimism: 'Always wanted
a smaller house, Jem Finch ... Just think, I'll have more room for my azaleas
now.' When the whole of Maycomb is madly excited over Tom's trial, without ever realising that it was not so much Tom as the white world on trial,
Miss Maudie does not lose her head: 'I am not. 'Tis morbid watching a poor
devil on trial for his life. Look at all those folks, it's like a Roman carnival.'

When children put all sorts of queer questions about Arthur Radley, she replies pat:

> 'Stephanie Crawford even told me, once she woke up in the middle of the night and found him looking in the window at her. I said what did you do, Stephanie, move over in the bed and make room for him? That shut her up awhile.'

She tells the Finch children:

> 'You are too young to understand it ... but sometimes the Bible in the hand of one man is worse than a whiskey bottle in the hand— oh, of your father.'

And here is the heart of the matter—the dichotomy between appearance and reality. Things are not what they seem. Both Arthur Radley and Tom Robinson, who are punished for no crimes they ever committed, are the representatives of all innocent victims. In fact, Radley stitching Jem's pants torn during the children's pranks against himself, leaving gifts for the children in the tree hole, throwing a blanket round Scout while she stood shivering in a dark, cold night watching the house on fire, and finally saving children's lives from the fatal attack of Bob Ewell, is more human than most of the Maycomb fold. He is not the blood-thirsty devil as pictured in the popular fantasy. And so is Tom, who was driven only by compassion to respond to Mayella's request for help. She had assaulted him. There was no rape. But in the court Bob Ewell shamelessly 'stood up and pointed his finger at Tom Robinson "I see that black nigger yonder ruttin' on my Mayella."' Ewell and evil are almost homophones. They are filthy parasites, a blot on society. This shows how culture has nothing to do with colour. The novelist's moral and emotional identification with the whole problem is so great that the verdict of the trial upsets her, too. For a moment she seems to be losing her grip on the story. The characters are on the brink of losing their identity, and the novelist, in her righteous anger, is on the point of reducing them to mere mouthpieces. For even the children stunned by the judgment fumble for words, and for a while the narrative is in danger of getting lost in the doldrums of discussion—dull, heavy, futile. This can be understood in the context of her having patterned the story after the model of a morality play with a distinct line of demarcation between good and evil, right and wrong, beautiful and ugly. Like Ewell, Cunningham, too, betrays his character through connotation. The finch, the family name of Atticus, means a songbird like

the mockingbird. It is the Finch family that pits itself against evil in defence
of good. Jem Calways (sounds like Gem) and Scout are names that do not fail
to evoke a sense of value and selfless service, whereas Jean, which is a variation of Joan, distantly clicks into our memory that angelical girl, Joan of Arc,
battling for a great cause.

To Kill a Mockingbird is a regional novel. Like Jane Austen, who does
not care to go beyond the district of Bath, or Thomas Hardy who hardly,
if ever, takes his story out of the confines of Wessex, Harper Lee sticks to
Maycomb in Alabama. The small world assumes a macrocosmic dimension and expands into immensity, holding an epic canvas against which is
enacted a movingly human drama of the jostling worlds—of children and
adults, of innocence and experience, of kindness and cruelty, of love and
hatred, of humour and pathos, and above all of appearance and reality—
all taking the reader to the root of human behaviour. Time does not have
a stop in Harper Lee's world, but it moves on lazily. The cycle of seasons
keeps on turning with the ever-returning summer, and life in Maycomb, 'a
tired old town', flows on in all its splendour and ugliness, joys and sor-
rows. Harper Lee, in her firm determination to keep away from the contemporary trend of experimentation without ever succumbing to the lure
of following the footsteps of novelists like Hemingway and Faulkner,
returns to the nineteenth century tradition of the well-made novel with
immense facility. If she at all betrays any influence, it is from the past
rather than the present—Jane Austen's morality and regionalism, Mark
Twain's blending of humour and pathos in the jostling worlds, Dickens's
humanitarianism and characterisation, Harriet Stowe's sentimental concern for the coloured folk. If by modernism we mean whatever that is anti-
traditional, Harper Lee is not a modern, though a contemporary novelist.
The contemporaneity of To Kill a Mockingbird is incidental, its universali-
ty essential. She tells the story with astonishing zest and yet a leisureliness
characteristic of the past age. For instance, about a century divides To Kill
a Mockingbird from Harriet Stowe's Uncle Tom's Cabin but there is no fundamental difference either about the content or the technique of the novels. In both we see an astonishing streak of sentimentality, an irresistible
love of melodrama and the same age-old pity for the underdog. But
Harper Lee has an unusual intensity of imagination which creates a world
more living than the one in which we live, so very solid, so easily recog-
nisable. It all looks so effortless, so very uncontrived. But it is painful to
see the way the harsh realities impinge mercilessly on the juvenile world
of innocence. Harper Lee has an intense ethical bias and there is about the
novel a definite moral fervour.

The novelist, in an unmistakable way, has viewed one of the most fundamental human problems with the essentially Christian terms of reference, and we see emerging from the novel a definite moral pattern embodying a scale of values. As we notice the instinctive humanising of the world of things we are also impressed by the way Harper Lee can reconcile art and morality. For *To Kill a Mockingbird* is not a work of propaganda, it is a work of art, not without a tragic view of life. The novelist has been able to combine humour and pathos in an astonishing way. But comedy and tragedy are, in the final analysis, two sides of the same coin. The novel bubbling with life and overflowing with human emotions is not without a tragic pattern involving a contest between good and evil. Atticus in his failure to defend the Negro victim, eventually hunted down while scaling the wall in quest of freedom, the innocent victim, and Arthur Boo, who is endowed with tender human emotions and compassion, but is nearly buried alive in the Radley House, which is a veritable sepulchre, simply because his father loved to wallow in the vanity fair, and the suffering Finch children, they all intensify the sense of waste involved in the eternal conflict. 'The hero of a tragedy,' observes Freud in *Totem and Taboo*, 'had to suffer; this is today still the essential content of a tragedy.' By that norm, *To Kill a Mockingbird* could be seen to hover on the frontier of a near-tragedy. The tragic mode is no longer a monopoly of the theatre. Like the epic that precedes it, the novel that succeeds it, too, can easily order itself into a comic or a tragic pattern. Particularly after the seventeenth century, tragedy seems to be steadily drifting towards the pocket theatre. *To Kill a Mockingbird* has the unity of place and action that should satisfy an Aristotle although there is no authority of the invisible here as in a Greek tragedy. With Atticus and his family at the narrative centre standing like a rock in a troubled sea of cruelty, hatred and injustice, we have an imitation of an action which is noble and of a certain magnitude. And the story, that is closed off on the melancholy note of the failure of good, also is not without its poetic justice through the nemesis that destroys the villain out to kill the Finch children. In fact, twice before the final catastrophe the story seems to be verging on its end. The first probable terminal is chapter twenty-one, when Tom is convicted and sentenced; the second is chapter twenty-six, when Tom is shot dead—not killed but set free from the coils of life, as it were—and there is nothing really left. But the novelist wants to bring the story to a rounded-off moral end. Like a symphony it starts off on a new movement after touching the lowest, almost inaudible key, and we have the crescendo of its finale. Here is exploration, or at least an honest attempt at exploration, of the whole truth which is lost in the polarities of life. But Harper Lee who lets us hear in the novel the 'still, sad music of humanity' is, immensely sentimental. Her love for melodrama is inexhaustible. Hence, although her view of human life is tragic, the treatment is sentimental, even melodramatic. However, though not a tragedy, it is since *Uncle Tom's Cabin* one of the most effective expressions of the voice of protest against the injustice to the Negro in the white world. Without militant championship of 'native sons' writing in a spirit of commitment, here is a woman novelist transmuting the raw material of the Negro predicament aesthetically. Like Jane Austen, Harper Lee is a moralist, and *To Kill a Mockingbird* almost approximates to Lionel Trilling's view on the novel:

> For our time the most effective agent of the moral imagination has been the novel of the last two hundred years. It was never, either aesthetically or morally, a perfect form ... But its greatness and its practical usefulness lay in its unremitting work of involving the reader himself in the moral life, inviting him to put his own motives under examination, suggesting that reality is not as his conventional education has led him to see it. It taught us, as no other genre ever did, the extent of human variety and the value of this variety. It was the literary form to which emotions of understanding and forgiveness were indigenous, as if by the definition of the form itself.
>
> (LIONEL TRILLING; *The Liberal Imagination*: London, 1951, p. 222)

As we read *To Kill a Mockingbird*, a thesis novel, we notice an unfailing moral order arising out of the flux of experience which is the evolution of human consciousness elaborated through the structure of events, without ever raising the age-old problem of art and morality. There is a complete cohesion of art and morality. And therein lies the novelist's success. She is a remarkable story-teller. The reader just glides through the novel abounding in humour and pathos, hopes and fears, love and hatred, humanity and brutality—all affording him a memorable human experience of journeying through sunshine and rain at once. *To Kill a Mockingbird* is indeed a criticism of life and that, too, a most disturbing criticism, but we hardly feel any tension between the novelist's creativity and social criticism and the tale of heroic struggle lingers in our memory as an unforgettable experience while its locale, Maycomb County—'*Ad Astra per Aspera*: from mud to the stars'—stretches itself beyond our everyday horizon as an old familiar world.

WILLIAM T. GOING

Store and Mockingbird:
Two Pulitzer Novels about Alabama

In 1933 and 1961, over a quarter of a century apart, T.S. Stribling's *The Store* and Harper Lee's *To Kill a Mockingbird* received one of the Pulitzer awards granted annually for distinguished fiction dealing preferably with the American scene. Placed side by side they comment revealingly not only on life in two of the state's small towns fifty years and three hundred miles apart but also on the changing techniques of Southern fiction.

Maycomb of 1932–1935, the county seat of Maycomb County, is the locale of *Mockingbird*. This fictional town is "some twenty miles east of Finch's Landing ... on the banks of the Alabama River" in the southwestern part of the state (Miss Lee somewhat obscures, intentionally or unintentionally, its exact location by mentioning a Saint Stephens river—"the Saint Stephens"— and implying that old Saint Stephens, the territorial capital of Alabama, was located on the Alabama River, when it actually stood on the Tombigbee). Monroeville, county seat of Monroe County and birthplace of Miss Lee, who is the same age as her heroine, Jean Louise Finch, is the model for Maycomb. The chief locale of *The Store* is Florence of 1884–1885 in the northwestern part of the state with a "long spindling bridge across [the] Tennessee" linking it with the rest of the state to the south.

The hub and center of both towns is the courthouse. In Maycomb the edifice, surrounded by live oaks, "sagged in the square"; it was of early

From *Essays on Alabama Literature*. © 1975 by William T. Going.

Victorian design with its south portico supported by Greek revival columns left over from "the original courthouse that burned in 1856." It is the setting for the climactic scene of Atticus Finch's defense of Tom Robinson, a Negro accused of the rape of a white woman. From the same balcony as Jean Louise, Miss Lee had watched her father, Amasa Lee, defend many a case. In Florence the courthouse, bordered by gnarled mulberry trees, is the setting for the opening chapters of *The Store*; here Governor Terry O'Shawn, former Florence lawyer, conducts a late summer rally for the candidacy of Grover Cleveland. Elevated "on the portico of the courthouse in the light of four oil lamps," the orator proclaims himself "a herald of a great Democrat and a great friend of the South." The final scene of the novel is also set on Courthouse Square. Colonel Vaiden "headed the stumbling mules into the Square. The crows swarmed around the gnarled mulberries along Intelligence Row. On three of these trees, in the center of the mob, swung three figures."

The oracles and keepers of local consciences in both towns are the editors of the newspapers: *The Florence Index* is owned and run by A. Gray Lacefield, scion of a family that once possessed a great plantation; in Maycomb Mr. Underwood, who lives across from the courthouse in rooms over his printing press, "had no use for any organization but *The Maycomb Tribune*, of which he was sole owner, editor, and printer." In both towns the social and spiritual life of Negroes and whites centers in churches. As for the whites, the Vaidens have changed their religion with the generations: old Simeon Vaiden of South Carolina had been converted to Methodism by Wesley himself, and his own son Jimmie was a hardshell Alabama Baptist, and his sons, Augustus and Miltiades, are Christian Campbellites. On a Sunday morning in 1884 in the bare interior, where his wife is the song leader without benefit of instrumental music, Augustus' mind follows the fortunes of a fly caught in a spider web; "he wondered if he had taken the hog its slop that morning." In Maycomb Auntie entertains her missionary circle, which always studies the Mrunas in darkest Africa, with elaborate refreshments of coffee, charlotte, and dewberry tarts. When Mr. Finch is attending the legislature in Montgomery, Calpurnia, the cook, takes the children to church with her. Here they make some marvelous discoveries: the Rev. Sykes locks the doors until the collection reaches the proper total to relieve the distress of Sister Robinson, and Zeebo, Calpurnia's son, lines out the hymns.

"Yeah, it's called linin'. They've done it that way as long as I can remember."

Jem said it looked like they could save the collection money for a year and get some hymn-books.
Calpurnia laughed. "Wouldn't do any good," she said. They can't read.... Can't but about four folks in First Purchase read.... I'm one of 'em."

Both communities have an interest in their educational institutions. Jean Louise, known to all as Scout, begins the first grade in Maycomb's public schools. Since Miss Caroline is a new teacher and from Winston County in north Alabama, which "in 1861 ... seceded from Alabama," she must be educated about the social strata of Maycomb. After she has been shocked by the dirt and cooties of Burris Ewell, Little Chuck Little, a perennial first-grader, comforts her: "Now don't you be afraid, you just go back to your desk and teach us some more." Scout learns to her consternation that she is not yet ready to read, though she has long enjoyed the *Mobile Register* while sitting in her father's lap in the evenings; she must also stop the writing Calpurnia has taught her on rainy days: "We don't write in the first grade, we print."

Miltiades Vaiden's nephew Jerry Catlin has come to Florence from his home in Tennessee to attend the Normal School, just as young Stribling did at the turn of the century. Jerry, who has been reading Ingersoll, refuses to attend compulsory chapel and learns some of the social cruelties operative on a small campus when Florence opinion reacts unfavorably to his uncle's cotton theft.

It is already apparent that the two novels concern family life. The Vaiden place, with its large log house near Connor's Landing and Waterloo, is presided over by Miltiades' spinster sister Cassandra, now that Augustus and Miltiades have moved to Florence, Marcia to Tennessee, Sylvester to Arkansas, and Lycurgus to Louisiana, Polycarp having died in 1865. But memories of old man Jimmie Vaiden and his forge still linger. In *Mockingbird* the home plantation at Finch's Landing on the Alabama is now run by Atticus's sister Alexandra and her husband. Memories of the family founder, old Simon Finch, the apothecary from Cornwall who had practiced medicine in Saint Stephens, still haunt the children's minds when they return to the Landing at Christmas. The mature Jean Louise, who is the story's narrator, now believes that everything goes back to Andrew Jackson, because if he "hadn't run the Creeks up the creek, Simon Finch would never have paddled up the Alabama." Though *Mockingbird* is involved with fewer characters and is not a part of a trilogy like *The Store*, it too conveys a sense of the family generations of the past.

Both T.S. Stribling and Harper Lee studied law at the University of
Alabama, and Stribling practiced a few years in Florence. For this reason as
well as for the excitement inherent in the American legal system where a
trial, unlike the European system, is a kind of contest with the judge as ref-
eree, both of these novels take on a heightened interest at the prospect of
legal action. Jem and Scout in *Mockingbird*, being children of a lawyer whose
wife has been dead some time, manifest great enthusiasm for courts of law
and principles of justice; Scout requires a legal explanation of the Alabama
concept of rape, and Jem learns to read his father's face in the courtroom.
Both children know that Tom Robinson has been condemned when they see
the jury file in and never once look Tom in the eye. But without question
Atticus's defense of Tom is a challenging appeal to all that is noble and right.
The Negroes who sit in the courtroom balcony pay him the silent tribute of
standing as he leaves the room. Scout, who has fallen asleep after she and Jem
slipped up to the colored balcony, is awakened by the Rev. Sykes, "Miss Jean
Louise, stand up. Your father's passin'."

The Store is complicated with many legal entanglements. The merchant
J. Handback took in twenty-five bales of cotton from the Vaidens in 1865 on
the very day he sought refuge in bankruptcy. Colonel Miltiades, after he had
gained the confidence of the merchant in 1884, appropriates five hundred
bales and sends them down the Tennessee to New Orleans via Cairo to collect his debt, rationalizing about the value of cotton in 1865 and the interest
he would have made on such a fortune during the intervening years. The
Colonel is brought to court for disturbing the peace when he and Handback
fight over the matter, but the case becomes highly involved when Handback
and the sheriff search his house for the money without due process and
thereby cause his wife Ponny, who knows nothing of these complicated
affairs, to give premature birth to a child and die. Finally on the day of the
Presidential election, the Colonel agrees to pay the Handbacks $10,000 as
"their full legal residue in the proceeds of said cotton [$48,751.37]"; in return
they will not proceed with a criminal prosecution against him lest he counter with a suit involving search without warrant and maluse. All of these tech-
nicalities are encouraged by Mr. Sandusky, a young man who reads law in
Governor O'Shawn's office and boards at Augustus Vaiden's.

The final episode of the novel that leads indirectly to Toussaint's lynching is caused by another legal tangle over the loss of a deed to the Lacefield
plantation that forces the Colonel to sell the mules and farm implements of
his Negro sharecroppers. But Toussaint Vaiden, descended from the Negro
stock on the old Vaiden place, is urged to legal recourse by his "educated"
wife Lucy and goes to court on the premise of a breach of the contract to see

him through the present cotton-growing season. The case goes before Judge Abernathy's chancery court with Toussaint being represented by the opportunist Sandusky, and Miltiades by the Governor himself, who says: "I consider this case so important, so constructive, so grave that it falls under the head of state papers, gentlemen. I will stop this kind of petty persecution of white landowners by Negro tenants permanently, I trust."

Not only do these novels reach climaxes in courtroom scenes; both contain characters involved in state politics and government. Atticus Finch is a state legislator: he is always reelected without opposition even though Maycomb County disapproves some of his forward-looking concepts of justice. He is the Governor's chief support during some of the emergency sessions of the depression when "there were sit-down strikes in Birmingham; bread lines in the cities grew longer, people in the county grew poorer." In *The Store* Gracie, a mulatto half-sister of Miltiades, is the mistress of the Reconstruction Governor Beekman and lives briefly in the Governor's mansion in Montgomery. When Governor O'Shawn fails to persuade the mob from their lynching, he obtains a reprieve until the four-o'clock train can take him out of Florence before the lynching occurs, thus leaving his reputation untarnished.

It is already evident from the incidents cited that Negroes play considerable roles in both novels. Calpurnia in *Mockingbird* and Gracie in *The Store* are fully developed characters. Both have long been associated with their respective white families, and both have been taught to read and write. Calpurnia is servant as well as mother to Jean Louise, who is given moral precepts whenever she asks questions like, "Why do you talk nigger-talk to the—to your folks when you know it's not right?" Cal replies: "It's right hard to say .... It's not necessary to tell all you know. It's not ladylike—in the second place, folks don't like to have somebody around knowin' more than they do."

Gracie has intuitive instincts and deep loyalties to the Vaiden family. When she is entrusted with the Colonel's $48,000 to hide from J. Handback, who comes to visit her on Saturday nights, she never hesitates nor does she question the Colonel's motives.

Negro characters also play minor roles in both novels. Zeebo, the town garbage collector, and the Rev. Sykes in *Mockingbird*—Fo' Spot, the river roustabout, and the Rev. Lump Mobray in *The Store*—are examples. In the latter Tony, Gracie's neighbor, exercises her motherly instincts as well as the small means available to her for getting her children trained for life. After her daughter Pammy Lee is suspected of becoming too familiar with young Jerry at Miss Drusilla's where she works, Tony admonishes:

"Well, you ain't goin' back to Miss Drusilla's no mo' aftah this, Pammy Lee.... you's a woman now. You's worth mo'n fifty cents a week. I'm gwi' sta't out in de mownin', lookin' fuh a place wid mo' pay fuh you. I'se gwi' send Jinny Lou up to Miss Dru's in yo' place ... an' let huh lea'n [her] to cook."

The poor whites who are either tenant farmers or ne'er-do-wells are usually jealous of the industrious Negroes near them. In both novels these men are the actual villains. It is true that the Colonel in *The Store* opposes "educating niggers" and that he treats them like children—his own children whom he can command at will—but he does not cheat them, short change them, and abuse them as does J. Handback. The merchant, however, is not overtly cruel as is Cady, the ignorant, shiftless sharecropper who burns the little Negro schoolhouse and leads the mob in lynching Toussaint. Ewell, who lives near the town dump in Maycomb, is the same type of character; he is frustrated by a decent Negro like Tom Robinson, and he forces his daughter Mayella to swear to lies, just as Cady forces his wife and daughter to support him in his feud against Toussaint. And this bottom rail of Southern society goes to even greater lengths of hate in both novels. Ewell finally tries to murder Atticus's children on a dark Halloween night, but he is prevented by Boo Radley, who happens to be lurking in the shadows. The Cadys in 1885 are more successful: they burn and lynch, and in the sequel, *Unfinished Cathedral*, it is Cady's son who dynamites part of that structure that kills Miltiades.

Because Maycomb was a "tired old town" in 1932 with its "streets turned to red slop" in rainy weather with "grass ... on the sidewalks," its outlook and social patterns seem little different from Florence of 1884. These were times of "vague optimism": "Maycomb County had recently been told that it had nothing to fear but fear itself." Something of the same tone pervaded Florence a half century earlier: many believed that "we're going to have a period of fine business" under Cleveland, that "great Democrat and great friend of the South." For this reason the background of the two novels seems quite similar. True, the fashionable "hug-me-tight" buggy of J. Handback had given way to Maycomb's Fords and Chevrolets; an alert, respected citizen with a little innocent help from his daughter could stop a lynching in 1935, when a Governor could not in 1885. But the fate of the Negro in each case was death: the South moved slowly.

Despite this similarity of small-town background *The Store* and *To Kill a Mockingbird* are quite different books. In *The Store*, according to the publishers, Doubleday, Doran, and Company, "Mr. Stribling took upon himself the task of painting a real picture of the South, and the North as it influenced the South, precisely as all these different forces were, and not as one might wish them to be." The novel is the middle member of a trilogy concerned with "Family History and the Destiny of a Nation," the other two being *The Forge* (the Vaidens during the Civil War) and *Unfinished Cathedral* (Miltiades as a wealthy twentieth-century banker). As Stribling himself has stated; his aim in the novels was historical: "Each generation quickly and completely forgets its forebears. I was filled with a profound sense of tragedy that my own family, my neighbors, the whole South surrounding one would be utterly lost in the onrushing flood of years. History will not rescue it from oblivion because history is too general to be human and too remote to be real."

To achieve so large a tapestry Stribling resorts to a heavily plotted novel. There are at least three separate, ingeniously dovetailed, struggles in *The Store*. The central plot belongs to Miltiades: his efforts to own a store like Handback's so that he may control plantations and sharecroppers, and thus restore a way of life that existed before the war. And in order to achieve this end he must have an antebellum home and an aristocratic wife. Though Miltiades succeeds relatively soon in breaking Handback's prowess by his bold cotton theft and public rationalization of collecting an old debt, his success leads him to the same sort of land-poor tyranny that Handback suffered, and it is not until the very end of the novel that the Colonel is accidentally saved from financial ruin, from the machinations of Handback's son, and from Sandusky's litigious subterfuges by the sudden discovery of the actual deeds that give him clear title to the Lacefield place.

To provide the proper setting for his financial comeback the Colonel seeks to marry his old sweetheart, Drusilla Lacefield Crowninshield, who jilted him before the war. Believing that Miltiades never really loved her so much as he loved the Lacefield name and that her daughter Sydna cherishes a kind of father-lover image in Miltiades, Drusilla refuses him. Nevertheless, the Colonel marries Sydna instead of her mother, and he sets about replacing the old square wooden columns on the Crowninshield "manor" with round stone ones.

The second plot belongs to Gracie, the mulatto half-sister of the Colonel, who is also the mother of his son Toussaint, whom the Colonel believes is the illegitimate son of the carpet-bag Governor Beekman. She is also the mistress of J. Handback, who has built her the little house in East Florence that he visits regularly. Gracie's loyalties are torn between family ties to the Vaidens and gratitude to Handback, who ultimately offers her marriage and escape to Louisiana, where she and Toussaint can pass as French or Caribbean. When she refuses because she has been too much involved with Miltiades' cotton theft, she foregoes her life-long wish to find a way to educate Toussaint and to take him out of a Negro environment. Handback commits suicide, but Gracie goes on struggling. Toussaint marries Lucy Lacefield, an "educated" Negro girl whose parents still live on the old Lacefield place; Gracie is installed by Miltiades in the Lacefield manor house where she, Toussaint, and Lucy farm on shares. At last their struggle with the Negro-hating Cady leads indirectly to Toussaint's suing Miltiades and the subsequent lynching, after which Gracie and Lucy flee north to the Ohio on the *Rapidan*, aided by Fo' Spot, who is rousting on the boat.

Nor is this all. A third plot belongs to Miltiades' nephew Jerry, who reads Ingersoll and studies Yoga: he is in love with Sydna Crowninshield, a few years his senior. His struggles to express his love as well as to maintain his anti-religious convictions at Florence Normal mark him a Vaiden. His roommate at Mrs. Rose Vaiden's boarding-house is O'Shawn's law clerk, Sandusky, whose rabid pursuit of legal complications links Jerry with all the other plots of the novel.

It has been necessary to outline these plots in order to demonstrate that even in a novel of 571 closely printed pages little additional action can be compressed within its scope. Stribling has always been skillful in designing and interweaving patterns of struggle. His long interest in adventure and detective fiction is evident. Even in his serious novels that preceded *The Store* Stribling uses many of the features dear to nineteenth-century novelists: withholding of relevant information until a more dramatic moment, designing "teasers" to entice the reader to the next chapter, and straining probability in the attempt to enmesh plot within plot. Such devices usually succeed with a first reading, but for the second they impede as well as reveal other weaknesses.

The chief of these—often the fault of all but the best historical fiction—is the lack of character motivation. Despite the numerous characters in *The Store*, only two are well drawn, Miltiades and Gracie. The others are interesting, at times vivid and picturesque, pathetic or amusing, but they are painted paper and cannot be turned sideways, cannot be questioned. Enough has already been said about Gracie and Miltiades to suggest the variety of situations they find themselves in. Though they seem living people whose problems can be vicariously shared, their motives for action are not always clear. An example at the beginning and end of the novel will illustrate this contention. When J. Handback mistakes Miltiades for the hardware drummer Bivins after Governor O'Shawn's speech for Cleveland, he asks the Colonel if he would mind delivering a message to Bivins at the hotel. When the Colonel inquires why he doesn't deliver it himself, Handback replies that Bivins would try to sell him more items than he needs. Apparently satisfied with this explanation from his old enemy, Miltiades agrees, and from this slim thread of a beginning the Colonel gains a position in Handback's store, steals his cotton and ultimately wrecks the merchant. This action on the part of both men who mortally hate each other is highly improbable. Since both have a sardonic fear of each other, the more one sees of their subsequent actions the less likely does he feel that either man would have been motivated to react in this way at this moment.

At the end of the novel, Gracie, who has always wanted to take Toussaint out of the Deep South and has never liked the idea of his marriage to the Negro Lucy, leaves on the *Rapidan* with her. Why we are never told. Gracie's journey is apparently financed by Fo' Spot, a Negro she never cared for. The reader is left to supply whatever motivation he can come by. Perhaps her deep grief for Toussaint is enough to drive her away. But Gracie never acts impulsively, and the terrifying final scene is almost ruined by this tag end of unmotivated action.

The host of minor characters in the novel—Landers, the Republican postmaster; Ponny, Miltiades' first wife; Captain Dargan of the *Zebulon D*; Bradley, the real estate agent; and Negroes like Andy, the porter at the Florence Hotel—are vivid and momentarily convincing. Stribling's ability to sketch a portrait in brief dialogue and pictorial gesture is impressive. But the lack of motivation for his main characters is often hidden behind this gallery of minor portraits and the onrush of events.

Perhaps his concern with the complexities of action also betrays Stribling in the realm of ideas just as it does in his character motivation. Robert Penn Warren in an essay, "T.S. Stribling: a Paragraph in the History of Critical Realism," points out that when this novelist turns from the contemporary to the historical scene, he brings along with him his same set of ideas and his same concepts of sociology. "For him almost any young white man who does not live in a large city is a hobbledehoy," like Jerry Catlin. Religion is a somewhat "greasy" affair; "it is impossible for a person to be devout without, at the same time, being a fool," like Augustus Vaiden and his pious, fussy wife Rose. In regard to race Stribling always brings "into collusion a noble Negro, or rather a mixed-breed, and a white society considerably less than noble." This is the theme of *Birthright*, dealing with a Harvard-educated Negro who returns to his native Tennessee, and it is a theme of *The Store*, dealing with Gracie, Toussaint, and Lucy.

There is nothing wrong with the thematic idea—it is surely a valid one—but Stribling in isolating it for examination glosses over the basic historical situation in the South of 1884: the real problems of how to handle the franchise, how to solve the shift in the labor scene, or how to replace the social pattern of the plantation. It is true that *The Store* touches on these issues, but always to the same purpose: except for a brutality and stupidity peculiar to the Southern white man, Stribling would have us believe that all these problems would have been solved long ago. A city, preferably a northern one, would immediately save Jerry from being a country hick, and there Toussaint and Gracie would already have been free and equal. In Stribling's pantheon there are no equitable Southern white men. They are all rather like J. Handback, who believes that a pound for a nigger is twelve ounces, or like Miltiades Vaiden, who would prolong the peonage of the plantation through the benign dictatorship of the store.

In other words, Stribling vitiates much of his fictional validity because he bends his characters to fit his ideas, and for this reason they never seem properly real. Stribling had read his V.L. Parrington, H.L. Mencken, and Sinclair Lewis too uncritically. Or, to put the matter another way, he reflects too unquestioningly the prevailing attitude of American liberalism of the 1920's.

Two additional traits combine in *The Store* to make it seem brittle and superficial. The point of view is nowhere artistically useful, and the style is often a kind of hasty journalese. Basically the omniscient perspective controls his narrative, but Stribling's delight in the short paragraph and pointed dialogue plunges the reader into an immediacy that is jarringly broken with regularity. When Miltiades rushes to Gracie's house to rescue his $48,000, he discovers that $300 is missing.

> "What did you take it for?" trembled the Colonel.
> "For—for Miss Ponny, Colonel Milt," breathed the woman.
> "Ponny! Ponny! What did Ponny want with three ..."
> "Oh Mas' Milt!" gasped Gracie, "to buy a coffin ... to buy a coffin for her and her little baby ......"
> And the quadroon began weeping, with a faint gasping sound, battling against her emotions like a white woman.

No valid objection can be made to the omniscient perspective, long a favorite with generations of storytellers. Sinclair Lewis, Stribling's mentor, often uses it with striking effect as in *Babbitt* where he begins a series of sections with the phrase, "At this moment in Zenith...." The trouble with

Stribling's use of the perspective is that he wants the best of the two worlds of godlike omniscience and of first-person immediacy both at the same time. Despite these faults that doubtless seem more obvious today than in the rather lean literary years of the early 1930's, *The Store* has a certain enduring vitality. In addition to a galloping narrative that does not entirely bolt into bypaths of improbabilities as is the case with *Unfinished Cathedral*, the novel has many moments that preserve the way of small-town life in Alabama and at the same time explicate a thematic concept. When Sydna is discussing the difficulty of understanding northerners, she says:

> "I can't possibly understand the taste of Yankees."
> "Why, darling, of course you can't," agreed Drusilla; "they're tradespeople."
> "Mother ... Colonel Milt runs a store!"
> "My dear, Miltiades has to run a store to keep his business going. It's not because he wants to run a store.... By the way, have you ever been in his store, Sydna?"
> "No, I haven't."
> "Well, it's a sight, and I consider that a great honor to the keeper, because it shows that he doesn't care a thing in the world about the store as a store."

When Stribling wrote *The Store*, he was fifty; he had taught school, practiced law, traveled widely, worked on several newspapers and magazines; he had written quantities of journalistic material, adventure stories, detective fiction, and at least five novels that had received considerable critical attention: *Birthright* (1922), *Teeftallow* (1926), *Bright Metal* (1928), *Backwater* (1930), and *The Forge* (1931). When Harper Lee wrote *To Kill a Mockingbird*, she was in her early thirties; she had studied law at the University of Alabama, worked in the reservation department of an international airline, and spent most of her time in New York recollecting the South and learning to write. She had worked hard on her first novel, which was some three years "churning through the editorial mills of the house of Lippincott," reported *News-Week*. The aspiring author had quit her desk job and "hived up" in a cold-water flat. The result is a remarkable achievement.

One of the things about Stribling that disturbed Robert Penn Warren in 1934 when he was writing about the new Pulitzer Prize winner was that the author "has never been interested in the dramatic possibilities of a superior white man brought into conflict with his native environment," a matter that has challenged many serious Southern novelists like William Faulkner and Caroline Gordon. A quarter of a century later Miss Lee has done precisely that for the Alabama scene. Even though it is usually easier to write about the spectacular, wicked man, Miss Lee has chosen the more difficult task of writing about the quiet, good man. Other novelists have been concerned with this type of man—the thoughtful, well-educated Southerner at quiet odds with his environment like the minor character Gavin Stevens in Faulkner's *Intruder in the Dust*. But Miss Lee has made him the central figure and hero of her novel and succeeded at the same time in writing an exciting and significant story.

The epigraph from Charles Lamb—"Lawyers, I suppose, were once children"—indicates the two aspects of *Mockingbird*, childhood and the law. The plot can be simply stated: Atticus Finch, one of Maycomb's leading attorneys, is the court-appointed defender of Tom Robinson, accused of raping Mayella Ewell, a daughter of the town's notorious poor white-trash family. In this struggle he is unsuccessful—at least the all-white jury finds Tom guilty, and he is killed escaping from prison before Atticus can gain a hearing on the appeal. But to a certain extent the case is not altogether lost; certain precedents have been set. Instead of a young lawyer who defends only for the record's sake Judge Taylor appoints a distinguished lawyer who chooses to fight obvious lies and racial hatred so that he and his children—and ultimately Maycomb itself—can remain honest and honorable people. No one except Atticus Finch ever kept a jury out so long on a case involving a Negro. And in the process of the trial Atticus's children have matured in the right way—at least in his eyes.

The struggle of the children toward maturity, however, occupies more space than Atticus's struggle to free Tom, the central episode. Through their escapades and subsequent entanglements with their father and neighbors like Miss Maudie Atkinson, Mrs. Henry Lafayette Dubose, and particularly the legends about Boo Radley, the town's boogie man, Jem and Scout learn what it means to come to man's estate. In Part I, an evocation of the happy days of summer play, the process is begun. With their friend Dill Harris from Meridian they enact the weird stories about Boo Radley—how he sits in his shuttered house all day and wanders about in the shadows of night looking in people's windows, how he once drove the scissors into his father's leg, how as a not-too-bright adolescent he had terrorized the county with a "gang" from Old Sarum. Might he even be dead in that solemn, silent house, the children wonder. Miss Maudie gives, as always, a forthright answer to that question: "I know he's alive, Jean Louise, because I haven't seen him carried out yet." Although Atticus forbids these "Boo Radley" games, the children go on playing—Scout being Mrs. Radley, who sweeps the porch and screams that Arthur (Boo's real name) is murdering them all with the scissors, Dill being old Mr. Radley, who walks silently down the street and coughs whenever he is spoken to, and Jem being the star actor, Boo himself as "he went under the front steps and shrieked and howled from time to time."

In the midst of these juvenile Gothic masques the children begin to learn something about the difference between gossip and truth. When Jem tears his pants and is forced to leave them behind on the wire fence during their night expedition to peek through the Radleys' shutters, he later finds them crudely mended, pressed, and hanging over the fence. When Miss Maudie's house burns during a cold night, all the neighborhood turns out to help and to watch. Scout, who is told to come no closer than the Radleys' gate, discovers that during the confusion a blanket has been thrown round her shoulders. Jem realizes that this thoughtful act was not performed by Mr. or Mrs. Radley, who have long been dead, and he saw Mr. Nathan, Boo's brother and "jailer," helping haul out Miss Maudie's mattress. It could have been only Boo.

One of the most interesting features of *Mockingbird* is the skill with which Miss Lee weaves these two struggles about childhood and the law together into one thematic idea. Like Stribling she does a neat workmanlike job of dovetailing her plots. When Scout attends her first day at school, the morning session is devoted to explaining the Cunningham family to Miss Caroline so that she will understand why she must not lend Walter any lunch money. The Cunninghams are poor but proud. When the Sunday night lynching party arrives at the jail, it is Jem and Scout, who, having slipped off from home, see their father calmly reading a newspaper by the light at the jail door, sitting in one of his office chairs. Hiding in the doorway of the Jitney Jungle, Scout rushes forward in time to disconcert the Cunningham mob by asking innocent questions about Walter, her classmate—her father had always taught her to talk to folks about the things that would interest them.

The afternoon session of Scout's first day at school had been taken up with Burris Ewell and his dirt and defiance of Miss Caroline. It is Burris's father who brings the charge of rape against Tom Robinson.

This neatness that makes for economy of character portrayal is successful when it avoids the appearance of too convenient coincidental circumstances—a fault that *Mockingbird* does not entirely escape. But in the more important aspect of thematic development the novel is successful. Carson McCullers and Truman Capote have written with insight about Southern childhood, and William Faulkner has traced the legal and moral injustices done the Negro just as Eudora Welty has underlined the quiet patience of the Negro's acceptance of his bleak world. Harper Lee has united these two concepts into the image of a little child—schooled in basic decencies by her father even though "ladylike" manners of the superficial sort that Aunt Alexandra admires are sometimes lacking—who turns the tide to stop the Sunday night lynching. After the trial when Jem cannot comprehend the injustice done Tom Robinson by the jury, he asks his father, "How could they do it, how could they?" Atticus replies, "I don't know, but they did it. They've done it before and they did it tonight and they'll do it again and when they do it—seems that only the children weep."

Almost all readers will agree that the first two-thirds of *Mockingbird* is excellent fiction; the difference of opinion will probably turn upon the events after the trial. The major incident here is the school pageant about the history of Maycomb County as written by Mrs. Merriweather; the performance is the town's attempt at "organized activity" on Halloween. On their way home from the pageant, Ewell attacks the Finch children to get even with Atticus for making him appear a complete and guilty fool at Tom's trial. Scout is saved from the knife by her wire costume representing a Maycomb County ham; Jem receives a painful broken arm. And Ewell is killed with his own knife by Boo Radley, who again lurks opportunely in the shadows. Later that night after visits from the doctor and the sheriff when Scout is allowed to walk home with Mr. Arthur, she stands for a moment on the Radley porch seeing the knothole in the tree where Boo had once left them pitiful little presents of chewing gum and Indian-head pennies. She half realizes as a child of nine, and now as an adult she more fully realizes, what their childish antics must have meant to a lonely, "imprisoned," mentally limited man like Mr. Arthur, and she recalls her father's word to Jem that "you never really know a man until you *stand* in his shoes and walk around in them. Just standing on the Radley porch was enough."

Thematically the aftermath of the injustice done Tom and the growing up of a boy and girl are brought together in the Halloween episode. The structural problem of joining Boo Radley and Tom Robinson into some sort of juxtaposition is solved, but the slapstick comedy of the school pageant and the grotesque coincidental tragedy and subsequent salvation are perilously close to the verge of melodrama—the same sort of melodrama that blights the novels of Stribling. To keep this section of *Mockingbird* from seeming altogether an anticlimax to the trial of Tom, it should at least have been denominated Part III. Then the story would have been set off into its three components of School and Summer Play, Tom Robinson's Trial, and Halloween Masquerade. Such a device would distribute the thirty-one chapters into the equal grouping of Miss Lee's apparent planning, and at the same time it would not force the Halloween tragi-comedy to seem quite so close to the climactic trial.

It is strange that the structural *forte* of *Mockingbird*, the point of view of the telling, is either misunderstood or misinterpreted by most of the initial reviewers of the novel. Phoebe Adams in the *Atlantic Monthly* calls it "frankly and completely impossible, being told in the first person by a six-year-old girl with the prose and style of a well-educated adult." Richard Sullivan in the *Chicago Tribune* is puzzled and only half understands: "The unaffected young narrator uses adult language to render the matter she deals with, but the point of view is cunningly restricted to that of a perceptive, independent child, who doesn't always understand fully what's happening, but who conveys completely, by implication, the weight and burden of the story." More careful reviewers like Granville Hicks in the *Saturday Review* and F.H. Lyell in the *New York Times* are more perceptive. The latter states the matter neatly: "Scout is the narrator, reflecting in maturity on childhood events of the mid-Thirties."

Maycomb and the South, then, are all seen through the eyes of Jean Louise, who speaks from the mature and witty vantage of an older woman recalling her father as well as her brother and their childhood days. This method is managed with so little ado that the average reader slips well into the story before he realizes that the best evidence that Atticus has reared an intellectually sophisticated daughter is that she remembers her formative years in significant detail and then narrates them with charm and wisdom. She has become the good daughter of a good man, who never let his children know what an expert marksman he was until he was forced to kill a mad dog on their street. Atticus did not like to shoot for the mere sport of it lest he kill a mockingbird like Tom Robinson or Boo Radley; and mockingbirds must be protected for their songs' sake.

This modification of a Jamesian technique of allowing the story to be seen only through the eyes of a main character but to be understood by the omniscient intelligence of Henry James is here exploited to bold advantage. The reader comes to learn the true meaning of Maycomb through the eyes of a child who now recollects with the wisdom of maturity. Along with Scout and Jem we may at first be puzzled why Atticus insists that Jem read every afternoon to old Mrs. Henry Lafayette Dubose in atonement for his cutting the tops off her camellia bushes after she taunted him about his father's being "no better than the niggers and trash he works for." But we soon learn with Scout that Atticus believed Jem would become aware of the real meaning of courage when he was forced to aid a dying old woman in breaking the narcotic habit she abhorred.

Jean Louise's evolving perception of the social milieu in her home town
as she grows up in it and as she recalls her own growing up involves the reader in an understanding of the various strata of Maycomb society and its
Southern significance. After Jem has brooded about the trial, he explains to
Scout that

> There's four kinds of folks in the world. There's the ordinary kind
> like us and the neighbors, there's the kind like the Cunninghams
> out in the woods, the kind like the Ewells down at the dump, and
> the Negroes.
>   "What about the Chinese, and the Cajuns down yonder in
> Baldwin County?"
>   "I mean in Maycomb County. The thing about it is, our kind
> of folks don't like the Cunninghams, and the Cunninghams don't
> like the Ewells, and the Ewells hate and despise the colored
> folks."
>   I told Jem if that was so, then why didn't Tom's jury, made up
> of folks like the Cunninghams, acquit Tom to spite the Ewells?

After considerable debate Scout concludes, "Naw, Jem, I think there's just
one kind of folks. Folks."

This naively sophisticated sociological rationalization is far more valid
and persuasive in its two-pronged approach. As mature readers we realize its
mature validity; as observers of children we delight in their alert reactions to
the unfolding events. The convolutions of the "mind of Henry James" have
given way to the immediacy and pithy wisdom of Jean Louise's first-person
narration.

Though Miss Lee may not have solved all her problems of style in the
dual approach of child eyes and mature heart, *Mockingbird* demonstrates the
powerful effect and economy of a well-conceived point of view as opposed to
the discursive, shifting omniscience of *The Store*. With the passage of years
from 1933 to 1961 James, Joyce, and Faulkner have been archetypical in
shaping perspectives for both writers and readers of fiction.

Neither Harper Lee nor T.S. Stribling is a novelist of innovations.
Stribling borrows heavily from the popular methods of Lewis and
Hergesheimer, and creates in *The Store* an Alabama panorama, lusty and
lurid, of the 1880's. Superficial in its sociology as well as in its narrative techniques, it nevertheless demonstrates the virile power of the tale of action in
a wealth of realistic background of gaslight, carriages, and pistols. In the
same year as *The Store* Faulkner published *Light in August*, also the story of a

man of mixed breed in conflict with the thoughtful and thoughtless society around him. Faulkner has shown the way for Southern fiction to grapple with its deep problems of race conflict. And William March later in the 1930's and the 1940's has called attention on the Alabama scene to the whole untapped reservoir of the average man—the shopkeepers and farmers around Reedyville—the people "like us," as Jem says.

Miss Lee, in a sense, has actually revealed more of Alabama history from the Simon Finches of old Saint Stephens to distrusted Republicans like the Misses Barber from Clanton than does Stribling in his much longer historical novel. The spirit of history is as important as the events of history, and Miss Lee presents Miss Caroline as an outsider from Winston County because she represents to this Maycomb community what every South Alabama child knew about north Alabama: a place "full of Liquor Interests, Big Mules, steel companies, Republicans, professors, and other persons of no background." Miss Lee has mastered an eclectic technique of a meaningful point of view along with validity of idea and freshness of material. She echoes Faulkner in her deep concern for the inchoate tragedy of the South, and like him she is not afraid to pursue the Gothic shadows of Edgar Allan Poe. But her eclecticism is her own: she has told a story of racial injustice from the point of view of thoughtful children with "open, unprejudiced, well-furnished minds of their own," as the *New York Times* has phrased it. And in Atticus Finch she has created the most memorable portrait in recent fiction of the just and equitable Southern liberal.

The symbols of *store* and *mockingbird* are true symbols of the South. The economy of the plantations was swallowed up in the economy of the store. But Timrod's mockingbird, creature of the strong and gentle song that rightly heard can save the land from its inbred violence, is a symbol at once more profound and poignant.

COLIN NICHOLSON

Hollywood and Race:
To Kill a Mockingbird

Nothing, it would seem, could be much faster than the ability of the reader's eye to move across the printed page, processing linguistic information, absorbing it and 'staging' it in the imagination. Almost instantaneously, the mind decodes the words on the page, translating complex messages into images, into imagined events. On the cinema screen, however, things move even faster. The viewer encounters several sign systems at once. These include spoken language, musical accompaniment and pictorial event and the viewer is bombarded with additional modes of communication. Novel readers thus exercise much greater control over their responses, and over the time taken to digest and respond to them, than do film spectators.

In the case of the literary and filmic texts of *To Kill a Mockingbird*, these differences of pace and control are in some ways intensified. Harper Lee's celebrated novel of the American South is leisurely, reasoned and reflective. As directed by Robert Mulligan, the film of the book moves with considerable speed, selecting and compressing incidents into a relatively short running time, so that several themes developed in the narrative space of the novel are necessarily compressed in the film's option to concentrate upon the central theme of racial hostility towards blacks by Southern whites. In the novel there are repeated image-patterns and themes which provide a context and a sense of depth for this central concern of racial prejudice. The

From *Cinema and Fiction: New Modes of Adapting, 1950–1990.* © 1992 by Edinburgh University Press.

care with which a family history is integrated into a wider sense of the history of the Southern States: the theme of family relationships, of journeying both literal and metaphorical out of childhood, of religious hypocrisy; all these, if they survive in the film, survive only at fleeting moments, and not as fundamental parts of the fabric of the story as they indubitably are in Lee's novel.

The novel is narrated by Jean Louise Finch, one of the central characters, from the perspective of an adult remembering events from her own childhood. As a child she was known as 'Scout', and because she had lived through these experiences *before* she begins to record them as an adult in written form, Scout reports for us more than she properly realises she is seeing. It is a familiar literary technique in first-person narration, and here, in the tension between what Scout saw as a child and what she understands as a remembering adult, we are able to follow the steps of her development from innocence to maturity. Since the focus of the novel is on Scout's brother, Jem, he becomes the main character, with the reader observing Scout's changing awareness through the characterisation of Jem and through her own relationship to him. In such ways, the Finch children, together with Dill, remain the centre of attention throughout the book.

The obvious and frequent corollary in American film of a remembering first-person narrator in fiction is the use of the 'voice-over' technique. When Scout first comes into view on screen, her adult voice is already speaking words on the sound-track which closely approximate to those used in the novel. But the star system of the Hollywood studio productions of the sixties changed the focus of the novel in crucial ways. In the screen version, Scout's father, Atticus Finch (Gregory Peck), becomes the central character. The American white male, cast here in the heroic figure of a progressive liberal lawyer fighting for the civil rights of a black man falsely accused of raping a young white woman, dominates the action. This shifts our attention onto the campaigning for, and survival of, the rights and principles of racial justice which are denied to the accused African-American, Tom Robinson. The film's concentration on the father, stressed throughout by the camera's constant attention to Peck, is seen particularly in the sequence where Atticus shoots the mad dog. The camera lingers on Jem's open-mouthed admiration for his father's mastery with guns. Atticus may be an American liberal, but even though his spectacles slip symbolically from his eyes as he aims the gun, he shares, in both film and book, the masculine prowess which a wider American culture considers to be important. As the all-powerful father-figure, Atticus displaces the children as the source of developing awareness.

Hence his dominance and authority on the screen narrow the film's scope and range.

The deeply ironic schoolroom discussion of American democracy and German fascism, which takes place in Chapter 26 of the novel, is only the most obvious case in point.[1] The smug complacency of Miss Gates does much to prepare the Finch children and the reader for the gap between Maycomb's opinion of itself as a town, and the stark actuality revealed by things which are to come. It contributes a considerable amount towards the experience and understanding of Jem and Scout, and provides a cutting counterpoint to their forthcoming live encounter with racism and persecution in the small Southern town. But all of this is omitted from the picture, as is the novel's extensive satire on religious hypocrisy. Another crucial omission is the novel's repeated reference to and detailed treatment of family structure and family life. From Dill's status as unwanted child to the repression in the Radley household and the Ewell poverty and violence, the greater narrative attention of the novel enables it to explore the often painful experience of family influences. In this respect the Finch family household proves the most interesting, with the black servant Calpurnia becoming accepted as a surrogate mother-figure, though there is no verbal reference in the film to the fact of her colour, and the children form relationships which cross over the immediate ties of blood-kinship.

In the film the viewer sees things immediately, through a camera which is always allied to Scout, the narrator's, perception. As a result there is an inevitable slackening of the narrative tension which generates some of the novel's most powerful effects. Conversely the immediacy of film enables Mulligan's picture to register the shock impact of unsettling experiences on the children. The novel, however, remains more powerful. Consideration of the image of the mockingbird might help us to understand the process whereby some things are lost in the transition to film mode. In the opening lines we read:

> When he was nearly thirteen, my brother Jem got his arm badly broken at the elbow. When it healed, and Jem's fears of never being able to play football were assuaged, he was seldom self-conscious about his injury. His left arm was somewhat shorter than his right; when he stood or walked, the back of his hand was at right-angles to his body, his thumb parallel to his thigh. He couldn't have cared less so long as he could pass and punt. (p. 9)

The careful attention to detail here suggests that this is a self-conscious piece of narrative foreshadowing, looking forward as it does to the vicious attack upon the Finch children by Bob Ewell, an attack which does not take place until the novel's penultimate chapter. Such things cast a shadow forward, as well as registering that this is, in fact, a discourse of memory, a personal history the outcome of which is known to the narrator, though not to the reader. But it is rather more than that, too.

Whereas in the film there is virtually only one mockingbird, that is to say only one victim, the accused Tom Robinson; in the novel several characters besides Jem Finch are at one time or another considered in that light. Much play is made, in the film's climactic courtroom scene, with the fact that Tom Robinson's left arm hung dead at his side, the result of an accident with a cotton-gin which meant that it was anyway impossible for him to have raped anyone in the way his supposed victim had described it. The novelistic foreshadowing, which suggests that Jem Finch is also in some sense a mockingbird and that his experiences of racism have damaged him and, in his transition from childhood to adulthood, left him permanently scarred, is passed over in the film. Images which give the novel a kind of depth and range, are omitted, leaving Atticus's courtroom remark to echo reductively in the film version: 'This case is as simple as black and white' (p. 207).

Nor can this be attributed solely to the inevitable selection and compression which must take place in the translation of a novel into film, since this film demonstrates an ability to find correlatives for the novel's backward-looking narrative structure. Quite apart from the voice-over technique of Jean-Louise's adult voice, the film makes suggestive and subtle uses of childhood images in its opening sequence as the credits roll and before the film narrative proper begins. As a visual equivalent to the novel's adult narrator re-creating the world of her own childhood beginnings, we watch a child's hands shaping the letters of the film's title—a kind of writing—and we see a child's hands drawing an image of a mockingbird. While this image is being made, the camera pans across a watch, symbol of time passing, and itself an image which recurs in the film. Then, the child drawing the bird tears the paper, 'killing' the mockingbird and leaving a jagged image of white on black; the camera continues to pan across the different toys and objects left by Boo Radley for the children to collect from the tree-knot outside the Radley house. Spilled from the toy-box which normally contains all of these items, we see a penknife, which foreshadows two subsequent events in Boo Radley's life: the attack upon his father, and much more significantly, his slaying of Bob Ewell at the time of the latter's attack upon Scout and Jem. We also see two carved figures, perhaps representing the two Finch children.

That toy-box forms a part of the film's own reference back upon itself in much the same way that the novel's narrative is a return to time past. On the evening of the day when Nathan Radley cements up the knot-hole in the tree, Jem shows Scout all of the objects which have been left for them by Boo. 'It was to be a long time before Jem and I talked about Boo again,' says the adult voice-over. Then a hand closes the toy-box which takes us back to the film's opening sequence. Such use of images suggests several possible ways in which film can find its own equivalents and correlatives for techniques of continuity, recall and foreshadowing used in narrative fiction.

Perhaps one of the most striking of these connects the small-town atmosphere of Maycomb ('a tired old town'), static and enclosed, with a particular tendency in the film's camera-work. On page 11 of the novel we read words which are remarkably close to the opening sentences of the film's screenplay: 'A day was twenty-four hours long but seemed longer. There was no hurry, for there was nowhere to go; nothing to buy and no money to buy it with'. This is taken almost word-perfect into the screenplay. The end of the novel's sentence—'nothing to see outside the boundaries of Maycomb County'—is omitted, perhaps because Hollywood sought a wider American audience for the film's narrowing of focus onto the theme of racial prejudice. But that oppressive, self-regarding community is explored in a variety of ways in the novel's leisurely space. Given the more intense demands of unity in film-time, such space is not available.

From the opening camera-shot, a shift from looking upwards to trees and outwards to the sky beyond, down onto the practically deserted streets of Maycomb, we gradually become aware that the severely restricted camera-movement throughout the film is having particular effects. When the children peer over the fence into the Radley house, the camera slides conspiratorially up behind them: as they move around the side of the house, the camera arcs upwards, to look down on them. In the courtroom scene the camera moves into close-up on Tom Robinson's face as he gives his evidence. Clever editing during the moment of Ewell's assault upon the children gives the impression of rapidity and confusion. And for the final shot, in a sense reversing the open movement down onto the streets of Maycomb, the camera tracks away from Jem's bedroom, and away from the Finch household. With the exception of these shaping movements, the camera is remarkably static during the film narrative; sometimes tracking slightly to the left or right, but more predominantly remaining fixed, unmoving. Even when Atticus drives from Maycomb proper to where Tom Robinson's wife Helen and the rest of the segregated Negro community live, we see only the car's departure and arrival. In all these ways, any sense of movement is kept to minimal levels, and the overall atmosphere of statis and enclosure reinforced.

Both novel and film suffer from being sentimentalised narratives. One reviewer of the film commented:

> Harper Lee's *To Kill a Mockingbird* is one of the best recent examples of the sentimental novel: the book designed principally to create warmth, which doesn't exclude ugliness but views it through generally optimistic eyes ... is not vigorous enough to celebrate life, but does enjoy it.[2]

The scene early in the film, where Jem and Scout discuss their dead mother while the camera lingers on Gregory Peck's listening expression out on the front-porch is a case in point. Or, perhaps to more obviously engineered effect, when, at the conclusion of the court scene, Scout tells us, 'I looked around. They were standing. All around us and in the balcony on the opposite wall, the Negroes were getting to their feet' (pp. 215–16). With Reverend Sykes's comment, film and novel indulge in the creation of sentimental emotion towards the idealising of Atticus Finch: 'Miss Jean Louise, stand up. Your Father's passin'.'

Moreover, both versions veer at other times—and frequently—towards the melodramatic, and on at least one occasion the film seems better able to keep a sense of greater realism, even at a moment of high melodrama. In the novel, during the scene when Jem, Scout and Dill arrive at the jailhouse where a lynch-mob has gathered, the staginess of the affair is accentuated: 'I sought once more for a familiar face, and at the centre of the semi-circle, I found one' (p. 156). It is Mr Cunningham, and Scout proceeds to address him on the matter of his entailment and concerning their family relationships in the closed community of Maycomb, reminding Mr Cunningham to say 'hey' to his son Walter on Scout's behalf. The unreality of the scene is further conveyed:

> when I slowly awoke to the fact that I was addressing the entire aggregation. The men were all looking at me, some had their mouths half-open. Atticus had stopped poking Jem: they were standing together beside Dill. Their attention amounted to fascination. (p. 157)

In the silence which follows Scout's speech, the novel records that she:

looked around and up at Mr Cunningham, whose face was equally impassive. Then he did a peculiar thing. He squatted down and took me by both shoulders. 'I'll tell him you said hey, little lady,' he said (p. 158) before leading the mob away.

Both film and novel wish to stress the creative goodness of childhood, even in such extremes of situation. Perhaps realising that when translated into visual terms such a transformation of Cunningham from angry potential lyncher into softened and caring father might stretch the bounds of credibility, the film opts for registering the acute embarrassment of Cunningham's sideways glance—he is obviously too disconcerted to face Scout directly while she is talking—before he mutters the response included in both versions. Within the margins of a highly melodramatic and unlikely resolution of the scene, the film is slightly more satisfying than the novel.

When, however, melodrama passes over into a more gothic mode, when aspects of mystery and of terror at the unknown form part of the narrative—the film often seems better able to convey a sense of threat, of suspense and of shadowy uncertainty. For the children involved, the figure of Boo Radley is one such gothic dimension, a character who in many ways typifies an identifiable strand in American fiction from the Southern States. Again, for the children, the Radley household figures as the equivalent of a gothic mansion:

> Inside the house lived a malevolent phantom. People said he existed, but Jem and I had never seen him. People said he went out at night when the moon was high, and peeped in windows ... A Negro would not pass the Radley place at night, he would cut across to the sidewalk opposite and whistle as he walked. (pp. 14–15)

Although this provides Harper Lee with ample opportunity for comic insight into the workings of childhood imagination and superstition, we also realise that the bogey figure of Boo Radley serves as a symbolic figure of more serious dimensions. Not only is he both sign and representative of an oppressive and inhibited society which, rather than face up to them, is far happier suppressing home truths that are shaming, he is also by that same token a mark of embarrassment to his own family as well as a signal of the repressive intolerance in a wider community.

Aided by Elmer Bernstein's musical score, the film's judicious use of light and shadow, and in particular its presentation of night sequences as the children pursue Dill's idea of 'making Boo Radley come out' (p. 14), catches this mood and feeling of the uncanny and the mysterious. When Jem stays at home on guard, while Atticus takes the black servant Calpurnia home (Calpurnia, of course, sitting on the back seat of the car), Jem sits in the swing chair on the front porch, hearing a screech-owl as shadows of leaves cast black and white patterns on his face. Frightened, he runs down the street after his father's car, shouting 'Atticus.' Outside the Radley house he hears their swing-chair creaking in the wind, and knocking against the woodwork. At this moment he finds the first of the objects left in the tree-knot by Boo. Hearing the sound of the screech-owl again, he takes to his heels and heads for home. The camera repeatedly plays upon that creaking swing-chair on the Radley porch, but even so, this whole aspect of the story is expertly condensed into that cinematic moment when in order to 'get a look at Boo Radley,' Jem, watched fearfully by Scout and Dill, crawls one evening onto the Radley porch. As he peeps through the window, he is approached by a figure casting a looming, threatening shadow which is seen first by the viewer watching the film, then by Scout and Dill, then again by the viewer. When a shadowy hand reaches out to touch Jem, all three children crouch in terror; the figure, starkly stage-lit to register black upon white, withdraws and the three children run for their lives. Symbolic overtone, as well as melodramatic event are registered together. And towards the film's close, Boo Radley, at Scout's invitation, does touch the unconscious Jem's forehead, bringing to the surface, and out into the open a relationship that had hitherto remained unclear and incomplete.

Boo Radley ends by helping the children at a decisive moment, and anyway makes them presents during the progress of the story, those presents with which the film opens. But the way in which Boo saves the children, and more importantly the reaction of the authorities to his intervention, brings us into an area where both texts appear to be complicit in the very values they seek to reform. Much more so than in the novel, the film makes great play with the court scene, devoting to it a disproportionate amount of playing time. It is the scene in which the central values of democratic justice and common decency come into conflict with racial prejudice so deeply rooted that it overturns utterly convincing evidence of Tom Robinson's innocence. But although there may be dramatic reasons for Atticus Finch's defence and celebration of America's legal procedures—after all, he is concerned primarily to sway the opinions of a jury whose biases he knows only too well— none the less the words he uses stand in sharp opposition to the actual practices of the court and its jurors.

In the major summing-up speech for the defence, some passages from the novel are altered in their sequence, but with minor exceptions the language is the same. Atticus Finch, played with style and conviction by Gregory Peck, asserts that 'there is one institution in which all men are created equal,' and he continues, 'in this country our courts are the great levellers' (p. 209). Then, of the integrity of the jury system, he claims 'that is no ideal to me, it is a living working reality. Gentlemen, a court is no better than any man of you sitting before me on this jury. A court is only as sound as its jury, and a jury is only as sound as the men who make it up' (pp. 209–10). The first irony which strikes us is the obvious one that no women could serve on juries in Alabama at that time (p. 225). To have black men serve was unthinkable. But the film makes a telling point in this respect. Although the three children, symbols of warmth, light and innocence, sit next to Reverend Sykes, the court is otherwise rigidly segregated. This is dramatically focused for us when the pronouncement is made: 'will the defendant please rise and face the jury.' What happens is that the camera does not turn to the jury, but to the people who are in fact Tom Robinson's peers and equals—the black community sitting up in the courtroom gallery. It is a brief shot, but it carries considerable cinematic weight in terms of its irony and social comment.

Given the horrors that overtake Tom Robinson after a guilty verdict is returned, the whole of the court scene creates serious problems for the readers' and viewers' attitudes towards the sentimental warmth with which much of the story unfolds. Overall, both novel and film serve to vindicate the liberal values of domestic and civic virtue which the Finch household represents. The reviewer for *Newsweek* makes the appropriate comment on this problem:

> In a seemingly leisurely way, the novel drifted through 121 pages of youthful adventure, and, only then, with the children solidly established did it turn into a rape case. The two discrete parts of the novel are telescoped in the film, however, and the result is to bring the trial out of the blurry background and into sharp focus. The trial weighed upon the novel, and in the film, where it is heavier, it is unsupportable. The narrator's voice returns at the end, full of warmth and love ... but we do not pay her the same kind of attention any more. We have seen that outrageous trial, and we can no longer share the warmth of her love.[3]

That sentimental warmth helps to create the conditions for a tidily 'happy' ending, an ending that further suggests that problems have been raised which the authoress, and following her the director Robert Mulligan, cannot finally resolve. Brendon Gill writing in *The New Yorker* makes the point:

> In the last few minutes of the picture, whatever intellectual and
> moral content it may be said to have contained is crudely tossed
> away in order to provide a 'happy' ending. Peck ... and the sher
> iff agree to pretend that a wicked white man who has been killed
> will be reported to have fallen on his own knife, thus sparing the
> man who killed him—admittedly a mental case, but the saviour
> of the lawyer's children—the humiliation of a public arraign
> ment. The moral of this can only be that while ignorant red
> necks mustn't take the law into their own hands, it's all right for
> *nice* people to do so.[4]

If Boo Radley has cast a shadow upon the development of the children throughout the unfolding story, the way in which his killing of Bob Ewell is covered up by those in authority leaves the unavoidable impression that for Maycomb, and by extension for Alabama more generally, 'Law' and its 'Order' are to be manipulated by those who, it is presumed, know best. *To Kill a Mockingbird* generates serious moral and social issues. But in order to bring them to a satisfying conclusion, film and book take refuge in the very suppression of truth and deception of a community which the assumed story has attempted to expose.

NOTES

1. All page references are to the *Pan* edition of the novel, and are given parenthetically in the text.
2. Stanley Kauffmann, *New Republic*, 2 February 1963, p. 30.
3. *Newsweek*, 18 February 1963, p. 93.
4. Brendan Gill, *The New Yorker*, 23 February 1963, p. 126.

FILMOGRAPHY

To Kill a Mockingbird (An Alan Pakula/Universal-International Production US 1962.) Starring Gregory Peck, Mary Badham, Philip Alford, John Megna, Frank Overton, Rosemary Murphy, Ruth White, Brock Peters; Narrated by Kim Stanley; Cinematography by Russell Harlan; Music by Elmer Bernstein; Screenplay by Horton Foote from the novel by Harper Lee; Directed by Robert Mulligan.

ERIC J. SUNDQUIST

Blues for Atticus Finch:
Scottsboro, Brown, and Harper Lee

Perceptions of the South as an American problem have long been shaped
by literary representations of the region created by authors on both sides of
the Mason-Dixon line. In many of the most influential works, race and racial
conflict have been at the heart of such representations, as indeed they have
been at the heart of American social history. Harriet Beecher Stowe and
Frederick Douglass, for example, are only the best known of numerous antebellum writers who waged war over slavery well before any shots were fired
in the Civil War. In the post-Reconstruction era, national views of America's
continuing racial dilemma and of the South alike were forcefully dictated by
the popularity of Joel Chandler Harris's folkloric plantation tales and
Thomas Dixon's racist novels celebrating the Ku Klux Klan, while black
writers such as Charles Chesnutt and W. E. B. Du Bois, as well as later figures of the Harlem Renaissance, looked to the South and the formative experience of slavery in recovering the roots of African-American experience and
arguing for black equality. And in employing antebellum time frames to
engage contemporary racial contentions that were clearly national as well as
regional in scope, Mark Twain established a paradigm of retrospective analysis followed by other writers who likewise subjected nostalgia for the plantation world to probing critique.

From *The South as an American Problem*. © 1995 by the University of Georgia Press.

More recently, the monumental achievement of William Faulkner and the pathbreaking modern work of Richard Wright, Ralph Ellison, and Toni Morrison, to cite the most obvious, have kept the South at the forefront of consciousness in the nation's long drama of guilt and redemption over its twin birth in revolutionary democracy and racial slavery. As in the case of the Civil War itself, however, so in the case of the literature devoted to the mid-twentieth-century civil rights movement—in which one might expect the most overt confrontation with the South as an American problem—there has been a marked tendency to work at the crisis of American racial equality obliquely, to experiment with allegorical displacements and baroque characterization. One has only to think, for example, of William Melvin Kelley's *A Different Drummer* or Alice Walker's *Meridian*, two of the best African-American novels inspired by the civil rights era, to notice what unorthodox strategies have seemed necessary to represent adequately the upheavals and psychic costs of the struggle for black equality. Important as these novels are, though, they seem marginalia to the stately oratory of Martin Luther King Jr., memoirs by movement participants such as Anne Moody or Bobby Seale, allied autobiography by Malcolm X, Claude Brown, or Maya Angelou, and the great range of black music that told the story in other modes. Beside the influence and legacy of such work, permanent statements in the form of fiction have not been as commanding as one might expect.

At the same time, there remains the peculiar, unavoidable presence of Harper Lee's *To Kill a Mockingbird*. Published in 1960, a model of conventional plot and character, the novel is the most widely read twentieth-century American work of fiction devoted to the issue of race. The novel was an immediate best-seller, and several generations of American children have studied the novel at least once before leaving secondary school. For this reason it has defined for much of the nation—indeed, for much of the world, especially through its film version—the South as an American problem, a region unto itself yet at the same time an incarnation of the racial conflict that belongs to the whole of the United States rather than to southern states alone. In addition, the novel has remained a particular touchstone of white liberalism. Former Clinton campaign strategist James Carville, for example, has recalled *To Kill a Mockingbird* as the most important book of his life for the change it effected in his view of racial justice: "I just knew, the minute I read it, that [Harper Lee] was right and I had been wrong." Likewise, in arguing against the Confederate iconography of the current Georgia state flag, Governor Zell Miller recently cited the famous scene in which Scout's innocent banter disperses the mob come to lynch Tom Robinson as a model for his appeal to the state general assembly as "fathers and mothers, neighbors and friends" who had been taught in Sunday school to do the right thing.[1]

Despite the importance of such testimony, it is nonetheless tempting to ascribe the book's immense popularity, especially at the time of its publication, to its indulgence in comforting sentimentality and to assume that its fawning readership was overwhelmingly white. Even if that were true, one would still have to account for the novel's recorded impact on those whose sense of the righteous sprang from other sources. In his memoir of the civil rights movement, for example, James Farmer, head of the Congress of Racial Equality, recalls that in 1961, while he was under arrest with other Freedom Riders in Jackson, Mississippi, Roy Wilkins brought in two books "as gifts to help [him] pass the prison hours," one of them *To Kill a Mockingbird*.[2] Farmer did not record his opinion of the novel, but the significance of the gesture as an index of the book's popular appeal at the height of the civil rights protest is obvious.

Even though the novel continues to have a widespread influence on the imagination of many young Americans, however, it is today something of a historical relic—or better, an icon whose emotive sway remains strangely powerful because it also remains unexamined. It is something of a mystery, moreover, that the book has failed to arouse the antagonism now often prompted by another great novelistic depiction of the South as a national problem, *Adventures of Huckleberry Finn*, which arguably uses the word *nigger* with more conscious irony than does *To Kill a Mockingbird* and whose antebellum framework and moral complexity ought to be a far greater bulwark against revisionist denunciation. For all its admirable moral earnestness and its inventory of the historical forces making up white liberal consciousness in the late 1950s, Lee's novel might well have been entitled "Driving Miss Scout." That its basic answers to the questions of racial injustice appear almost irrelevant to the late-twentieth-century United States makes its cultural impact the more crucial to understand, not least because the novel pursues its ethical instruction with a cunning simplicity while at the same time implying that there *are* no simple answers, perhaps no answers at all.

In showing America's mid-century racial ambivalence in full bloom, *To Kill a Mockingbird* sweeps back through historical events whose culmination is in the watershed years of the late 1950s and early 1960s but that can hardly be understood within so narrow a time frame. Lee's novel is a document of historical crisis enfolded within a problem in literary representation, which in turn is built upon the interrelation between her strategies of fictive representation and the question of legal representation that is an issue in the novel itself and in the real world of jurisprudence and constitutional law to which Scout Finch's narrative frequently alludes. The novel offers an anatomy of segregation at the moment of its legal destruction. Insofar as it is a story that provisionally foresees the end of a long, bewildering, and violent phase of American history, it is a story of the South, the primary arena of desegregation, as a distillation of the nation, the atavistic and the everyday concentrated into a parable that brings no certainty that the end of segregation will be the end of racism.

* * *

Given its enduring appeal to deep wells of white American innocence, it may seem at first glance surprising how blunt is *To Kill a Mockingbird*'s examination of the South's "rape complex," as Wilbur Cash once called it. As a portrait of the South of the 1930s, the novel might be taken simply as a confirmation of the archetypal defense of lynching offered in the Senate by Alabama's J. Thomas Heflin: "Whenever a negro crosses this dead line between the white and negro races and lays his black hand on a white woman he deserves to die."[3] It could better be argued, however, that the appeal of the book, whose story is focused, after all, on the psychological and physical maturation of a young white girl with whom readers of the 1950s and 1960s are expected to identify, lies in its portrayal of a contemporary episode of the southern sexual "disease"[4] and in its invocation of the specter of "mongrelization" that was once more appearing in the oratorical and editorial protests that fueled southern reaction to *Brown v. Board of Education*. Behind the veneer of Scout Finch's first-person naïveté, Lee's novel defies, without destroying, conventional white southern fears of black sexuality, which drove the South, said Lillian Smith, to superimpose the semiotics of Jim Crow upon the white female body: "Now, parts of your body are segregated areas which you must stay away from and keep others away from. These areas you touch only when necessary. In other words, you cannot associate freely with them any more than you can associate freely with colored children."[5] Smith's characteristically acerbic description of the ethos of segregation brings together the two strong vectors of Lee's novel—its focus on childhood, the battleground of desegregation, and the rhetorical power of white womanhood, long the weapon of choice in racist arguments against equality.

Throughout the South *Brown* provoked new hysteria of the sort recorded in Mississippi circuit court judge Tom Brady's infamous broadside "Black Monday" (so called for the day the *Brown* opinion was issued), in which he summoned up the specter of alien invasion ("Communism disguised as 'new democracy' is still communism, and tyranny masquerading as liberalism is still tyranny") and prophesied that desegregation would unleash a new black threat to "the loveliest and the purest of God's creatures ... [the] well-bred, cultured Southern white woman or her blue-eyed, golden-haired little girl." Sedition and the threat of racial corruption were everywhere: the year before Lee's novel was published, an Alabama state legislator who objected to the plot of a children's book entitled *The Rabbit's Wedding*, in which a white rabbit marries a black rabbit, succeeded not only in banning the subversive book from state libraries but in having copies burned as well.[6] Against the grain of its ineffable goodness *To Kill a Mockingbird* includes as well this powerful undertow of southern resistance and, in its half-disguise of violent racial realities, inscribes in an equally dangerous children's story the nightmare of America's own growing up.

The capital rape case of Tom Robinson tried by Atticus Finch occurs in 1935, set in a small-town Alabama courtroom that would inevitably have been reverberating with the impact of the ongoing trials of the young black men known as the Scottsboro Boys. Perhaps the most notorious modern criminal trials with race not technically but nonetheless fundamentally at issue, the ordeal of the young men charged with the rape of two white women, in a sequence of trials lasting from 1931 to 1937, put the South under sensational national scrutiny matched only by that aroused by the 1955 murder in Money, Mississippi, of Emmett Till, a fourteen-year-old Chicago boy accused of being fresh with a local white woman. Although it is conceivable that Lee's character Tom Robinson was inspired by the death sentence given a real-life black Alabama man named Tom Robinson in 1930 for his part in defending his family from a lynch mob, a story recounted in Arthur Raper's *Tragedy of Lynching*,[7] actual parallels to Tom's case were readily available, and Scottsboro was only the most egregious evidence that the kinds of justice administered by southern mobs and southern courts were often indistinguishable. From the southern point of view Scottsboro was a call to arms. Vanderbilt historian Frank Owsley, for instance, identified the Yankee intrusion into the sacred body of the South prompted by Scottsboro with the prior infamies of abolitionism and Reconstruction, when radical whites had encouraged black men "to commit universal pillage, murder and rape."[8] Outside the South, though, Scottsboro was emblematic of southern injustice and a litmus test of sectional paranoia, as was the Till case a generation later.

With mounting tension over civil rights activism augmented by the exoneration of Till's white killers, *To Kill a Mockingbird* was written, and subsequently read, in an atmosphere charged on the one hand by the impact of *Brown* and on the other by publicity about the revival of Judge Lynch in the

South. Yet by dwelling on the narrative recollection of time past—"when enough years had gone by to enable us to look back on them," Scout tells us in setting the context for the book's action on the first page (3)—the plot deliberately casts backward to the era of Scottsboro, and Lee could easily have replaced her own epigraph from Charles Lamb ("Lawyers, I suppose, were children once") with Langston Hughes's "The Town of Scottsboro," one of several poems he devoted to the cause:

> Scottsboro's just a little place:
> No shame is writ across its face—
> Its court, too weak to stand against a mob,
> Its people's heart, too small to hold a sob.[9]

Hughes's Scottsboro might as well be Maycomb, where Tom Robinson is tried and quickly sentenced to death, or Sumner, Mississippi, where Till's murderers were tried and just as quickly acquitted. This doubled legal time frame is but one of several ways in which Lee, like Mark Twain before her, lays one era upon another in the retrospective narrative of Scout Finch, who looks back to a time when "people moved slowly ... took their time about everything," when "there was no hurry, for there was nowhere to go" (5). Scout's nostalgia tells us about the operation of temporality in autobiography, about Lee's share in the long southern tradition of antimodernism, and about the power of mourning, commingled with defiance, in the reservoir of southern memory. But it tells us, more to the point, that we are reading at every moment an allegory of the South's own temporality and its public philosophy of race relations: "Go slow."

   To Kill a Mockingbird is a novel of childhood, but one saturated in narrative consciousness of deeper regional and national time. Although it is not, strictly speaking, a historical novel, its careful deployment of familial genealogy, state history, and the romantic stereotypes of southern "breeding" create a context in which the pressure of contemporary time, with its threatened destruction of a white southern way of life, becomes urgent. The novel harks back to the 1930s both to move the mounting fear and violence surrounding desegregation into an arena of safer contemplation and to remind us, through a merciless string of moral lessons, that the children of Atticus Finch are the only hope for a future world of racial justice. Framed by the Boo Radley story, the book's racial "nightmare" (144) is to a noticeable degree made peripheral for young readers to the gothic tale of the "malevolent phantom" Boo (8) and the revenge of Bob Ewell. But Boo Radley's story is at the same time a means to displace into more conventional gothic territory the Finch children's encounter with "blackness" as it is defined by the white South and, more broadly, by white America. Associated from the outset with animal mutilation and black superstition (9), and with the laughter of Negroes passing in the night (55), Boo functions transparently as a harbinger of violated taboos and a displaced phantasm of racial fear, ultimately unmasked as the gentle, domesticated "gray ghost" of harmonious integration (13–14, 280). The novel's concluding Halloween sequence, with its brilliant prelude of the school pageant devoted to Alabama history and personified products of Dixie agriculture (dressed as a ham, Scout survives Bob Ewell's attack), tells us that the true danger comes from "white trash" ("Boo" evolves into the insidious "Bob"); and it offers the illusion that racial hysteria—the Klan, night-riding mobs, the White Citizens Council—can be likewise unmasked, humiliated, and brought to justice once the South disposes of its childish fears and moves forward into the post-*Brown* world.

To Kill a Mockingbird is a masterpiece of indirection that allows young readers to face racism through the deflecting screen of a frightening adventure story, just as it allows American readers to face racism through a tale that deflects the problem to the South. Embedded in an episodic story of wit and charm, and pursued through a series of remembered events that often channel serious racial issues into a puzzle of half-truths, children's games and pranks, and devious piety, the novel's lessons are as often held in abeyance as they are driven home by Lee's analogical strategies and her temporal displacement of the book's action into the lives of a pre-*Brown* generation. From the very outset of the novel Scout's reminders that we are reading a tale of the Depression-era South have the effect of suspending our judgment. The New Deal, however it may have helped southern blacks economically, posed little challenge to Jim Crow; though key civil rights legislative and judicial policy dates from the decade, the practice of segregation, and often of mob rule, remained largely untouched by the awakening of southern liberalism.[10]

There is thus everywhere available to the reader as an explanation of the book's dramatized racism and miscarriages of justice the argument that its action belongs to a bygone era. One effect of the temporal displacement, in fact, is to anchor the novel's social crises in a remembered world of general economic deprivation and cultural isolation. The Finch family is comparatively well off, of course, but the region's impoverished small farmers and sharecroppers, whether black or white, live still in the "shadow of the plantation," to borrow the title of Charles Johnson's important study of Black Belt Alabama in the 1930s, "dulled and blocked in by a backwardness which is a fatal heritage of the system itself."[11] Indeed, To Kill a Mockingbird itself so clearly harks back to the tradition of liberal exposés of southern racism, whose classic texts may be dated from the 1930s—works such as Johnson's *Shadow of the Plantation* (1934), Raper's *The Tragedy of Lynching* (1933), John Dollard's *Caste and Class in a Southern Town* (1937), Wilbur Cash's *The Mind of the South* (1941), and climaxing in a book with an even broader canvas, Gunnar Myrdal's monumental *An American Dilemma* (1944)—that the novel might almost be read as a kind of recapitulatory tribute to the tradition. Be that as it may, *Brown v. Board of Education* irrevocably changed things, and any novel dating from the rising crest of the civil rights movement must bear the consequences of its own nostalgia for a simpler, slower time, especially when that nostalgia is as tightly interwoven with the narrative's moral fabric as in the case of *To Kill a Mockingbird*.

* * *

The novel dwells on the problem of education, its relationship to the force of law, and the Finch children's assimilation to a network of southern social codes.[12] Combined with the contrast between the useless public schooling available to Scout and Jem and the righteous moral lessons they learn from Atticus, from their black cook Calpurnia, and from their regular witness of Maycomb's injustice, the book's nostalgia is a means to probe anxiety about desegregation in the post-*Brown* South and to remind its audience how fully the 1930s impinged upon the 1950s. Recalling a 1938 trip into rural Georgia, journalist Ralph McGill, a southern liberal in the Atticus Finch mold, might well have been describing both the pathetic Maycomb school portrayed by Lee and her implied judgment of the consequences for the South of its resistance to *Brown*. "There were poor schools in other regions of America," wrote McGill in 1963,

> but none had so many as the Southeast. And nowhere were there so many as shabby, barren, unpainted, bedraggled, disgracing their state and their country's flag raised daily on the school grounds.... That the South should hold on so desperately, with such pathetic, almost preposterous pride, to customs, traditions, and a so-called way of life that kept them and their children from equal opportunity, which is the basic promise of their country, seemed even more irrational.[13]

When Harper Lee, like McGill, renders Alabama's compulsory education a farcical enterprise (30), she does so not simply to reflect upon the failures of time past, when black faces left no trace in the classroom. She also does so, one can suppose, in order to estimate the nation's contemporary legitimate interest in a federalized social practice that is, according to *Brown*, "the very foundation of good citizenship ... a principal instrument in awakening the child to cultural values, in preparing him for later professional training, and in helping him to adjust normally to his environment."[14]

Equal education, said *Brown*, was the key to valued and meaningful membership in the nation, and the Court's decision made schools the crucible of change. Emmett Till's murder in 1955, the vicious treatment accorded the black students who integrated Central High School in Little Rock in 1957, and the abuse heaped upon African-American and white students in various communities who launched sit-in protests over the same period of time were reminders that the effects of *Brown*, good and ill alike, were to be felt especially by a younger generation, by children. In the commonsense words of McGill, *Brown* "was a decision about children. That's what the wise and moderate, long-overdue words of the nine justices were all about—the rights and opportunities of American children" and the principle that "the Constitution of the United States is as concerned with the rights of children as with those of their parents." In his most famous address, the speech made at the Lincoln Memorial on the occasion of the 1963 March on Washington, Martin Luther King Jr. likewise dreamed of that day when, "down in Alabama, with its vicious racists, with its governor having his lips dripping with the words of interposition and nullification.... little black boys and black girls [would] be able to join hands with little white boys and white girls as sisters and brothers."[15] The preoccupation of *To Kill a Mockingbird* with the moral education of children, its beguiling proposition that juries, police forces, and whole communities of sympathetic children (220, 157, 213) would make for a more just world, and, most famously, Scout's naive routing of the lynch mob that has come to drag Tom Robinson from jail—all are calculated to substantiate the ethical authority driving *Brown*, which said simply that all American children have an inalienable right to *equal* education.

In addition to dwelling for obvious reasons on the lasting impact upon children of segregation—creating in them, said the Court, "a lasting feeling of inferiority as to their status in the community that may affect their hearts and minds in a way unlikely ever to be undone"—the language of *Brown* also underscored the issue of temporality in its calculation of what *equal* meant in 1954. Whether to legitimize its heterodox appeal to social science rather than constitutional jurisprudence or simply to emphasize the long capitulation of federal rule to local southern practice, the opinion written by Chief Justice Earl Warren noted that "we cannot turn the clock back to 1868 when the [Fourteenth] Amendment was adopted, or even to 1896 when *Plessy v. Ferguson* was written." What Warren's formulation sought to do was justify the Court's dismissing historical interpretations of the Fourteenth Amendment as inconclusive and thus pave the way, not for a carefully reasoned destruction of separate but equal as a doctrine, but instead for a clean break with the constitutional past. *Brown* dealt with the racist underpinnings of *Plessy* by saying, in essence, that they were no longer relevant to the moral life of the mid-twentieth-century United States.[16] The peculiar nature of the *Brown* opinion was itself evidence that Warren had correctly foreseen the massive resistance that would arise in the South; and the notorious language of the Court's 1955 decree of implementation—"at the earliest practicable date ... with all deliberate speed"—did not so much temporize as turn the issue over to executive and legislative enforcement, putting the spotlight on southern recalcitrance even as it gave it de facto sanction.[17]

But by what date, and with what speed? Five score years after the Emancipation Proclamation, King declared that he had stood in the lengthening shadow of Abraham Lincoln's failed dream quite long enough; and he admonished his vast audience that it was "no time to engage in the luxury of cooling off or to take the tranquilizing drug of gradualism." The gap between going slow and outright resistance was, in King's experience, painfully narrow, and since well before emancipation and the Civil War gradualism had served as a pretext for inaction and regression of the sort announced in the 1956 manifesto of resistance signed by many southern congressmen. Whereas *To Kill a Mockingbird* shot to the top of the nation's bestseller lists and was quickly adapted into its favorite movie, by 1960 only 6 percent of southern public schools had complied with *Brown*. Perhaps no one had a better sense of the likely cruelty of "deliberate speed" than Thurgood Marshall, the NAACP's lead attorney in the arguments for *Brown*. In the wake of the white rioting that accompanied Autherine Lucy's attempt in 1956 to desegregate the University of Alabama (Harper Lee's alma mater), Marshall was asked if he did not believe in gradualism, to which he laconically replied: "The Emancipation Proclamation was issued in 1863, ninety-odd years ago. I believe in gradualism, and I also believe that ninety-odd years is pretty gradual."[18]

In his conversation with Jem after the miscarriage of justice that results in Tom Robinson's conviction, Atticus puts his own estimation of the crisis then on the horizon two decades away in a more pragmatic and revealing way: "Don't fool yourselves—it's all adding up and one of these days we're going to pay the bill for it. I hope it's not in you children's time" (221). Here as elsewhere, Atticus's assessment conflates the novel's time frames, at once forecasting the post-*Brown* world and yet delaying any resolution of its spreading political turmoil and street violence. Speaking from the other side of the color line, James Baldwin would similarly remark: "A bill is coming in that I fear America is not prepared to pay." However, his counsel to black Americans, whom he placed at the center of "this dreadful storm, this vast confusion," was to be ready to risk all—"eviction, imprisonment, torture, death"—in order to eradicate racism. "For the sake of one's children," Baldwin argued, "in order to minimize the bill that *they* must pay, one must be careful not to take refuge in any delusion—and the value placed on the color of the skin is always and everywhere and forever a delusion."[19] Although he too recognizes racism as a delusion, Atticus Finch stops short of asking for dramatic sacrifice in the name of justice. In fact, although he pleads directly to the readers of 1960, warning of a day of racial cataclysm rather than one of harmonious justice, Atticus, like Lee, seems satisfied with the "baby-step" (216) taken toward racial justice and appears to hope for a postponement of the fire next time.

In its constant dialectic between the era of Scottsboro and the era of mounting civil rights strife, the novel contains the unsettling prediction, so to speak, that the white southern children of the 1930s will have grown up into the white southern parents of the 1950s—supporters of interposition and massive resistance, members of the White Citizens Councils, those who spit on the Little Rock students or mobbed Autherine Lucy at Alabama and James Meredith at the University of Mississippi. Because Scout and Jem are, respectively, eight and twelve years old in 1935, they would be thirty-three and thirty-seven in 1960, in all likelihood parents faced with the decision of whether to support or resist school desegregation. The temptation for white readers to identify with the Finch children of the 1930s is thus counterpointed by the risk, nowhere clearly lessened by the novel's own predictions about their adult lives, that Scout and Jem may not have done the right thing when faced with a world of desegregation. Likewise, the book's minimal attempts to enter into African-American life, while they may be chalked up to the effects of Scout's limited point of view, which at times is manifestly racist—he's "just a Negro," she remarks to Dill when the latter weeps over Tom's abuse by the prosecutor (199)—or to Lee's attempt, comparable to that of Harriet Beecher Stowe in *Uncle Tom's Cabin*, to speak first of all to white America, or the moderate white South, must also be counted, if not as a failure of nerve, at least as an internalization of Jim Crow. In its sympathetic portrayal of Calpurnia and Tom, as well as a few secondary black characters, the novel was without question a step ahead of most popular white fiction of its era. Yet the whole psychological design of the narrative—its subliminal violation of racial (and gender) taboos and its guarded but nonetheless fierce satire on what Lee calls the "pink cotton penitentiary" of white southern womanhood (136)—sacrifices the legitimate exploration of an African-American perspective in order to enforce its searching critique of white liberalism in crisis. Of necessity, and with a diminution of power that would only become completely clear in historical retrospect, its narrative marginalization of black life functions as a form of segregation whose effect is to focus our attention not on region or state alone but on the nation come at last to its own southern crossroads.

*   *   *

Atticus Finch has been studied by attorneys for the quality of his moral character,[20] and his cinematic portrayal by Gregory Peck as a man of great tenderness and justice is so ingrained in American consciousness as to make him nearly impossible to imagine otherwise. If there is little question as to Atticus's integrity, however, his actions and his defense of Tom Robinson are seldom seen in any sort of historical context; and his own participation in the book's evasion of the hardest moral questions is usually ignored in favor of his commanding pedagogy. It is surely not hard to imagine that Atticus Finch, whether as portrayed by Peck or not, would be more easily recognized than Thurgood Marshall by the vast majority of Americans. Presented as the southern "good father," standing as he does in nearly mythic contrast to bad public fathers such as George Wallace, Ross Barnett, and Orval Faubus, Atticus is depicted as a grand hero to the book's black community, who stand in silent reverence as he passes from the courtroom after his futile but heroic defense of Tom (211).

Atticus Finch is a good lawyer, then, and a gentleman, but he is not a crusader. He takes Tom Robinson's case because he is appointed counsel (as required by a 1930s statute in Alabama capital cases), is a man of professional ethics, and appears, moreover, to believe in defending Tom, even though he has no illusions about winning a rape case involving a black man and a white woman. Atticus ends his defense of Tom Robinson with a ringing declaration that the court of Maycomb County has available to it the same measure of justice one might seek from the United States Supreme Court—"in this country our courts are the great levelers, and in our courts all men are created equal" (205), he reminds his jury—but there is never one moment of doubt as to the verdict that will be returned. Scout puts it best: "Tom was a dead man the minute Mayella Ewell opened her mouth and screamed" (241). Against the certainty of defeat, Atticus Finch's heroic effort is all the more moving. In his integrity, humility, and common sense, Atticus is almost certainly meant to provide an alternative to the cranky fulminations about "Sambo," states' rights, and the Cold War voiced by Faulkner's liberal attorney, Gavin Stevens, in *Intruder in the Dust*. At the same time, however, Atticus too remains a man of the South, a moderately liberal insider. How else could he function as the symbolic conscience of his family and the white townspeople, those "with background" who privately "say that fair play is not marked White Only," who wish him to do the right thing on their behalf, but who otherwise scorn him as a "nigger-lover" (83–86, 108), who excuse themselves from jury duty, thus turning the decision over to "white trash," and who uphold at all human cost the grandiose myth of southern white womanhood (236)?

The course of Tom's ordeal and Atticus's defense is artfully constructed to exacerbate two mirroring paradoxes. First, Tom is placed in a deadly trap when he must either give in to Mayella Ewell's sexual advances or resist her, and then when he must either recant his story or accuse a white woman of lying. Driven to the impudence of declaring his fear that, no matter what he does, he will end up the victim of a judicial system in which mobs and juries are indistinguishable—"scared I'd hafta face up to what I didn't do," he meekly but archly replies to the prosecutor (198)—Tom is the personification of the daily apprehension that John Dollard found to be widespread among southern African Americans in the 1930s: "Every Negro in the South knows that he is under a kind of sentence of death; he does not know when his turn will come, it may never come, but it may also be at any time."[21] The second paradox, which is Scout's, the reader's, and finally the book's, is perfectly summed up in Atticus's admonition to his daughter, who has sought to defend him from the scorn of town and family alike: "[T]his time we aren't fighting the Yankees, we're fighting our friends. But remember this, no matter how bitter things get, they're still our friends and this is still our home" (76). The peculiar political morality that pervades the novel is incarnate in this expression of near paralysis, which at once identifies the race crisis as a *southern* problem—a matter of states' rights, ideally immune to renewed federal intervention—and describes it in terms that make decisive local action unthinkable. Even though Atticus Finch's own heroism may work to obscure this element of the book's lesson, the novel is, in fact, perfectly in accord with the southern view that the meaning of *Brown* was to be worked out internally. Just as the South closed ranks against the nation at the outset of desegregation—a reaction heightened by Mississippi's being thrust into the national spotlight by the Till case—so *To Kill a Mockingbird* carefully narrows the terms on which changed race relations are going to be brought about in the South.

Atticus's moral courage forms a critical part of the novel's deceptive surface. Whether to shield his children from the pain of racism or to shield Lee's southern readers from a confrontation with their own recalcitrance, Atticus, for all his devotion to the truth, sometimes lies. He employs indirection in order to teach his children about Maycomb's racial hysteria and the true meaning of courage, but he himself engages in evasion when he contends, for instance, that the Ku Klux Klan is a thing of the past ("way back about nineteen-twenty"), a burlesque show of cowards easily humiliated by the Jewish storeowner they attempt to intimidate in their sheeted costumes purchased from the merchant himself (147).[22] Such moments are not distinct from the book's construction of analogies for moral courage in the face of ingrained communal racism—for example, Atticus's killing of the rabid dog or Mrs. Dubose's breaking free of her morphine addiction—but rather part of it. Indirection and displacement govern both the novel's moral pedagogy and, in the end, its moral stalemate. The ethical example of Atticus Finch is heightened in exact ratio to the novel's insistence that, so far as Maycomb and Alabama are concerned, it is both inimitable and incomplete.

In the wake of losing Tom Robinson's case, Atticus suffers personal anguish and bitterness, but he reminds the children on this occasion and others that both juries and mobs in every little southern town are always composed of "people you know," of "reasonable men in everyday life," of "our friends" (157, 220, 146) and that racial injustice is a southern problem that must be solved from within by right-thinking white people. Atticus does not characterize the verdict as "spitting on the tomb of Abraham Lincoln,"[23] nor does he say of the jury: "If you ever saw those lantern-jawed creatures, those bigots whose mouths are slits in their faces, whose eyes pop out like a frog's, whose chins drip tobacco juice, bewhiskered and filthy, you would not ask how they can do it."[24] These remarks, which belong to Samuel Leibowitz, the principal defense attorney in several of the Scottsboro trials, cut through the decorous sanctimony of *To Kill a Mockingbird* and constitute as sharp an intervention into the novel as the comparable public reaction, outside the South, to the exoneration of the murderers of Emmett Till.

Vilified as the tool of the "Jew money from New York" that one prosecutor, during trial, said was bankrolling the representation of the Scottsboro Nine by the NAACP and the Communist Party,[25] the flamboyant Leibowitz came into the case in 1933, after its most significant development. His appearance as counsel was predicated on the case against Ozie Powell having been remanded back to Alabama after the historic Supreme Court reversal of the initial verdict in *Powell v. Alabama* in 1932. The Scottsboro cases are central to the novel not simply because Tom Robinson's trial is set perforce in their context, and not simply because the similarities between the accusations by, and cross-examinations of, the respective complaining white women, Victoria Price and Mayella Ewell, are of special note, but, more important, because *Powell* puts before us the very question of representation—of speaking or acting on behalf of another. In guaranteeing a constitutional right to counsel in certain capital cases, *Powell* for the first time partially incorporated the Sixth Amendment into the Fourteenth, thus nationalizing right to counsel as a matter of due process. The radical Left branded the decision a mere ruse to obtain an unchallengeable conviction on retrial, with the *Daily Worker* declaring that "the Supreme Court ha[d] taken great care to instruct the Alabama authorities how 'properly' to carry through such lynch schemes."[26] But *Powell* was arguably one of the most important decisions by the Court in the decades leading up to *Brown*, a contribution not only to criminal justice but to civil rights. Although the restrictions of *Powell* would not be entirely erased until *Gideon v. Wainright* in 1962 (which extended the federal constitutional guarantee of right to counsel to noncapital felony cases as well), the Court's opinion initiated a federal attack on previously insulated procedures of state criminal law and started a gradual revolution in constitutional restraints based on the Fourteenth Amendment that would continue through the century.[27] In the realm of criminal law *Powell* therefore nationalized rights under the Fourteenth Amendment in a way comparable to the education cases, beginning with *Missouri ex rel. Gaines v. Canada* in 1938, that opened the way to *Brown v. Board of Education* and finally destroyed the states' capacity to maintain legal Jim Crow.

By comparison to the role of education in *To Kill a Mockingbird*, right to counsel seems an abstruse issue—and one not overtly racialized. More critical might appear the other major Supreme Court decision to come out of the Scottsboro cases, *Norris v. Alabama*, which again overturned the convictions on the grounds that eligible African Americans had been systematically excluded from the jury pool. Like *Powell*, *Norris* further accelerated the dismantling of the post-Reconstruction rulings that had so long governed the immunity of state authority in determining civil rights protection.[28] Because it was decided in April 1935, in fact, *Norris* would have been at hand had Atticus Finch chosen to challenge the composition of the Maycomb County jury, arguing, for example, that Calpurnia, who teaches her son reading out of Blackstone's *Commentaries* (125), is a fit juror. But it is safe to assume that his efforts would have been as futile as those of Leibowitz at the lower court level. (One Scottsboro defendant, Haywood Patterson, whose case was remanded on a technicality at the same time as that of Clarence

Norris, accurately described his unsympathetic all-white jury as "a nest of possums.")[29] Even though it has no such explicit racial dimension, *Powell* was nevertheless racialized in fact. The Court's opinion, written by George Sutherland, adverts to racial realism in its second sentence: "The petitioners, hereinafter referred to as defendants, are negroes charged with the crime of rape, committed upon the persons of two white girls."[30] The Court recognized, as the opinion indicates in several other instances, that the South's "rape complex" was more than a minor factor in the denial of due process.

Like Tom Robinson's case, the Scottsboro cases and the appeals leading to *Powell* magnified the simple question put to Atticus by Scout when she innocently asks: "What's rape?" (135). Atticus gives what to Scout is a bafflingly legalistic answer, one of the several occasions on which his own dicta for truth and honesty are violated. *To Kill a Mockingbird* gives two answers, one indicative of Scout's unlikely transcendence of the suffocating strictures of white southern womanhood, the other indicative of the comparable trap laid by the novel's historical frame of reference. To judge from Scout's acculturation over the course of the book, the South's inexhaustible penchant for ultimately referring every racial question to the mystical body of the white woman is not eviscerated in the novel but, along with Maycomb's racial and class stratifications and the moral cowardice of the vast majority of its citizens, left more or less in place. In the fiercely satiric missionary tea sequence, for example, Scout must learn to be a "lady" amidst the rank hypocrisy of the town's leading ladies, who complain that their black servants have become sulky in the aftermath of Tom's conviction, condemn not Mayella Ewell but Helen Robinson of immorality, and tediously invoke the specter of the black rapist ("there's no lady safe in her bed these nights" [232]). She must learn to be a lady by swallowing her grief and protest when news of Tom's death during a prison escape arrives in the very midst of this excruciating scene. Scout registers, without protesting, her partial kinship with Tom's incarceration and readies herself to "enter this world, where on its surface fragrant ladies rocked slowly, fanned gently, and drank cool water," as she later recalls, without telling us from the vantage of retrospect whether, in fact, she has ever escaped that world (233).[31]

Both the novel and Scottsboro asked what meaning "rape" might have if it were only a rhetorical justification for lynching and lesser forms of prejudice or for sectional resistance to the nationalization of constitutional rights. Past a certain stage in the Scottsboro case, as in that of Tom Robinson, no one could doubt the defendants' innocence; the question, rather, was the interpretation of "rape" as a political disguise in the large wardrobe of southern racism and the judicial procedure employed to codify a predetermined guilt. The facts of *Powell* might have arisen in any number of criminal cases, but black-on-white rape cases in some parts of the Jim Crow South were often guarantees of the denial of due process—if the accused even got to arraignment and trial. Anticipating the Till case two decades later, the initial Scottsboro case was distinguished by the fact that the court was anxious to preserve the appearance of due process and avert a mob's vigilante justice. The anti-lynching crusader Jessie Ames rightly noted, however, that a lynching of the defendants was avoided only "at the expense of the integrity of the law."[32]

It is a tragic feature of the initial Scottsboro trial, then, that its speedy procedure at once averted (even if it actually reproduced) mob rule, created various outrageous abridgments of due process, ultimately resulted in key Supreme Court guarantees of criminal and civil rights, and yet brought justice to none of the accused. As Atticus's futile defense of Tom Robinson proves, the beneficial effects of *Powell* were not immediately apparent in the courtrooms of Alabama. The case bears on the novel not because it affects Tom's case, however, but because it makes clear how right to counsel and strategies of literary representation are related. The right of black men and women to adequate representation in courts of criminal law usually meant, certainly in the segregated South, representation by white counsel—that is, representation by a white voice and argument of the kind idealized in the portrayal of Atticus Finch. That is to say, because the novel's power is tied to the national culture's propensity to embrace such liberal heroics, we must take note of its immersion in a legal moment at which the constricted frame of reference defining Tom Robinson's right to be represented could not help but enforce Harper Lee's moral appeal to white paternalism at the same time that it underscored her implicit insistence that the nationalization of civil rights, like that of criminal rights, could not be accomplished by judicial fiat. On key fronts in the battle over the Fourteenth Amendment, *To Kill a Mockingbird* thus describes exactly why the South would remain an American problem so long as it refused to admit that federal oversight and the Constitution took precedence over state and local custom.

In this respect, the mechanism by which Atticus's defense of Tom Robinson overlaps with Scottsboro at two points is worth special attention.

Samuel Leibowitz outraged the Alabama courtroom audience, the southern press, and several judges by his scathing dismantling of the testimony of Victoria Price, the principal witness after Ruby Bates recanted her story. His cross-examination called into question Price's virtue (he proved she had been a prostitute), her sexual experiences at the time in question (he showed she had voluntary intercourse with a white man less than twenty-four hours before the purported gang rape), and the state's worthless medical case (he forced examining doctors to admit that the evidence was useless: no motile sperm; no semen on her clothing; no vaginal injuries; and no scratches on her back, despite her claim of having been raped by six young men while lying bare-backed in a train car loaded with chert). For her part, Victoria Price, who at first took apparent pleasure in what seemed at times a chatty recounting of the events, became increasingly sullen and vituperative in response to Leibowitz's grilling, not least when he feigned politeness.[33]

But neither his argument nor the evidence itself mattered. What Leibowitz failed to estimate correctly was that the trial, in the end, was about the South's right, as one prosecutor put it, to "protect the sacred secret parts of ... the fair womanhood of this great State."[34] He miscalculated as well the degree to which Communism and the advocacy of black rights easily merged in the ritual scenario of violated southern womanhood. For instance, a 1934 leaflet issued by the Birmingham White Legion asked: "How would you like to awaken one morning to find your wife or daughter attacked by a Negro or a Communist?"[35] In the course of the first round of appeals, the Alabama State Supreme Court, although its motives may have been less than honest, rejected the adducement of Victoria Price's reputation as a prostitute, just as it rejected the appeal on the right-to-counsel and jury pool issues as well. If the Court observed a distinction important to women's rights, however, it too put the South's rape complex on display. Dismissing the appellants' complaint about the undue speed of the trial, the Court cited the celerity with which the assassin of President McKinley had been tried and executed in 1901. It applauded swift justice and, taking a page out of the speeches of Benjamin Tillman and the novels of Thomas Dixon, contended that "some things may happen to one worse than death." "[I]f the evidence is to be believed, one of these things happened to this defenseless woman, Victoria Price."[36] Or, as another prosecutor had replied in the second trial, when Leibowitz objected to his ranting about "niggers" and rape: "I ain't said nothin' wrong. Your Honor knows I always make the same speech in every nigger rape case." The judge in question concurred; and when he gave his instructions to the jury in a subsequent trial, he snarled out the word "r-r-rapist" in a gruesome tone.[37]

Although he takes none of Leibowitz's personal pride in doing so, Atticus Finch also politely but thoroughly humiliates Mayella Ewell on the stand, shredding her testimony, proving that she has been beaten (and probably raped) by her father, Bob Ewell, and in the process laying the ground for an appeal even as he virtually guarantees his client's conviction by the local jury. His brilliant cross-examination of Mayella more or less obviates the jury's verdict, which is predicated upon the simple assertion by a white woman and her father that a "black nigger" has been "ruttin" on her (173). Lee, of course, does not call into question Mayella's veracity by undermining her reputation for chastity but instead takes the greater risk—for which Tom must pay the heavier price—of making evident her own attempt to seduce an African-American man. It is necessary to the novel's excruciating effect that Mayella Ewell be a more sympathetic victim and a more compelling witness than Victoria Price. But it is also necessary that, like Victoria Price and like Carolyn Bryant, the principal defense witness in the trial of Emmett Till's killers, she lie in order to protect her father and to uphold the scaffolding of Maycomb County's rape complex. In Mayella's case, fittingly, there can be no medical evidence of rape because no doctor was called; but Atticus uses the evidence of her beating to prove that Robert E. Lee Ewell (to cite her father's actual name), not Tom Robinson, is guilty. He does so in a way important both to the novel's invocation of Scottsboro and to its own tactical usurpation of black voice, act, and identity.

Because he is disabled, his left arm shriveled from a cotton gin accident, Tom cannot have produced Mayella's injuries. There may be a particular allusion to Scottsboro here in that evidence brought forth in proof of the young men's innocence included the fact that one was crippled by syphilis to the point of sexual incapacity and another was nearly blind. All were poorly educated, and four of the nine were said to be mentally impaired. None of this necessarily counts against a charge of rape, of course, but as the Supreme Court reiterated in its *Powell* opinion,[38] it counts mightily in the rationale for right to counsel as a part of due process, for the physical or mental deficiency of the defendants was made a key part of the appeals in *Powell* both to undermine the probability of guilt and to bolster the more far-reaching constitutional argument. The cost to the humanity of the defendants, however, was not insignificant—no less so than the cost to our accurate perception of Emmett Till's humanity imposed by William Faulkner in a 1956 interview: "Maybe the purpose of this sorry and tragic error committed in my native Mississippi by two white adults on an afflicted Negro child is to prove to us whether or not we deserve to survive."[39] In what way Till was "afflicted" or how his murder might be construed as simply an "error" Faulkner, with his characteristic mixture of sympathetic insight and reactionary detachment, did not explain. Like Faulkner's peculiar construction of Till as a potential sacrificial victim, the question of physical or mental deficiency in the *Powell* decision bears analogically on the representation of blackness in *To Kill a Mockingbird*. It is not enough for Tom Robinson to be innocent. He must be unquestionably a "quiet, respectable, humble Negro" (192, 204). He must be pathetically innocent—a victim of Mayella's desperate loneliness and abuse, a strong man but emotionally incapable of resistance or violence, and comparable, as the novel's central metaphor puts it, to those innocent songbirds whose only job, a form of minstrelsy, is to "make music for us to enjoy ... [to] sing their hearts out for us" (90).

In making Tom Robinson a contemporary version of Uncle Tom, the novel silences him and largely deletes from view his life and that of his family, but its reasons for doing so are not simplistic or one-dimensional. Lee's strategy of indirection sets in motion a dialectic between Atticus's voluble, nearly sacrosanct white voice and Tom's proscribed, muted black voice, and again between the 1930s, the world of Scottsboro and *Powell*, and the 1950s, the world of Selma and *Brown*. Of course the justification for Tom's own diffidence in the white man's world is clear enough if we call to mind the testimony of another Alabama sharecropper of the 1930s, Ned Cobb, whose story, under the pseudonym Nate Shaw, was recorded in the magnificent oral history *All God's Dangers*. In 1932, the same year as Scottsboro, Cobb was brought to trial for resisting sheriff's deputies who had come to confiscate illegally a neighbor's cotton crop. Recounting his own farcical one-day trial in the moving vernacular of his narrative—with its colloquial but still telling use of the term *nigger*—Cobb created an indelible picture of the legal and social silence imposed upon African Americans in his day:

> The nigger was disrecognized; the white man in this country had everything fixed and mapped out. Didn't allow no niggers to stand arm and arm together. The rule worked just like it had always worked: they was against me definitely just like they was against those Scottsboro boys.... The trials was just a sham, just a sham, both of em. I might tell em everything just like it was but they'd kick against me in court, in regards to my color, unless it come up this way: now a nigger could go in court and testify against his own color in favor of the white man, and his word was took. But when it come to speakin out in his own defense, niggers weren't heard in court. White folks is white folks, niggers is niggers, and a nigger's word never has went worth a penny unless some white man backed it up and told the same thing that the nigger told and was willin to stand up for the nigger. But if another white man spoke against the nigger and against the white man that was supportin him, why, they'd call that first white man "nigger-lover" and they wouldn't believe a word he said.[40]

We must imagine that, could Tom speak for himself, his interpretation of Alabama justice (if not his language) might be pretty close to Ned Cobb's. Because it filters Tom's story through the legal representation of Atticus Finch and the storytelling representation of Scout Finch, however, *To Kill a Mockingbird* denies Tom even this much of a voice in his story and therefore precludes a full portrait of the African-American struggle for justice. Here too, moreover, the novel's nostalgia screens out the urgency of the moment in which Lee was writing, for its frame of reference—its frame of representation, one might say—is not the world of Ned Cobb alone but also the world of Emmett Till.

*   *   *

Thirty years and two thousand miles away from Tom Robinson, Eldridge Cleaver, minister of information for the Black Panthers, composed a harsh, violent refutation of the white South's racial fantasies when he recalled his 1955 breakdown in Soledad Prison upon learning of Emmett Till's lynching. His rage against yet another perversion of justice, said Cleaver, was the catalyst for his new philosophy that rape could be made into an "insurrectionary act," one explicable in the lines from his poem "To a White Girl":

> Your white meat
> Is nightmare food.
> White is
> The skin of Evil.
> You're my Moby Dick,
> White Witch,
> Symbol of the rope and hanging tree,
> Of the burning cross.[41]

Whatever injustice is answered by his rage, Cleaver's theory of rape was abhorrent. Yet his militant seizure of the historical myth of black male sexuality and his verse, in part an amalgam of James Weldon Johnson, Jean Toomer, Langston Hughes, and others, are a fair index of the conservatism of Harper Lee's novel—its palpable attempt both to register the reappearance of the South's rape complex in the Till case and to displace it into the time past of Scottsboro, to fold it into Scout's narrative but at the same time banish it to a nightmare from which the South might yet awake.

Cleaver was one of many African Americans, from Muhammad Ali to Henry Hampton, producer of *Eyes on the Prize*, who dated their civil rights

activism—or, as in the case of Cleaver, their outlaw radicalism—to an awareness of the Till case. Medgar Evers, field secretary for the NAACP, risked his
life to gather evidence and witnesses against Till's killers, and Anne Moody
remembered that Till's murder made her hate both the whites responsible
for the crime (the murder *and* the trial) and the blacks who did not rise
against such injustice.[42] The Till case left an equal measure of well-directed
activism and boiling debate in its wake for more than two decades to come,
with Susan Brownmiller and Angela Davis, among others, making it a point
of departure for their critiques of the conjunction of racism and sexism and
Toni Morrison choosing it as the subject for her only play, *Dreaming
Emmett*.[43]

The most elaborate African-American response to Emmett Till was
James Baldwin's 1964 play *Blues for Mister Charlie*. As Baldwin recognized,
the special heinousness of the case came less from the self-evident miscarriage of justice or the gruesome publicity of the violence done Till (his mother demanded an open casket at his Chicago funeral, and photos of the disfig-
ured corpse ran in *Jet* magazine) than from the cold-blooded display of
southern defiance in the aftermath of the acquittal. In a famous 1957 interview conducted by William Bradford Huie for *Look* magazine, Till's murderers had freely admitted killing the boy and explained their actions in stereotypical terms. J. W. Milam argued that he and Roy Bryant had only intended to whip Till for his alleged insult to Bryant's wife and send him back to
Chicago; but when Till purportedly bragged about his white girlfriends in
the North, Milam did the only thing he could: "I counted pictures o' *three*
white gals in his pocketbook before I burned it. What else could I do [but kill
him]? No use lettin' him get no bigger!"[44] In reply to such white supremacist arrogance, Baldwin created not a cringing black victim but a smart-talk-
ing black man, born in the South but with a racial consciousness galvanized
by life in the North, whose own brashness calls the white man's rhetorical
bluff, mocking both the racist history of the Delta economy ("Coke! Me and
my man been toting barges and lifting bales, that's right, we been slaving, and
we need a little cool") and the white man's sexual anxiety ("The master race!
You let me in that tired white chick's drawers, she'll know who's the master
race!").[45] Baldwin, one might say, sought to provide a bridge from Bigger
Thomas to Stokely Carmichael and Eldridge Cleaver, from the impotent
rage of the pre-*Brown* years to the militant youth leadership, and increasing
radicalism, of the civil rights movement when the Student Nonviolent
Coordinating Committee and Black Power came to the fore.

Despite fascinating, surreal elements of stagecraft, Baldwin's play
labors to conceptualize either white racists or white liberals in provocative

terms, as though Baldwin simply found their fear unfathomable. His spokesman for liberal outrage, the journalist Parnell James, is no more effectual than Harper Lee's B. B. Underwood, who bangs out frantic editorials on racial injustice but secretly despises blacks. In *Blues for Mister Charlie*, no Atticus Finch appears, and Richard, like Emmett Till, is murdered in cold blood, albeit in deliberately stylized stage drama suffused with a sense of ritual repetition and debilitating weariness. But African-American characters speak at length and with passion in the play: Baldwin, like Cleaver, Moody, and others, found in Emmett Till a sufficient catalyst for his own reconstruction of the governing mythos of the white South, different in degree but not in kind from the governing mythos of white America.

From the perspective of the light it sheds on *To Kill a Mockingbird*, however, surely the most remarkable response to Till's death is Gwendolyn Brooks's sharp, strong refutation of the murder and its archive of white southern hatred in her poem "A Bronzeville Mother Loiters in Mississippi. Meanwhile, a Mississippi Mother Burns Bacon." Speaking from within the consciousness of one of the white killers' wives, Brooks imagines the growing revulsion the woman feels as the terror of her husband's act overtakes her. The illusion of his racial heroism shatters as she imagines Till's death even as her husband's bestial hands and lips clutch at her for satisfaction of his desire:

> She heard no hoof-beat of the horse and saw no flash of the shining steel.
> He pulled her face around to meet
> His, and there it was, close close,
> For the first time in all those days and nights.
> His mouth, wet and red,
> So very, very, very red,
> Closed over hers.

In the extended metaphor of the Fine Prince come to rescue his wife, the "milk-white maid," from the Dark Villain, Brooks rewrites a scene epitomized in *Birth of a Nation* but common to the racial rescue fantasies that made the Till travesty possible. Just as the mythology of heroism collapses into the truth of night riders and the Klan, so the protection against rape collapses into the expression of rape, its blood-red desire suffocating the woman's screams but linking her irrevocably to Till's mother:

> But his mouth would not go away and neither would the
> Decapitated exclamation points in that Other Woman's eyes.[46]

If it is generous to Carolyn Bryant (who, at least in public and in court, displayed no such conscience or cross-racial sisterhood), Brooks's poem, published in the same year as *To Kill a Mockingbird*, provides a further means to imagine Scout Finch grown up, for Brooks's daring leap into a counterracial and historical reality, because it has no parallel in the carefully circumscribed narrative of Scout Finch, forces us to ask if Harper Lee's adult narrator is capable of speaking in such a voice. It is a possibility that the novel neither denies nor confirms. Even if it is generated by the fictive adult consciousness of the 1950s, however, Scout's voice remains that of the child of the 1930s, which has the inevitable effect of placing it into a sectional as well as a temporal trap, at once lessening the moral force of its judgment and defining the novel itself as a manifestation of the South as an American problem. That such various representations of African-American self-assertion as those of Cleaver, Baldwin, and Brooks coexisted historically with *To Kill a Mockingbird*—but of course failed to reach even a fraction of Lee's vast audience—is a reminder that Atticus and Scout Finch may be less characters in a novel than the embodiment of the nation's profound, continuing, and frequently self-deluding need for racial salvation. If Harper Lee stops short of turning Tom's sacrifice into such a perfect agency for white redemption—as Faulkner had done with the sacrifice of Joe Christmas in his own Scottsboro-era novel, *Light in August*—the novel's desperate strategy of retrospection in effect stalls for time while black leaders capable of pushing beyond the spent forces of massive resistance and the liberal endgame of Atticus Finch come to the fore. As much as the farcical trial of Tom Robinson, of course, the conclusion of the novel also demonstrates that the law—most of all, the Constitution or the Supreme Court—may be incapable of rendering justice. The lesson latent within Atticus's willingness to cover up Boo's part in the killing of Bob Ewell is that circumvention of the law, even violent civil disobedience, may be necessary in order to create even an approximation of justice—though it remains a real question at the end of Scout's narrative whether the way of life in Maycomb has changed at all.

Tom Robinson's disabled arm is his legal alibi, but it is also the author's alibi—in the one case useless but in the other, for that very reason, perfect. Atticus must not only speak for him but also appropriate into his own ethical heroism Tom's masculinity and dignity as a black man, his very identity, much as the book itself appropriates Tom's African-American world to the ethical heroism of its white liberal argument. The reiterated moral of the novel—that to understand a person you must stand in his shoes or, better yet, "climb into his skin and walk around in it" (157, 218, 30)—is, in fact, called into question by its principal strategy of representation, which is in turn bound tightly to the limited, ventriloquized voice that African Americans are granted in the legal and customary world of the novel that belongs as much to 1950s America as it does to 1930s Alabama. *Powell v. Alabama* gave criminal defendants the right to legal representation as passionate and valuable as that afforded Tom Robinson by Atticus Finch. But in its very assault on states' rights and, by implication, on the doctrine of segregation, *Powell* also underlined the fact that the triumph of white liberalism might not be the end of racism.

It was Harper Lee's fortune to write at a moment when white America was ready for fictive salvation, and the risk she took cost her widespread scorn in the South for betraying her region and its way of life; but it was also her fate to write at a moment when other voices were being heard—in boycotts and demonstrations, in demands for enforcement of the law—and when other options for literary representation of the struggle for black justice were readily apparent. Just as the reach of Atticus Finch's integrity is circumscribed by his admonition that moral action must respect the prejudices of "our friends" and ultimately abide by local ethics, so the novel's undeniable power is circumscribed by its own narrative strategies.

It is no mistake, perhaps, that the white children of *To Kill a Mockingbird* never grow up. In Scout's retrospective narration, they remain ever poised for the hypothesis of desegregation. With the promised land of the post-*Brown* world ever on the horizon, Scout and Jem are timeless inheritors of the liberal vision even as Atticus Finch is its timeless exponent. Yet in choosing to contain Tom's story—the story of the black South—within the carefully controlled narrative consciousness of Scout and the idealized grandeur of Atticus Finch, Lee subordinated lasting vision to a moral expediency that remains familiar enough in late-twentieth-century America, as the racial problems of the South have become more commonly recognized as national problems. Locked into the paired narrative capacities of Atticus and Scout, Tom Robinson, and the social and historical African-American world for which he stands, are left without a true voice in their own representation, living still, in every rereading of the novel, under the South's death sentence and returning us to the admonition of James Baldwin in his essay on Faulkner and desegregation: "Any real change implies the breakup of the world as one has always known it, the loss of all that gave one an identity, the end of safety.... There is never time in the future in which we will work out our salvation. The challenge is in the moment, the time is always now."[47]

NOTES

For helpful comments on this essay I would like to express my gratitude to colleagues in the 1992–93 faculty seminar sponsored by the Robert Penn Warren Center for the Humanities at Vanderbilt University and to audiences at Dartmouth College, West Virginia University, the University of Michigan, Northwestern University, the University of Southern California, the University of California at Riverside, and the Bread Loaf School of English. For research assistance, also supported by Vanderbilt University, I would like to thank Lisa Siefker Long.

1. James Carville, quoted in Garry Wills, "From the Campaign Trail: Clinton's Hell-Raiser," *New Yorker*, October 12, 1992, 93; Zell Miller, quoted in Celestine Sibley, "Miller Unfurls a Call for Justice and Honor," *Atlanta Constitution*, January 13, 1993, B, 2.

2. James Farmer, *Lay Bare the Heart: An Autobiography of the Civil Rights Movement* (New York, 1985), 14.

3. W. J. Cash, *The Mind of the South* (1941; reprint, New York, 1960), 117–19; J. Thomas Heflin, quoted in Harvard Sitkoff, *A New Deal for Blacks: The Emergence of Civil Rights as a National Issue* (New York, 1978), 267.

4. Harper Lee, *To Kill a Mockingbird* (1960; reprint, New York, 1982), 88. Further citations will be included in the text.

5. Lillian Smith, *Killers of the Dream*, rev. ed. (New York, 1961), 87.

6. Tom Brady, "Black Monday," in *The Eyes on the Prize Civil Rights Reader*, ed. Clayborne Carson et al. (New York, 1991), 93; Stephen J. Whitfield, *A Death in the Delta: The Story of Emmett Till* (Baltimore, 1988), vii, 10; David R. Goldfield, *Black, White, and Southern: Race Relations and Southern Culture, 1940 to the Present* (Baton Rouge, 1990), 76, 87.

7. Arthur Raper, *The Tragedy of Lynching* (Chapel Hill, 1933), 59–65; but cf. Robin D. G. Kelley, *Hammer and Hoe*: Alabama Communists during the Great Depression (Chapel Hill, 1990), who identifies the man as Tom Robertson, 81.

8. Frank L. Owsley, "Scottsboro: Third Crusade; Sequel to Abolitionism and Reconstruction," *American Review* 1 (January 1933): 267.

9. Langston Hughes, *Scottsboro Limited: Four Poems and a Play in Verse* (New York, 1932), n.p. It is noteworthy that the two best novels that may be said to be "about" Scottsboro, *To Kill a Mockingbird* and Arna Bontemps's *Black Thunder* (1936), a historical novel centered on the Richmond, Virginia, slave uprising led by Gabriel Prosser in 1800, speak pointedly to its principal issues without even mentioning the case.

10. Sitkoff, *New Deal for Blacks*, 102–215 passim; Morton Sosna, *In Search of the Silent South: Southern Liberals and the Race Issue* (New York, 1977), 60–87.

11. Charles S. Johnson, *Shadow of the Plantation* (1934; reprint, Chicago, 1969), 212.

12. Claudia Johnson, "The Secret Courts of Men's Hearts: Code and Law in Harper Lee's *To Kill a Mockingbird*," *Studies in American Fiction* 19 (Autumn 1991): 129–39.

13. Ralph McGill, *The South and the Southerner* (1963; reprint, Athens, Ga., 1992), 244.

14. *Brown v. Board of Education*, 347 U.S. 493 (1954).

15. McGill, *South and the Southerner*, 245; Martin Luther King Jr., *A Testament of Hope: The Essential Writings and Speeches of Martin Luther King, Jr.*, ed. James M. Washington (San Francisco, 1986), 219.

16. *Brown v. Board of Education*, 347 U.S. 494, 492 (1954); Andrew Kull, *The Color-Blind Constitution* (Cambridge, Mass., 1992), 151–63; Richard Kluger, *Simple Justice: The History of Brown v. Board of Education and Black America's Struggle for Equality* (New York, 1976), 700–714.

17 *Brown v. Board of Education*, 349 U.S. 300–301 (1955). On massive resistance and the long-term effects of *Brown*, see, for example, Numan V. Bartley, *The Rise of Massive Resistance: Race and Politics in the South during the 1950s* (Baton Rouge, 1969), and Michael J. Klarman, "How *Brown* Changed Race Relations: The Backlash Thesis," *Journal of American History* 81 (June 1994): 81–118.

18. King, *Testament of Hope*, 218; Thurgood Marshall, in *Eyes on the Prize*, Henry Hampton, producer, PBS Television.

19. James Baldwin, *The Fire Next Time* (New York, 1964), 138–40.

20. See Thomas L. Schaffer, "The Moral Theology of Atticus Finch," *University of Pittsburgh Law Review* 42 (Winter 1981): 181–224, and Timothy L. Hall, "Moral Character, the Practice of Law, and Legal Education," *Mississippi Law Journal* 60 (Winter 1990): 511–54.

21. John Dollard, *Caste and Class in a Southern Town* (New Haven, 1937), 359.

22. This deflection of attention from the Klan is all the more striking in view of Lee's transparent use of the rise of Hitler and European anti-Semitism as an ironic counterpoint to southern racism and the hypocrisy of American "democracy" (244–47). In the 1930s, despite black attempts to exploit parallels between racism and fascism, the white South routinely suppressed any conscious recognition of the suitability of the comparison. See Johnpeter Horst Grill and Robert L. Jenkins, "The Nazis and the American South in the 1930s: A Mirror Image?" *Journal of Southern History* 58 (November 1992): 667–94.

23. Quoted in Quentin Reynolds, *Courtroom: The Story of Samuel S. Leibowitz* (New York, 1950), 275.

24. Quoted in Dan T. Carter, *Scottsboro: A Tragedy of the American South*, rev. ed. (Chapel Hill, 1991), 244; Allan K. Chalmers, *They Shall Be Free* (New York, 1951), 51.

25. Carter, *Scottsboro*, 235.

26. *Daily Worker* quoted in Sitkoff, *New Deal for Blacks*, 225.

27. Francis A. Allen, "The Supreme Court and State Criminal Justice," *Wayne Law Review* 4 (summer 1958): 192–95; William Beaney, *The Right to Counsel in American Courts* (Ann Arbor, 1955), 151–57; Anthony Lewis, *Gideon's Trumpet* (1964; reprint, New York, 1989), 112–13, 197–220; David Fellman, *The Defendant's Rights Today* (Madison, Wis., 1976), 211–12.

28. *Norris v. Alabama*, 294 U.S. 587 (1935); Carter, *Scottsboro*, 322–24; Sitkoff, *New Deal for Blacks*, 227–28.

29. Haywood Patterson and Earl Conrad, *Scottsboro Boy* (New York, 1950), 37; Carter, *Scottsboro*, 324.

30. *Powell v. Alabama*, 287 U.S. 49 (1932).

31. The context of the scene, the ladies' sanctimonious discussion of African missions, only heightens Lee's great irony by bringing the black anticolonialist movements of the late 1950s into dialogue with America's civil rights movement. The church's failed mission in Africa—its participation in buttressing colonial depredations—is made comparable by Lee to the Christian hypocrisy of the Jim Crow South, each domain of white supremacist ideology an extension of the other.

32. Quoted in Sosna, *In Search of the Silent South*, 36.

33. Carter, *Scottsboro*, 81, 205.

34. Carter, *Scottsboro*, 344–45.

35. Kelley, *Hammer and Hoe*, 79.

36. *Weems v. State*, 224 *Alabama Reports* 526, 528, 536, 551 (1932).

37. Reynolds, *Courtroom*, 283–84; Carter, *Scottsboro*, 346.

38. Carter, *Scottsboro*, 45–46, 221–22; *Powell v. Alabama*, 52, 58, 69, 71.

39. William Faulkner, *Lion in the Garden: Interviews with William Faulkner*, ed. James B. Meriwether and Michael Millgate (Lincoln, 1968), 254.

40. Theodore Rosengarten, *All God's Dangers: The Life of Nate Shaw* (New York, 1974), 340.

41. Eldridge Cleaver, *Soul on Ice* (New York, 1968), 11–14.

42. Anne Moody, *Coming of Age in Mississippi* (New York, 1968), 129, 187; Whitfield, *Death in the Delta*, 58–59, 85–126.

43. Whitfield, *Death in the Delta*, 110–15.

44. William Bradford Huie, "What's Happened to the Emmett Till Killers?" *Look*, January 22, 1957, 64. See also Whitfield, *Death in the Delta*, 33–69, and William M. Simpson, "Reflections on a Murder: The Emmett Till Case," in *Southern Miscellany: Essays in History in Honor of Glover Moore*, ed. Frank Allen Dennis (Jackson, Miss., 1981), 177–200.

45. James Baldwin, *Blues for Mister Charlie* (New York, 1964), 98, 102.

46. Gwendolyn Brooks, "A Bronzeville Mother Loiters in Mississippi. Meanwhile, a Mississippi Mother Burns Bacon," in *Selected Poems* (New York, 1963), 75–80.

47. James Baldwin, "Faulkner and Desegregation," *Nobody Knows My Name* (New York, 1961), 100, 106.

DEAN SHACKELFORD

The Female Voice in To Kill a Mockingbird: Narrative Strategies in Film and Novel

Aunt Alexandra was fanatical on the subject of my attire. I could not possibly hope to be a lady if I wore breeches; when I said I could do nothing in a dress, she said I wasn't supposed to be doing anything that required pants. Aunt Alexandra's vision of my deportment involved playing with small stoves, tea sets, and wearing the Add-A-Pearl necklace she gave me when I was born; furthermore, I should be a ray of sunshine in my father's lonely life. I suggested that one could be a ray of sunshine in pants just as well, but Aunty said that one had to behave like a sunbeam, that I was born good but had grown progressively worse every year. She hurt my feelings and set my teeth permanently on edge, but when I asked Atticus about it, he said there were already enough sunbeams in the family and to go about my business, he didn't mind me much the way I was.[1]

This passage reveals the importance of female voice and gender in Harper Lee's popular Pulitzer Prize-winning novel, To Kill a Mockingbird, first published in 1960. The novel portrays a young girl's love for her father and brother and the experience of childhood during the Great Depression in a racist, segregated society which uses superficial and materialistic values to judge outsiders, including the powerful character Boo Radley.

From *Mississippi Quarterly* 50, no. 1. ©1996 by Mississippi State University.

In 1962, a successful screen version of the novel (starring Gregory Peck) appeared. However, the screenplay, written by Horton Foote, an accomplished Southern writer, abandons, for the most part, the novel's first-person narration by Scout (in the motion picture, a first-person angle of vision functions primarily to provide transitions and shifts in time and place). As a result, the film is centered more on the children's father, Atticus Finch, and the adult world in which Scout and Jem feel alien. As several commentators have noted, the film seems centered on the racial issue much more than on other, equally successful dimensions of the novel. Clearly, part of the novel's success has to do with the adult-as-child perspective. Lee, recalling her own childhood, projects the image of an adult reflecting on her past and attempting to recreate the experience through a female child's point of view.

That the film shifts perspectives from the book's primary concern with the female protagonist and her perceptions to the male father figure and the adult male world is noteworthy. While trying to remain faithful to the importance of childhood and children in the novel, Foote's objective narration is interrupted only occasionally with the first-person narration of a woman, who is presumably the older, now adult Scout. However, the novel is very much about the experience of growing up as a female in a South with very narrow definitions of gender roles and acceptable behavior. Because this dimension of the novel is largely missing from the film's narrative, the film version of *To Kill a Mockingbird* may be seen as a betrayal of the novel's full feminist implications—a compromise of the novel's full power.

Granted, when a film adaptation is made, the screenwriter need not be faithful to the original text. As Robert Giddings, Keith Selby, and Chris Wensley note in their important book *Screening the Novel*, a filmmaker's approaches to adapting a literary work may range from one of almost complete faithfulness to the story to one which uses the original as an outline for a totally different work on film.[2] Foote's adaptation seems to fall somewhere in between these extremes, with the film decidedly faithful to certain aspects of the novel. His story clearly conveys the novel's general mood; it is obvious he wishes to remain close to the general subject matter of life in the South during the Great Depression and its atmosphere of racial prejudice and Jim Crow. Reflecting on the film, Harper Lee herself states, "For me, Maycomb is there, its people are there: in two short hours one lives a childhood and lives it with Atticus Finch, whose view of life was the heart of the novel."[3]

Though admittedly Atticus Finch is at the heart of the film and novel, there are some clear and notable discrepancies between the two versions that alter the unique perspective of the novel considerably—despite what Lee herself has commented. Only about 15% of the novel is devoted to Tom

Robinson's rape trial, whereas in the film, the running time is more than 30% of a two-hour film. Unlike the book, the film is primarily centered on the rape trial and the racism of Maycomb which has made it possible—not surprising considering it was made during what was to become the turbulent period of the 1960s when racial issues were of interest to Hollywood and the country as a whole. Significant, though, are the reviewers and critics who believe this issue, rather than the female child's perspectives on an adult male world, is the novel's main concern and as a result admire the film for its faithfulness to the original.

Many teachers of the novel and film also emphasize this issue to the neglect of other equally important issues. In 1963 and again in the year of the film's twenty-fifth anniversary, the Education Department of Warner Books issued Joseph Mersand's study guide on the novel, one section of which is an essay subtitled "A Sociological Study in Black and White." Turning the novel into sociology, many readers miss other aspects of Lee's vision. In an early critical article, Edgar Schuster notes that the racial dimensions of the novel have been overemphasized, especially by high school students who read it, and he offers possible strategies for teaching students the novel's other central issues, which he lists as "Jem's physiological and psychological growth" (mentioning Scout's growth in this regard only briefly as if it is a side issue), the caste system of Maycomb, the title motif, education, and superstition.[4] What is so striking about Schuster's interpretation is his failure to acknowledge that the issue of Scout's gender is crucial to an understanding not only of the novel but also of Scout's identification with her father.[5] As feminists often note, male readers sometimes take female perspectives and turn them into commentaries from a male point of view. Because the novel and film center so much on Atticus, he, rather than Scout, becomes the focus.

With regard to the film, I do not mean to suggest that Foote has not attempted to make some references to Scout's problems with gender identity. When he does, however, the audience is very likely unable to make the connections as adequately as careful readers of the novel might. Of particular interest are two scenes from the film which also appear in the novel. During one of their summers with Dill, Jem insults Scout as the three of them approach the Radley home and Scout whines, fearful of what may happen. As in the novel, he tells her she is getting to be more like a girl every day, the implication being that boys are courageous and non-fearful and girls are weak and afraid (a point which is refuted when Jem's fears of Boo Radley and the dark are demonstrated). Nevertheless, what is most important in the scene is Scout's reaction. Knowing that being called a girl is an insult and that

being female is valued less than being male in her small Southern town, she
suddenly becomes brave in order to remain acceptable to her brother.

In another scene, as Scout passes by Mrs. Dubose's house and says
"hey," she is reprimanded for poor manners unbecoming of a Southern lady.
This scene occurs in both film and novel. However, in the novel Lee clarifies that the presumed insult to Mrs. Dubose originates with Mrs. Dubose's
assumptions as a Southern lady, a role which Scout, in the novel especially,
is reluctant to assume. The film's lack of a consistent female voice makes this
scene as well as others seem unnecessary and extraneous. This is only one
example of the way in which the superior narrative strategy of the novel
points out the weakness of the objective, male-centered narration of the
film.

One scene from the film concerning girlhood does not appear in the
novel. Careful not to suggest that the Finches are churchgoers (for what
reason?), as they are in the novel, Foote creates a scene which attempts to
demonstrate Scout's ambivalence about being female. As Scout becomes
old enough to enter school, she despises the thought of wearing a dress.
When she appears from her room to eat breakfast before attending school
for the first time, Jem ridicules her while Atticus, Miss Maudie, and
Calpurnia admire her. Scout comments: "I still don't see why I have to
wear a darn old dress."[6] A weakness of the film in this regard is that until
this scene, there has been little indication that Scout strongly dislikes
wearing dresses, let alone has fears of growing up as a female. The novel
makes it clear that Scout prefers her overalls to wearing dresses, which is
perhaps why Foote found it necessary to create this particular scene.
However, the previous two crucial scenes, while faithful to the novel's
general concerns with gender, create loose ends in the film which do not
contribute to the success of the narration and which compromise the
novel's feminist center.

The intermittent efforts to focus on the female narrator's perspective
prove unsuccessful in revealing the work's feminist dimensions. As the film
opens, the audience sees the hands of a small girl, presumably Scout, color-
ing.[7] After the credits, a woman's voice, described by Amy Lawrence as a
"disembodied voice exiled from the image," is heard reflecting on her perceptions of Maycomb."[8] By introducing the audience to the social and spatial context, this first-person narrator provides a frame for the whole. The
audience at this point, without having read the novel first, may not, however, recognize who the speaker is. As Scout appears playing in the yard, the
viewer is left to assume that the voice-over opening the film is the female
character speaking as a grown woman. The camera zooms down to reveal

Scout and soon thereafter shifts to the standard objective narration of most films. When the disembodied narrator is heard again, she reflects on Scout's views of Atticus after he insists she will have to return to school; yet, despite what her teacher says, father and daughter will continue reading each night the way they always have. Here the voice-over is designed to emphasize the heroic stature of Atticus and perhaps even to suggest that one reason for Scout's identification with him is his freedom of thought and action: "There just didn't seem to be anyone or thing Atticus couldn't explain. Though it wasn't a talent that would arouse the admiration of any of our friends. Jem and I had to admit he was very good at that but that was all he was good at, we thought" (Foote, p. 35). This intrusion becomes little more than a transition into the next scene, in which Atticus shoots the mad dog.

In the next intrusion the female voice interrupts the objective narration when, at school, Scout fights Cecil Jacobs for calling Atticus a "nigger lover." She states: "Atticus had promised me he would wear me out if he ever heard of me fightin' any more. I was far too old and too big for such childish things, and the sooner I learned to hold in, the better off everybody would be. I soon forgot ... Cecil Jacobs made me forget" (Foote, p. 42). Here again, the first-person narration provides coherence, allowing the scene of Scout's fight with Cecil Jacobs to be shortened and placing emphasis on the relationship between Atticus and Scout. The subtext of their conversation could perhaps be viewed as a reflection of traditional views that women should not be too aggressive or physical, but this scene, coupled with earlier scenes reflecting social values, is not couched in terms of Scout's transgressive behavior as a woman-to-be. The female voice in the film is not used to demonstrate the book's concern with female identity; rather, it reinforces the male-centered society which Atticus represents and which the film is gradually moving toward in focusing on the trial of Tom Robinson.

Another instance during which the female narrator intrudes on the objective, male-centered gaze of the camera occurs when Jem and Scout discuss the presents Boo Radley leaves for them in the knot-hole. At this point in the film, the attempt to convey the book's female narrative center falls completely apart. Not until after the very long trial scene does the camera emphasize the children's perceptions or the female narrator's angle of vision again. Instead, the audience is in the adult male world of the courtroom, with mature male authority as the center of attention. Immediately after the trial, the film seems most concerned with Jem's reactions to the trial, Jem's recognition of the injustice of the verdict in the Tom Robinson case, and Jem's desire to accompany his father when he tells Helen Robinson that Tom has been killed.

Scout is unable to observe directly the last event, and, as a result, the narration is inconsistent—by and large from the rape trial to the end of the film. The film does, however, make use of voice-over narration twice more. In the first instance, the female narrator again provides the transition in time and place to move from the previous scene, the revelation of Tom Robinson's death to his wife, into the confrontation between Atticus and Bob Ewell. As the camera focuses on an autumn scene with Scout dressed in a white dress, Jean Louise prepares the audience for the climax, which soon follows: "By October things had settled down again. I still looked for Boo every time I went by the Radley place. This night my mind was filled with Halloween. There was to be a pageant representing our county's agricultural products. I was to be a ham. Jem said he would escort me to the school auditorium. Thus began our longest journey together" (Foote, p. 72). Following this passage is the climactic scene, when Bob Ewell attacks Scout and Jem and Boo Radley successfully rescues them.

Shortly thereafter, the camera focuses on Scout's recognition of Boo as the protector and savior of Jem and her, and for the remainder of the film, the narration, arguably for the first time, is centered entirely on Scout's perception of the adult male world. She hears Heck Tate and Atticus debate over what to do about exposing the truth that Boo has killed Ewell while defending the children. The movement of the camera and her facial expression clearly indicate that Scout sees the meaning behind the adult's desires to protect Boo from the provincial Maycomb community which has marginalized him—and this scene signifies Scout's initiation into the world of adulthood.

As the film draws to a close, Scout, still in her overalls which will not be tolerated much longer in this society, walks Boo home. For the last time the audience hears the female voice:

> Neighbors bring food with death, and flowers with sickness, and little things in between. Boo was our neighbor. He gave us two soap dolls, a broken watch, and chain, a knife, and our lives. One time Atticus said you never really knew a man until you stood in his shoes and walked around in them. Just standin' on the Radley porch was enough .... The summer that had begun so long ago ended, another summer had taken its place, and a fall, and Boo Radley had come out.... I was to think of these days many times;—of Jem, and Dill and Boo Radley, and Tom Robinson ... and Atticus. He would be in Jem's room all night. And he would be there when, Jem waked up in the morning. (Foote, pp. 79–80)

The film ends, when, through a window, Scout is seen climbing into Atticus's lap while he sits near Jem. The camera gradually moves leftward away from the two characters in the window to a long shot of the house. By the end, then, the film has shifted perspective back to the female voice, fully identified the narrator as the older Scout (Jean Louise), and focused on the center of Scout's existence, her father (a patriarchal focus). The inconsistent emphasis on Scout and her perceptions makes the film seem disjointed.

Noting the patriarchal center of the film, Amy Lawrence suggests the possibility for a feminist reading. She argues that the disembodied narrator—as well as the author, Harper Lee, and the characters of Scout and Mayella Ewell—provides a "disjointed subjectivity" on film which is characteristic of "the experience of women in patriarchy" (p. 184). Such "disjointed subjectivity" is, however, missing from the novel, which centers on Scout's perceptions of being female in a male-dominated South. The novel's female-centered narration provides an opportunity for Lee to comment on her own childlike perceptions as well as her recognition of the problems of growing up female in the South. The feminine voice, while present in the film, receives far too little emphasis.

In the novel the narrative voice allows readers to comprehend what the film does not explain. Though some critics have attacked Lee's narration as weak and suggested that the use of first person creates problems with perspective because the major participant, first-person narrator must appear almost in all scenes, the novel's consistent use of first person makes it much clearer than the film that the reader is seeing all the events through a female child's eyes. Once the children enter the courtroom in the film, the center of attention is the adult world of Atticus Finch and the rape trial—not, as the book is able to suggest, the children's perceptions of the events which unravel before them.

Although it is clear in the film that Scout is a tomboy and that she will probably grow out of this stage in her life (witness the very feminine and Southern drawl of the female narrator, who, though not seen, conveys the image of a conventional Southern lady), the film, which does not openly challenge the perspective of white heterosexuals (male or female) nearly to the degree the novel does, does not make Scout's ambivalence about being a female in an adult male world clear enough. Because the novel's narrative vision is consistently first person throughout and as a result focused on the older Scout's perceptions of her growing-up years, the female voice is unquestionably heard and the narration is focused on the world of Maycomb which she must inevitably enter as she matures.

Furthermore, a number of significant questions about gender are raised in the novel: Is Scout (and, by implication, all females) an outsider looking on an adult male world which she knows she will be unable to enter as she grows into womanhood? Is her identification with Atticus due not only to her love and devotion for a father but also to his maleness, a power and freedom she suspects she will not be allowed to possess within the confines of provincial Southern society? Or is her identification with Atticus due to his androgynous nature (playing the role of mother and father to her and demonstrating stereotypically feminine traits: being conciliatory, passive, tolerant, and partially rejecting the traditional masculine admiration for violence, guns, and honor)? All three of these questions may lead to possible, even complementary readings which would explain Scout's extreme identification with her father.

As in the passage quoted at the beginning of this essay , the novel focuses on Scout's tomboyishness as it relates to her developing sense of a female self. Also evident throughout the novel is Scout's devotion to her father's opinions. Atticus seems content with her the way she is; only when others force him to do so does he concern himself with traditional stereotypes of the Southern female. Especially significant with regard to Scout's growing sense of womanhood is the novel's very important character, Aunt Alexandra, Atticus's sister, who is left out of the film entirely. Early in the novel, readers are made aware of Scout's antipathy for her aunt, who wishes to mold her into a Southern lady. Other female authority figures with whom Scout has difficulty agreeing are her first-grade teacher, Miss Fisher, and Calpurnia, the family cook, babysitter, and surrogate mother figure. When the females in authority interfere with Scout's perceptions concerning her father and their relationship, she immediately rebels, a rebellion which Atticus does not usually discourage—signifying her strong identification with male authority and her recognition that the female authority figures threaten the unique relationship which she has with her father and which empowers her as an individual.

Exactly why Scout identifies with Atticus so much may have as much to do with his own individuality and inner strength as the fact that he is a single parent and father. Since the mother of Scout and Jem is dead, Atticus has assumed the full responsibility of playing mother and father whenever possible—though admittedly he employs Calpurnia and allows Alexandra to move in with them to give the children, particularly Scout, a female role model. However, Atticus is far from a stereotypical Southern male. Despite his position as a respected male authority figure in Maycomb, he seems oblivious to traditional expectations concerning masculinity (for himself) and femininity (for Scout). The children in fact see him as rather unmanly: "When Jem and I asked him why he was so old, he said he got started late, which we felt reflected on his abilities and his masculinity" (p. 93). Jem is also upset because Atticus will not play tackle football. Mrs. Dubose criticizes Atticus for not remarrying, which is very possibly a subtle comment on his lack of virility. Later the children learn of his abilities at marksmanship, at bravery in watching the lynch mob ready to attack Tom Robinson, and at the defense of the same man. Perhaps this is Lee's way of suggesting that individuals must be allowed to develop their own sense of self without regard to rigid definitions of gender and social roles.

Scout's identification with Atticus may also be rooted in her recognition of the superficiality and limitations of being a Southern female. Mrs. Dubose once tells her: "'You should be in a dress and camisole, young lady! You'll grow up waiting on tables if somebody doesn't change your ways...'" (p. 106). This is one of many instances in the novel through which the first-person narrator reveals Lee's criticism of Southern women and their narrow-mindedness concerning gender roles. Even Atticus ridicules the women's attitudes. In one instance he informs Alexandra that he favors "'Southern womanhood as much as anybody, but not for preserving polite fiction at the expense of human life'" (p. 149). When Scout is "indignant" that women cannot serve on juries, Atticus jokingly says, "I guess it's to protect our frail ladies from sordid cases like Tom's. Besides ... I doubt if we'd ever get a complete case tried—the ladies'd be interrupting to ask questions" (p. 224). This seemingly sexist passage may in fact be the opposite; having established clearly that Atticus does not take many Southern codes seriously, Lee recognizes the irony in Atticus's statement that women, including his own independent-minded daughter, are "frail."

Admittedly, few women characters in the novel are very pleasant, with the exceptions of Miss Maudie Atkinson, the Finches' neighbor, and Calpurnia. Through the first-person female voice, Southern women are ridiculed as gossips, provincials, weaklings, extremists, even racists—calling to mind the criticism of Southern manners in the fiction of Flannery O'Connor. Of Scout's superficial Aunt Alexandra, Lee writes: "... Aunt Alexandra was one of the last of her kind: she has river-boat, boarding-school manners; let any moral come along and she would uphold it; she was born in the objective case; she was an incurable gossip" (p. 131). Scout's feelings for Alexandra, who is concerned with family heritage, position, and conformity to traditional gender roles, do alter somewhat as she begins to see Alexandra as a woman who means well and loves her and her father, and as she begins to accept certain aspects of being a Southern female. As Jem and Dill exclude her from their games, Scout gradually learns more about the alien world of being a female through sitting on the porch with Miss Maudie and observing Calpurnia work in the kitchen, which makes her begin "to think there was more skill involved in being a girl" than she has previously thought (p. 118). Nevertheless, the book makes it clear that the adult Scout, who narrates the novel and who has presumably now assumed the feminine name Jean Louise for good, is still ambivalent at best concerning the traditional Southern lady.

Of special importance with regard to Scout's growing perceptions of herself as a female is the meeting of the missionary society women, a scene which, like Aunt Alexandra's character, is completely omitted from the film. Alexandra sees herself as a grand host. Through observing the missionary women, Scout, in Austenian fashion, is able to satirize the superficialities and prejudices of Southern women with whom she is unwilling to identify in order to become that alien being called woman. Dressed in "my pink Sunday dress, shoes, and a petticoat," Scout attends a meeting shortly after Tom Robinson's death, knowing that her aunt makes her participate as "part of ... her campaign to teach me to be a lady" (p. 232). Commenting on the women, Scout says, "Rather nervous, I took a seat beside Miss Maudie and wondered why ladies put on their hats to go across the street. Ladies in bunches always filled me with vague apprehension and a firm desire to be elsewhere ..." (p. 232).

As the meeting begins, the ladies ridicule Scout for frequently wearing pants and inform her that she cannot become a member of the elite, genteel group of Southern ladyhood unless she mends her ways. Miss Stephanie Crawford, the town gossip, mocks Scout by asking her if she wants to grow up to be a lawyer, a comment to which Scout, coached by Aunt Alexandra, says, "Not me, just a lady" (p. 233)—with the obvious social satire evident. Scout clearly does not want to become a lady. Suspicious, Miss Stephanie replies, "'Well, you won't get very far until you start wearing dresses more often'" (p. 233). Immediately thereafter, Lee exposes even further the provincialism and superficiality of the group's appearance of gentility, piety, and morality. Mrs. Grace Meriwether's comments on "'those poor Mrunas'" who live "'in that jungle'" and need Christian salvation reflect a smug, colonialist attitude toward other races. When the women begin conversing about blacks in America, their bigotry—and Scout's disgust with it—becomes obvious.

Rather than the community of gentility and racism represented in the women of Maycomb, Scout clearly prefers the world of her father, as this passage reveals: "... I wondered at the world of women .... There was no doubt about it, I must soon enter this world, where on its surface fragrant ladies rocked slowly, fanned gently, and drank cool water" (p. 236). The female role is far too frivolous and unimportant for Scout to identify with. Furthermore, she says, "But I was more at home in my father's world. People like Mr. Heck Tate did not trap you with innocent questions to make fun of you .... Ladies seemed to live in faint horror of men, seemed unwilling to approve wholeheartedly of them. But I liked them .... [N]o matter how undelectable they were, ... they weren't 'hypocrites'" (p. 236). This obviously idealized and childlike portrayal of men nevertheless gets at the core of Scout's conflict. In a world in which men seem to have the advantages and seem to be more fair-minded and less intolerant than women with their petty concerns and superficial dress codes, why should she conform to the notion of Southern ladyhood? Ironically, Scout, unlike the reader, is unable to recognize the effects of female powerlessness which may be largely responsible for the attitudes of Southern ladies. If they cannot control the everyday business and legal affairs of their society, they can at least impose their code of manners and morality.

To Scout, Atticus and his world represent freedom and power. Atticus is the key representative of the male power which Scout wishes to obtain even though she is growing up as a Southern female. More important, Lee demonstrates that Scout is gradually becoming a feminist in the South, for, with the use of first-person narration, she indicates that Scout/Jean Louise still maintains the ambivalence about being a Southern lady she possessed as a child. She seeks to become empowered with the freedoms the men in her society seem to possess without question and without resorting to trivial and superficial concerns such as wearing a dress and appearing genteel.

Harper Lee's fundamental criticism of gender roles for women (and to a lesser extent for men) may be evident especially in her novel's identification with outsider figures such as Tom Robinson, Mayella Ewell, and Boo Radley. Curiously enough, the outsider figures with whom the novelist identifies most are also males. Tom Robinson, the male African American who has been disempowered and annihilated by a fundamentally racist, white male society, and Boo Radley, the reclusive and eccentric neighbor about whom legends of his danger to the fragile Southern society circulate regularly, are the two "mockingbirds" of the title. Ironically, they are unable to mock society's roles for them and as a result take the consequences of living on the margins—Tom, through his death; Boo, through his return to the protection of a desolate isolated existence.

Throughout the novel, however, the female voice has emphasized Scout's growing distance from her provincial Southern society and her identification with her father, a symbol of the empowered. Like her father, Atticus, Scout, too, is unable to be a "mockingbird" of society and as a result, in coming to know Boo Radley as a real human being at novel's end, she recognizes the empowerment of being the other as she consents to remain an outsider unable to accept society's unwillingness to seek and know before it judges. And it is perhaps this element of the female voice in Harper Lee's *To Kill a Mockingbird* which most makes Horton Foote's screen adaptation largely a compromise of the novel's full power.

NOTES

1. Harper Lee, *To Kill a Mockingbird* (New York: Popular Library, 1962), pp. 85–86.

2. *Screening the Novel: The Theory and Practice of Literary Dramatization* (New York: St. Martin's Press, 1990), pp. 10–12.

3. Joseph Mersand, *Studies in the Mass Media: To Kill a Mockingbird: 25th Anniversary Brochure and Study Guide* (Urbana, Illinois: NCTE, 1963, 1988), p. 18.

4. Edgar H. Schuster, "Discovering Theme and Structure in the Novel," *English Journal*, 52 (1963), p. 507.

5. The earliest reviewers generally bypass the novel's concerns about being a young female in the South—even when they mention the work's autobiographical dimensions. Recent critics, most notably Harold Bloom and Claudia Durst Johnson, still fail to acknowledge the heavily feminist dimensions of the novel. See Harold Bloom, ed., Harper Lee's *To Kill a Mockingbird: A Contemporary Literary Views Book* (Broomall, Pennsylvania: Chelsea House, 1996). In her useful casebook on and introductory critical study of the novel, Johnson includes the gender issue but still focuses primarily on the novel's concerns about race relations in the South. See Claudia Durst Johnson, ed. *Understanding To Kill a Mockingbird: A Student Casebook to Issues, Sources, and Historic Documents* (Westport, Connecticut; Greenwood Press, 1994); and Claudia Durst Johnson, *To Kill a Mockingbird: Threatening Boundaries* (New York: Twayne, 1994). The appearance of the Bloom and Johnson books may indicate a growing interest in the novel as a serious work of literature rather than merely a canonical novel for high school students.

6. Horton Foote, *To Kill a Mockingbird*, in *Three Screenplays: To Kill a Mockingbird, Tender Mercies, and The Trip to Bountiful* (New York; Grove Press, 1989), p. 30.

7. Universal Studios, *To Kill a Mockingbird*. Directed by Robert Mulligan; produced by Alan Pakula; screenplay by Horton Foote.

8. Amy Lawrence, *Echo and Narcissus: Women's Voices in Classical Hollywood Cinema* (Berkeley: University of California Press, 1991), p. 170.

PATRICK CHURA

Prolepsis and Anachronism:
Emmett Till and the Historicity of
To Kill a Mockingbird

T hough there is a strong consensus that *To Kill a Mockingbird* is deeply ori-
ented within the history of the Depression era, no analysis has attempted to
separate the historical conditions of the moment of the text's production in
the mid 1950s from the historical present of the novel, the mid 1930s. Such
analysis is revealing, first because under scrutiny the novel's 1930s history is
exposed as at times quite flawed in its presentation of facts. The WPA, for
example, did not exist until 1935, but it is mentioned in the novel's fourth
chapter, which is set in 1933. Eleanor Roosevelt did not violate segregation
law by sitting with black audience members at the Southern Conference on
Human Welfare in Birmingham until 1938, but this event is mentioned by
Mrs. Merriweather during the fall of 1935. More important than these several occasional chronological lapses, however, is the novel's participation in
racial and social ideology that characterized not the Depression era but the
early civil rights era. Because the text's 1930s history is superficial, the novel
is best understood as an amalgam or cross-historical montage, its "historical
present" diluted by the influence of events and ideology concurrent with its
period of production. The 1954 *Brown v. Board of Education* decision, for
example, stimulated a national debate in which Lee's novel participates and
upon which it offers forceful commentary. As fundamental a presence in *To
Kill a Mockingbird* is the structural and ideological detail of the Emmett Till

From *Southern Literary Journal.* © 2000 by University of North Carolina Press.

trial of 1955,[1] which upon close consideration seems unquestionably to have provided a workable model for aspects of Lee's fictional Tom Robinson trial. In other words, racial events and ideology of the 1950s—the period concurrent with the novel's production—leach into the depiction of Lee's 1930s history, orienting large sections the text not to the Depression era but to social conditions of the civil rights era. The mid 1950s/early civil rights era is therefore the context from which the novel is best understood as the intersection of cultural and literary ideology.

Lee herself hints at the contradictions contained within conflicting historical periodization when she informs the reader early in the novel that its events are depicted from a somewhat distant perspective, "when enough years had gone by to enable us to look back on them" (3). Simply because neither the author nor even Scout, her first person narrator and authorial surrogate, can experience the 1930s within the 1930s but must interpret from a later moment invested with its own discrete historical perspective, historical prolepsis—the representation or assumption of a future act or development as if presently existing or accomplished—is inevitable, and it is an indication that Lee's 1930s historical background, though developed in some detail, should not be allowed to obscure the real conditions which governed the text's production in the years from roughly 1955 to 1959.

Central issues of Harper Lee's fictional Tom Robinson case, along with cultural tensions ascendant in the aftermath of the May 17, 1954 *Brown v. Board of Education* decision, are located in the story of Emmett Till, a 14-year-old boy from Chicago who was brutally murdered by two white men in the Mississippi Delta on August 28, 1955 for allegedly whistling at a white woman in a store in Money, Mississippi. There is a long list of similarities both circumstantial and deeply ideological between the 1955 lynching of Emmett Till and Lee's account of the conviction and murder of Tom Robinson, similarities which point to the common origin of both texts in a particularly troubled period in the southern history of race.

During the mid to late 1950s, race relations in the Deep South were of course defined and dominated by the *Brown* decision, which negated the doctrine of "separate but equal" that had since *Plessy v. Ferguson* been the basis of the South's segregated way of life. Prior to the 1954 decision, what Benjamin Muse has called an "unwholesome stability" (1) had prevailed in the South, depriving nearly all blacks of the right to vote and adhering to strict and inviolable *de facto* and *de jure* segregation of the races in all areas of social life in which mixing of any kind could result in the suggestion of social equality.

The business of "keeping the negro in his place" (Muse 39) had for centuries been a major concern in the South, but *Brown v. Board of Education* greatly exacerbated the southern fears relating to racial mixing, amalgamation, and expectations of social equality for blacks, creating what Newby terms a "a new racism" (10) that directly responded to the Supreme Court's authority by "recasting old ideas to meet a new national mood" (10). In the immediate aftermath of decision, the Deep South exhibited the paranoia of a closed society that could not distinguish the defense of a " 'few social areas' from the entire structure of white supremacy" (Whitfield 11). The preservation of white patriarchy "seemed to require the suppression of even the most insignificant challenges to authority" (11). The rising influence and activism of the NAACP resulted not only in the formation of the White Citizens Councils but production and dissemination of inflammatory anti-integration literature, organization of anti-integration rallies, intimidation of the small number of blacks who had registered to vote, condemnation of the "liberals and do-gooders" in the both the South and in Washington, and the implicit call for violent resistance to the idea of school integration.

Foremost among all latent and overtly expressed fears that were directly intensified by the *Brown* decision was that surrounding interracial sex. Gunnar Myrdal's exhaustive 1947 study of southern culture had asked white southerners to choose among six categories in gauging what they believed blacks most desired by asserting their civil rights. First in ranking came "intermarriage and sex intercourse with whites" (Myrdal 58). It is indisputable that the *Brown* decision, ostensibly about school desegregation, was actually understood by many in the South as a dangerous amelioration of deadly serious taboos regarding sexual relations between black males and white females. According to Whitaker, "Nowhere does the fear based on sex show up more clearly than in the disputes surrounding the 1954 Supreme Court decision" (12). Myrdal states emphatically, "Sex was the principle around which the whole structure of segregation ... was organized. And it was because of sex that racial segregation ... was intended to permeate every aspect of society" (589). Whitaker concurs in explaining that the "main worry" notably heightened and reified by the *Brown* decision was "the mixed relations between the races, especially relations that might lead to sex affairs or marriage" (13). As the rhetoric of the Citizens Councils clearly indicates,[2] the twin fears of amalgamation and miscegenation resulting from "mixed relations" between blacks and whites rested ultimately on the idea that "marriage or sexual intimacy with blacks would degrade and eventually extinguish Anglo-Saxon civilization itself" (Whitfield 1–2).

In the context of the *Brown* decision, mixed schooling therefore meant much more than the implication of social equality. President Eisenhower may have inadvertently verbalized some of the deepest fears of southerners when he explained in 1954 that segregationists "were not bad people. All they are concerned about is to see that their sweet little girls are not required to sit in schools along side some big overgrown negroes" (qtd. in Whitfield 72). Based as it is on what was in the South at this time an exceptionally offensive concept—that of sexually mature black men in close proximity to white females—this sentiment surfaces frequently in ideology of the post-*Brown* era. In his research into the period, Whitfield encountered these representative Southern views: "A negro of 14 may be in the fourth grade with a white girl of 10 or 11, and the negro is a fully developed man, sexually" (9). "You make a negro believe he is equal ... and the first thing he wants is a white woman" (9). Not surprisingly in this atmosphere, the lurid and provocative image of the "black rapist," though it had existed in southern code and southern white mythology as early as the 1880s,[3] was now resurrected in the southern consciousness and rhetoric (Whitfield 3).

The September 1955 trial of Roy Bryant and J.W. Milam for the murder of Emmett Till in retribution for allegedly whistling at and talking in a suggestive way to Carolyn Bryant was front page news throughout the country. When Bryant and Milam were found not guilty by an all-white, all-male jury that deliberated only 67 minutes—"it would have been a quicker decision, said the foreman, if we hadn't stopped to drink a bottle of pop" (Halberstam 441)—Milam and Bryant "stood acquitted in Mississippi and convicted by most of the nation" (441).

Graciously responding to my queries, Harper Lee has indicated that she was not in Mississippi in 1955 and was not present at the Emmett Till trial. But in order to be cognizant of the Till case and its meaning, she did not have to be. The Emmett Till trial, now forgotten by many, surprisingly absent from some recent histories, often ignored as one of the galvanizing events of the early civil rights movement, was in 1955 "probably the most widely publicized trial of the century" (Whitaker 148). Halberstam has termed it "an international incident" (432), "... the first great media event of the civil rights movement" (437). As the daughter of a well-known southern attorney and a one-time law student from a family with a considerable legal background,[4] Harper Lee may be presumed to have taken an interest in the Till case, which was immediately identified as a monumental legal benchmark.[5] In 1975, for example, the founder of the Citizens Councils attempted to identify the moment when the civil rights movement began: "It all started probably with a case of a young Negro boy named Emmett Till getting killed for offending some white woman ... that made every newspaper on the face of the earth ..." (Whitaker 148). Largely due to what most historians refer to as a decline of "faith in legalism" at the unconscionable verdict of the Till trial, blacks in the South were moved to attempt more concrete forms of protest. Within four months after Till's death, Alabama blacks were staging the Montgomery bus boycott—the first major battle in the civil rights era war against racial injustice.

Commonalities in the Emmett Till trial and the trial of Tom Robinson in *To Kill a Mockingbird* have been suggested but nowhere investigated. It was, for example, at a 1995 celebration of the thirty-fifth anniversary of the publication of *To Kill a Mockingbird* that journalist Charlayne Hunter-Gault (the first black student to enroll at the University of Georgia), perhaps unaware that, inexplicably, no constructive connection between the story of Tom Robinson and that of Emmett Till had ever even been investigated anywhere, described the Emmett Till story as "perhaps the closest my generation had come to the experience of Tom Robinson" (*TKM: Then and Now*).

The two cases are linked by numerous similarities of circumstance. Both cases combine the dual icons of the "black rapist" and concomitant fear of black male sexuality with mythologized "vulnerable and sacred" southern womanhood. Both cases involve alleged transgressions of the strict inviolable mores barring social and sexual contact between black males and white females of any social class, for which, in both cases, the penalty is death for the black offender. Both cases are heard by all-white, all-male juries consisting primarily of southern farmers. Both cases result in verdicts that preserve tenaciously held racial doctrine of the white power structure at the expense of justice and in the face of overwhelming contradictory evidence. In both cases a community of potentially fair-minded middle-class whites is required, against its initial leanings and for reasons perceived as the lesser of two evils, to support the obviously false testimony of a pair of otherwise-despised poor whites. In both cases, a courageous attorney and a fair-minded judge tacitly cooperate in a futile attempt to ensure justice. In both cases, the black victim is a diminished physical specimen of a fully grown man. In both cases, the press or media emerge as a force for racial justice. In both cases, the concept of child murder figures prominently in the calculus of revenge for the racial and social shame of a class of poor Southern whites.

The list of similarities could go on, eventually extending even into relatively minor surface details, such as the fact that Emmett Till was killed on August 28, 1955, and that his body was found on August 31, dates which turn out to be practically identical to the date of Tom Robinson's death, which took place when "August was on the brink of September" (228). Moreover, deeper connections are likewise discernible in a study of the cases as symbolic texts. Described by numerous historians as having a "muscular build," fourteen-year-old eighth-grader Emmett Till is not only comparable to the "muscular" but crippled Tom Robinson, but as an out-of-place, culturally displaced child, he fits well into Harper Lee's symbolic "mockingbird" category which encompasses the concepts of innocence, victimization, and wrongful persecution. Emmett Till's murderers, the half-brothers Roy Bryant and J.W. "Big" Milam, are described by Whitaker as a "tightly knit family" (107) that resembles the Ewells, whose joint testimony condemns Tom Robinson. Also like the Ewells, Bryant and Milam were "poor whites" or "rednecks" who provoked reactions of fear and disgust among both blacks and other whites in the local community. To the Ewells and Bryant-Milam, the term "white trash" (144) used by Whitaker is equally applicable. "People who knew Milam and Bryant," Whitaker notes, "disliked them and were afraid of them" (144). In interviews conducted by Whitaker in the early 1960s, Milam and Bryant were "invariably referred to as 'peckerwoods,' 'white trash' and other terms of similar disapprobation" (144). Like both Milam and Bryant, Bob Ewell had served in the military and is described by Lee as "the veteran of an obscure war" (217), whose inclination to violence is at one point in the novel explained by Lee's narrator as a vestige of his war experience. Commissioned in battle in Europe during World War II, Milam, thirty-six years old, was "especially proud of his war record" (Whitaker 108) and has been described by all primary sources as having learned to relish violence through his military service.

Tom Robinson's physical handicap of a crippled left arm—the arm having been "caught in a cotton gin" at the age of twelve—is emphasized in Lee's novel as a factor which should have resulted in acquittal or at least serious doubt not only concerning Tom Robinson's ability to choke and rape Mayella Ewell but to produce the kind of injuries she suffers on the right side of her face. In the circumstances surrounding the Till case, another kind of handicap, this time a "speech defect ... a stutter, the result of non-paralytic polio at the age of three" (Whitfield 15) is raised as a possible exonerating factor for the kind of transgression Till is alleged to have committed. Both in the immediate frenzy of press reports surrounding the murder and in interviews as recent as 1987, Mrs. Bradley claimed that her son's alleged "wolf whistle" was actually a manifestation of his stuttering problem:

He had particular trouble with b's and m's ... He was trying to say "bubble gum," but he got stuck. So he whistled.... I taught him, whenever he had trouble stuttering, to blow it out ... I can see him try to say "bubble gum" and blowing or whistling in Mrs. Bryant's presence.[6]

Immediately after Till's body was found, Till's uncle, Moses Wright, had also explained that Till "had polio when he was three and he couldn't talk plain. You could hardly understand him."[7] Till's speech defect as an extenuating factor in the case was accepted by parties other than Mrs. Bradley as late as 1962, when NAACP Regional Secretary Ruby Hurley, asked for clarification of the issue by Hugh Whitaker during his research into the case, gave what Whitaker terms the "official NAACP version" of the event. Ms. Hurley explained that Till's "only crime was the alleged 'whistling' at a woman. The 'whistling' was a defect in his speech as a result of a polio attack" (Whitaker 133).

Though these explanations may strain credulity, they were and are a part of the still unresolved confusion over what actually took place at the Bryant store that August evening in 1955. The term by which the Till case came to be known—the "wolf whistle" case—emphasizes the centrality of the possible speech defect as an exculpatory detail that clearly resembles Tom Robinson's similarly exonerating physical defect.

The bodies of both Emmett Till and Tom Robinson were horribly mutilated by excessive racially provoked violence intended to send a message about the seriousness of the alleged transgression and the tenacity with which existing social codes would be defended by the white power structure. Till's swollen decomposed body could be identified only by the ring he wore and was "badly mutilated.... The body had apparently been beaten severely, and there was a hole the size of a bullet above the right ear" (Whitaker 118). Tom Robinson is shot seventeen times by prison guards—his death ostensibly the result of an attempt to flee from the Enfield Prison during an outdoor exercise period. Though Tom Robinson is said to have run toward the fence "in a blind raving charge" (235) and failed to stop after the guards had "fired a few shots into the air" (235), the killing, referred to later in the novel by Mr. Underwood as a "senseless slaughter" (241) is almost certainly racially motivated. Atticus is told that the guards shot Tom "just as he went over the fence" (235), but Scout's response of uncontrollable shaking when she hears the news is caused by her knowledge that the exercise yard at Enfield is "the size of a football field" (236) together with the fact that Tom had "seventeen bullet holes in him" and that, as Atticus explains, "they didn't have to shoot him that much" (235). Though it would have been futile and perhaps impossible in the racial climate of the era to legally challenge or investigate the cause and motives of Tom Robinson's killing, beginning with the question of the number of shots used to kill him, the death as described from the guards' account appears dubious and not entirely logical. Scout's shaking results probably from the visual image of the killing she is able to create for herself from having earlier had the Enfield Prison exercise yard "pointed out" to her by Atticus. The size of the yard, the picture of a man with the use of only one arm attempting to climb the fence, the claim by the guards that Tom had nearly escaped, the seventeen shots used to stop him—all suggest a killing with a motive other than simply preventing Tom from fleeing. Lee's text unquestionably permits if not compels a reading of the event as a cold-blooded, racially motivated murder quite similar to the murder of Emmett Till.

A number of the leading figures in the Till case have obvious counterparts in *To Kill a Mockingbird*. Attorney Gerald Chatham, the prosecutor in the Till case, resembles Atticus Finch, and his efforts throughout the case are by several historical accounts described as "a valiant but futile effort to see justice done" (Whitaker 153). The circumstances in which Chatham and Atticus Finch found themselves, as attorneys fighting a losing battle against communal racist feelings and a verdict that is a foregone conclusion, are of course strikingly similar. Though according to Whitfield much of the transcript of the trial has been lost, several sources extol the "stirring oratory" (Whitaker 153) of Chatham and assistant Robert B. Smith's closing arguments. What little survives of the actual text of the arguments includes Smith's allusion to the "guarantees of life, liberty and the pursuit of happiness" (Whitfield 41) from the same sentence of the Declaration of Independence to which Atticus alludes in his closing argument in the Robinson case when he reminds the jury that "all men are created equal" (205). Whitaker compares Chatham to William Jennings Bryan and notes that after Chatham's closing argument, "all other summations were an 'anti-climax'" (153). After the trial and its verdict, the southern black press praised the work of Chatham and, as Whitaker explains, "wrote encouragingly" (162) of his and his assistant prosecutor's performance in a way that recalls the respectful tributes paid to Atticus by the local black community after the Tom Robinson trail. All accounts of the trial agree that Chatham and Smith had made their case "ably and diligently" (Whitaker 162), and they are repeatedly described as having "done their utmost ... despite having no assistance from the sheriff or police investigators in obtaining evidence" (162).

The fact that Gerald Chatham died of a heart attack at the age of 50, only one year after the Emmett Till trial, and that Chatham's relatives, when interviewed by Whitaker, felt "that the exertion in this trail hastened his death" (162) recalls several comments made in *To Kill a Mockingbird* about Atticus by Aunt Alexandra. At the news of Tom Robinson's killing, Alexandra reacts with anger to the town's seeming disregard for the health of her brother: "I just want to know when this will ever end … It tears him to pieces … it tears him to pieces … They're perfectly willing to let him wreck his health doing what they're afraid to do" (236). For Chatham as for Atticus, one momentous case became a self-defining moment; though Chatham had had a long career in law, his obituary referred only to "the Emmett Till case" in summarizing his public life (Whitaker 163).

Chatham and presiding judge in the Till case Curtis Swango seemed to work toward a common purpose in much the same way Harper Lee's Atticus Finch and Judge Taylor tacitly cooperate. As in the Robinson case, there is in the language surrounding the Till case the suggestion of collusion or at least mutual support between the justice-seeking lawyer and the sympathetic judge. To all observers of the Till trial, including Halberstam, it appeared that Chatham and Judge Curtis Swango, like Atticus Finch and Judge Taylor, "were set to do all they could in the hope that, by some miracle" a just verdict could be rendered (Whitaker 147). Describing Judge Taylor's way of looking at Bob Ewell during the latter's testimony "as if he were a three-legged chicken or a square egg" (250), Atticus remarks "Don't tell me judges don't try to prejudice juries" (250). Asked by Jem "who in this town did one thing to help Tom Robinson?" (215), Miss Maudie replies "People like Judge Taylor" (215). In a similar way, defense attorneys Kellum and Breland described Judge Curtis Swango as "bending over backward" to aid the case against Milam and Bryant.[8] And the fact that Atticus had been selected by Judge Taylor as Tom Robinson's defender is clearly linked to his desire to ensure the case is given a chance. When Scout suddenly realizes that "Maxwell Green should have had Tom Robinson's case" (215) and that the appointment of Atticus was meant to ensure a vigorous defense and is therefore, as Miss Maudie explains, "no accident" (216), the extent of Judge Taylor's own "bending over backward" for Tom Robinson is apparent.

Judge Swango's determination to keep the proceedings as fair as possible was obvious at several key moments and "won the respect of all (presumably all non-racist observers) who attended the trial" (Whitaker 163; my parentheses). Aware of the damaging effect that testimony by Carolyn Bryant might have on the all-white jury in the case, for example, Swango ruled the testimony of Mrs. Roy Bryant unrelated to the murder and thus inadmissible.

Whitfield quotes black congressman Charles Diggs, who attended the Till trial, as being impressed with the "fairness of Judge Swango" (45). *The Nation* praised Swango and Chatham for their "devotion throughout this occasion ... to justice" (Whitaker 45). That Judge Swango was reelected in the year after the Till trial is a fact curiously reminiscent of Atticus' own reelection to the Alabama state legislature in the term following his efforts on behalf of Tom Robinson.

The story of the determined rejection of Roy Bryant and J.W. Milam by their community in the aftermath of the Till trial closely parallels community attitudes toward Bob Ewell after the Robinson trial. After the Robinson case, having had "his brief burst of fame" (248), Bob Ewell not only "acquired and lost a job in a matter of days ... fired from the WPA for laziness" (248)—a fact which is acknowledged by the narrator as "unique in the annals of the nineteen-thirties" (248)—but he is ostracized by the same community that had felt the need to support him in his accusations against Tom Robinson. When Aunt Alexandra wonders why Ewell, having "had his way in court" (250) continues to harbor a grudge, Atticus explains: "I think I understand ... It might be because he knows in his heart that few people in Maycomb really believed his and Mayella's yarns. He thought he'd be a hero, but all he got for his pain was ... was, okay, we'll convict this Negro but get back to your dump" (250). "I destroyed his last shred of credibility in that trial," (218) Atticus asserts. The strong aversion among Maycomb citizens for Ewell is shown most directly by Link Deas, who defends Helen Robinson from Ewell's harassment and aggressively humiliates Ewell to keep him from trying it again.

In much the same way, Roy Bryant and J.W. Milam were rejected by both white and black elements of their community after the Till trail. The Milam-Bryant family had owned a chain of small country stores which catered almost exclusively to blacks. Immediately after the Till incident, these stores were boycotted, and all had to be closed or sold within fifteen months. Attempting then to make a living as a farmer, Milam tried but was unable to rent land for the 1956 crop year (Whitaker 160). Bryant also "had trouble finding work" (160), and "finding themselves not accepted in the Mississippi Delta" (160) Bryant and his family moved to Texas in 1957. Like Bob Ewell, both Milam and Bryant were feared, distrusted and shunned by the citizens who had stood up for them and "swarmed to [their] defense" (160) in the Till case. The underlying feelings in southern society toward men like Ewell, Milam, and Bryant is thus a subject of some interest and complexity. They are seen at various times and by various observers both as defenders of the race, "keeping the niggers in line" and "protecting women from the lust of negro men" (Whitfield 30), but outside this role they are scorned and ostracized for reasons of class. Initially denounced in the press and unable to find lawyers who would defend them, Milam and Bryant were eventually represented *pro bono* when opinion swung in their favor and the community of the Delta, in a strongly self-defensive reaction to what it perceived as Northern press bias against Mississippi, decided to rally around two of "its own."

Till's mother, Mrs. Mamie Bradley, is linked in an intriguing way to Helen Robinson, the wife of Tom Robinson. Though Sheriff Clarence Strider had ordered the immediate burial of Till's body in Mississippi, Mrs. Bradley had requested that the body be sent back to Chicago, where she received it in the Illinois Central terminal from which her son had left for his vacation two weeks earlier (Whitfield xiii). The scene was witnessed by a crowd of family friends and media, and there is a famous UPI photo that was taken in Chicago upon the arrival of the casket bearing Emmett Till's body. As the casket was unloaded and presented to her, Mrs. Bradley cried "Lord, Take my soul," and collapsed (Whitfield xiii). The expression of horror and pain on her face, the crate containing the casket in the foreground, and the three clergymen pressing near Mrs. Bradley to raise her limp, paralyzed body appeared in newspapers across the country in early September 1955. In *To Kill a Mockingbird*, a strongly analogous scene in which Helen Robinson is informed by Atticus that her husband has been killed, is witnessed and described by Dill: "Scout ... she just fell down in the dirt. Just fell down in the dirt, like a giant with a big foot just came along and stepped on her ... Like you'd step on an ant" (240). The near match of the two scenes, strongly suggestive of a possible influence in terms of both situation and the emotional context, has been previously overlooked.

The press became a catalyst in the growth of the civil rights movement, and one of its major roles became that of a defender and chronicler of injustice, clearly taking the side of social progress and arguing powerfully the case of the oppressed. Covering the Till trial in 1955, Halberstam had reflected "This was something different ... for the first time there was a national agenda on civil rights" (437). "Something new was being created, the civil rights beat it was called, for this new and aggressive young press corps" (441). Under the gaze of these progress-minded reporters primarily from the North but including some southerners, it would be impossible to hide crimes like the Till murder in remote corners of the South. After the Till verdict, "newspapers around the world reacted with editorials of condemnation" (Whitaker 157). The Till case was unique not only for the extent and the energy of the press coverage, but also for the slow sea changes it exposed in the southern media. Though the Scottsboro trials in the 1930s had excited considerable media interest, the lurid details of alleged gang rape and the provocative testimony of two alleged white prostitutes that were part of that of that case are cited by Whitaker as obvious factors. The Till case for the first time saw a noticeable majority of media take a strongly progressive stance on issues of civil rights. Many Mississippi and Alabama newspapers would eventually support the verdict exonerating Bryant and Milam, but this is readable as a gesture of self-defense against the strength of the condemnation leveled against Mississippi by the rest of the world after the verdict. The equal applicability to the Till case of Atticus' discernment of "the shadow of a beginning" (221) of racial progress is here clearly reflected.

In Lee's novel, the role of the press as a determined advocate of civil rights appears symbolically in the form of Mr. B.B. Underwood, owner, publisher, and editor of the *Maycomb Tribune*. It is Mr. Underwood, for example, "leaning out his window above the *Maycomb Tribune* office" with "a double barreled shotgun" (155), who backs up Atticus in his confrontation with the lynch mob in Chapter 15. "Had you covered all the time, Atticus," shouts Mr. Underwood as the mob disperses. Described as "a profane little man, whose father ... had christened Braxton Bragg, a name he had done his best to live down" (156), Mr. Underwood is a figure of the New South who puts aside risks to himself to write and publish a passionate denunciation of Tom Robinson's murder. In his editorial, referred to by the narrator in Chapter 25, "Mr. Underwood was at his most bitter, and he couldn't have cared less who canceled advertising subscriptions ... He likened Tom's death to the senseless slaughter of songbirds by hunters and children, and Maycomb thought he was trying to write an editorial poetical enough to be reprinted in *The Montgomery Adviser*" (241).

Among the most profound examples of mutually illuminating influence between the Till story and Lee's novel is the central presence in both of the concept of child murder. Not surprisingly, "child murder" was an immediate and persistent theme of outrage in the Till case. NAACP Executive Secretary Roy Wilkins, for example, gave what came to be a frequently repeated synopsis of the Till incident: "It would appear that the state of Mississippi has decided to maintain white supremacy by murdering children."[9] In a well-known statement of September 1955, William Faulkner called Emmett Till "an afflicted Northern child" and then used the case to indict American society in general: "... if we in America have reached the point in our desperate culture when we must murder children, no matter for what reason or what color, we don't deserve to survive, and probably won't" (qtd. in Wexler 63). The climactic scene of *To Kill a Mockingbird*, in which Scout and Jem are attacked by Bob Ewell in revenge for their father's role in the Robinson trial, replicates the motive and pattern of the crime against Emmett Till. After the attack, Sheriff Heck Tate's caustic description of Bob Ewell as "brave enough to kill children" (269) applies equally to Emmett Till's murderers, who are likewise compelled to retaliate for public humiliation by a deviant sense of southern honor. That Bob Ewell meant to kill Scout and Jem is unequivocally established by Sheriff Tate, who finds Scout's chicken wire Halloween costume "crushed to a pulp" (269) with a gash where Ewell's knife had struck at her. The costume "probably saved her life ... Bob Ewell meant business" (269) Tate concludes.

In accordance with a vestigial remnant of the Southern social code made applicable in postbellum culture to poor whites, if Roy Bryant had failed to act after Till's alleged remarks to his wife, "the shame would be his" (Whitaker 77). Furthermore, as Whitfield and others have asserted, Bryant's sense of honor was threatened in large part by the fact that the matter had inevitably become public—that local blacks and other whites were talking about the incident in the Bryant store. There were therefore two distinct motives compelling Bryant and Milam to act. One was obviously racial, but the other has more to do with public familial shame and loss of honor. Once this is acknowledged, Bob Ewell's violent retaliation, sensed by Jem and Scout but not by Atticus, who inexplicably discounts the threat Ewell poses, is more easily explained. Had Ewell stood still after Tom Robinson's death, he would have satisfied only the racial half of the revenge equation. His need to strike out at the source of his public disgrace is as compelling. For Bryant-Milam the locus of racial and public humiliation was black child Emmett Till. For Bob Ewell, the death of Tom Robinson satisfied a racial vendetta, but Ewell's public humiliation also called for retaliation of some form against Atticus, even if the victims were children. Such exegesis also throws light on the entire novel's indisputable thematic preoccupation with ideas of child-centered innocence profoundly applicable to the Emmett Till story. The novel's motto, for example, reads "Lawyers, I suppose, were children once" and Mr. Underwood's Chapter 25 editorial is written "so children could understand" (241). When the Robinson verdict is announced, Atticus remarks, "seems that only the children weep" (213).

Considered together, the actual and intended child murders located respectively in the Till case and Lee's novel emphasize the degradation of a deeply insecure segment of southern society that could produce such perverse malice, whose poverty-corrupted antebellum social code of gentlemanly honor had become horrifically deviant in response of the fundamental challenge to its identificatory foundational principles presented by racial integration. The stark terms of Lee's representation of child murder during a period when a readership would almost certainly have been cognizant of the central issues of the Till case justifies a view of Lee's text as not only reflective of but engaged with and responsive to a civil rights era ideological agenda.

It is surprising that deeper connections between the Till case and Lee's Tom Robinson case have not previously been pursued. It may be that the issue never grew into a full-fledged study simply because as a murder trial Till's case could not on the surface be easily classified with Tom Robinson's. But the extremely psychologically charged and polarizing issues in both cases are identical: sexual relations of black males and white females, the stereo-type of the black rapist, and the weight of such ideology in southern society. Mrs. Farrow's remark in the aftermath of the Robinson trial in *To Kill a Mockingbird* that "there's no lady safe in her bed these nights" (232) is an uncannily accurate version of the tensions dominating both cases. And the comment made by Scout's teacher Miss Gates as she leaves the courthouse after the Robinson verdict replicates with remarkable precision a typical fear-driven response to concerns over black social progress from the post-*Brown* era in a way that actually seems more descriptive of Emmett Till than of Tom Robinson: "... it's time somebody taught 'em a lesson. They were gettin' way above themselves, an' the next thing they think they can do is marry us" (247). It was Emmett Till, after all, who is alleged to have suggested that he had already "been with white girls" (Whitfield 17) and asked Carolyn Bryant for a date, and who is reported to have shown both whites and blacks the wal-let photo of his white girlfriend. Among the "traditions and customs of the South" that were involved in these cases, Whitaker correctly cites "Southern feelings with respect to the relationship of sex to the caste system of segre-gation" (ix) as most important, but the general ideology of segregation is also put forth in anger by Mrs. Merriweather in Chapter 24 of Lee's text: "People up there set 'em free, but you don't see 'em settin' at the table with 'em. At least we don't have the deceit to say to 'em yes you're as good as we are but stay away from us. Down here we just say you live your way and we'll live ours" (234). These views are inarguably the most accurate description of the social context in which both the Till and Robinson cases were deeply embed-ded. Charlayne Hunter-Gault's seemingly casual analogy linking the fiction-al Tom Robinson trial to the Emmett Till story is therefore amply justified.

It was in this atmosphere of provocative racial tension and salient race-sex anxiety concurrent with frequent trips in the mid 1950s between New York and her home in Monroeville, Alabama, that Harper Lee worked at the manuscript that was to become *To Kill a Mockingbird*. The conflict over the

Brown decision, the nearby Emmett Till case, the racist literature distributed by the Citizens Councils, the first black bus boycott and the beginning of the civil rights movement in Montgomery in 1956 were conspicuous features of a state of near fixation by national and regional media on southern racial issues. The result is a novel that seems unquestionably to have passed through the transforming alembic of such powerful ideology.

That Lee's text wages explicit battles over meaning and sends liminal signals with which a readership immersed in conditions concurrent with the novel's 1960 publication could be expected to passionately respond is not surprising. But perhaps because, as Stephen Greenblatt has noted, a work's reception is "located in an intermediate zone of social transaction, a betwixt and between" (*Learning to Curse* 11), the transaction between author and reader is never certain. Interestingly, most immediate responses to Lee's novel chose either to acknowledge the text's serious participation in its social milieu or to completely discount the text as historically uninvolved and almost frivolous. In its period of initial reception, the novel is described as "in no way a sociological novel. It underlines no cause" (R. Sullivan), a "humorous book ... wholesome as a dozen fresh eggs" and "an absolutely accurate picture of small town southern life in the 30s" (Waller) while simultaneously being touted as "a novel of strong contemporary national significance that deserves serious attention" (R. Sullivan). One interpretive key to the novel therefore lies in an identification of its periodicity, which has been, I would argue, the source of an ambiguity in a critical reception described by one of the novel's primary researchers as "baffling" (Johnson 24). Though Lee herself hinted in a 1961 interview that her setting "could have been the Mississippi Delta ..." (Deitch), a locale with implicit significance within the novel's period of reception as the spark that ignited the civil rights movement, most critics have chosen to develop in the novel a set of concerns particular to the 1930s and the Depression era. In this way, the text itself seems to have a acquired a type of "mobility" described by Greenblatt as characteristic of enduring works of art that problematize the distinction between literary and non-literary texts while presenting mixed strains of ideology, and which are thus able to be reevaluated within the social context of each historical frame of reference by which they are touched (*Learning to Curse* 11).

The range of responses elicited by *To Kill a Mockingbird* also reflects a lingering uncertainty about whether Lee's text is essentially subversive or orthodox in its central insights—a confusion that is only partially explicable as a function of the novel's publication during a period when definitions of subversive and orthodox racial views were in flux. Explaining the dialectic between Shakespeare's art and an Elizabethan state authority censorial of subversive ideas regarding religious and political power, Greenblatt has described a process by which "subversive insights are generated in the midst of apparently orthodox texts and simultaneously contained by those texts, contained so efficiently that the society's licensing and policing apparatus is not directly engaged" ("Invisible Bullets" 41). Though Greenblatt views this condition as "an historical phenomenon, the particular mode of this particular (Elizabethan) culture" (57), I would argue that something very much like this "submissive subversiveness" in which "a disturbing vista ... is glimpsed only to be immediately closed off" (52) occurs as well in Lee's novel.

The novel's denouement, for example, presents and endorses a conspiracy between Atticus and Sheriff Heck Tate that contradicts both characters' earlier strict adherence to legal procedure in the Tom Robinson case. By the terms of an improvised, legally subversive[10] agreement, Arthur Radley's intervention on behalf of the Finch children and the killing of Bob Ewell in defense of the children are concealed with the false explanation that "Bob Ewell fell on his knife." A *deus ex machina* personified in Boo Radley is thus allowed not only to intervene, to intervene anonymously, to intervene with impunity, but also to render compensatory justice, his actions sanctioned by both the sheriff and Maycomb's leading attorney. Not only will there be no investigation, legal charges or trial relating to Bob Ewell's death, but the circumstances of the death, including even the identity of the Arthur Radley as the salvific intercessor, will be suppressed. "There's a black boy dead for no reason, and the man responsible for it's dead," Heck Tate argues, "Let the dead the bury the dead this time, Mr. Finch. Let the dead bury the dead" (276). Atticus and Sheriff Tate then both acknowledge the killing of Bob Ewell not simply as a rescue of the Finch children but as symbolic retribution for the death of Tom Robinson.

Greenblatt's paradigm for Renaissance authority and its subversion—subversion created in order to be contained—is here re-presented with perhaps the one notable caveat that the subversion here "contained" by mutual agreement of Atticus, Heck Tate and later Scout is also implicitly sanctioned by the text as a viable situational response. That Arthur Radley killed Bob Ewell will not become public knowledge, and so the conspiracy to circumvent the ideological apparatus of the justice system is contained by and within a value system that judges not on the basis of legal syntax, but on an individualized concept of guilt or innocence that repudiates considerations of race or class. Thus the subversion presented by Lee departs from Greenblatt's Renaissance form only in that the "disturbing vista" that is "glimpsed only to be immediately closed off" presented in the former is orthodox and conservative (obedience to legal code over a personal value system), while that contained or closed off in the latter is liberal and hetero-dox. Such exegesis speaks volumes about the essential leanings of the era in which Lee wrote and published—an era in which forms of racial orthodoxy were constantly elided as the legal process either advanced the cause of civil rights —as in the *Brown* decision—or denied racial justice—as in the Emmett Till case. The Emmett Till case is often cited as a major factor in a collective erosion of faith in legalism—a disillusionment that called for nonviolent extralegal subversion—the source and eventual *modus vivendi* of the civil rights movement. In their commerce with both Emmett Till and Tom Robinson, legal remedies fail and are therefore elided into extralegal solutions. The substitute version of justice endorsed in *To Kill a Mockingbird* therefore implies the viability of a form of retribution for racial violence while exposing the limitations of legal redress for such violence, suggesting the efficacy of a particular kind of conscience-driven extralegal solution to extant racial conditions. Not without first creating and containing subver-sion, the plot strands involving Boo Radley and Tom Robinson are woven together in a way that constructs a form of moral consensus concerning the dividing line between law-bound adherence and individual subversive behavior.

Of importance also is the fact that the suppression of truth regarding Bob Ewell's death is accepted by Atticus in clear contradiction to the legal code by which his whole professional and personal life has been structured. The change of heart—in which his whole sense of himself is at stake—con-stitutes significant growth in Atticus, who is now able to see the inefficacy of legalism. Atticus had earlier publicly affirmed his faith that "our courts are our great levelers" and that equal justice was "no ideal to me, it is a living, working reality" (205)—but the law that had failed Tom Robinson here attains a sudden protean flexibility, the logic of which amounts to a demysti-fication of the legal system and its predictable machinations. In the falsity that hovers around the declaration of Atticus to Scout that "Mr. Ewell fell on his knife," the reader is invited to suspend judgment and implicated in the rationalization. When Atticus asks his daughter, "Can you possibly under-stand?" Scout's "Yes sir, I understand" (276) is offered with her passionate reassurance that a greater good is contained in the version of events that is not literally but symbolically true: "Mr. Tate was right ... it'd be sort of like shootin' a mockingbird, wouldn't it?" (276). The private withdrawal of Atticus into this acknowledgment is intertwined with the great public crisis into which the period had been led by the *Brown* decision and the murder of Emmett Till, a crisis that gave rise to serious national questions about the efficacy of court sponsored racial justice.

By the end of Lee's novel then, the limitations of a particular and high-ly historically relevant ideological apparatus have been exposed, and the law is, even for Atticus, reduced to a ritual in which absolute faith is no longer possible. Through this process we perceive the potential instability of the structure of legal order in the South on the verge of the violent convulsions that attended the civil rights era. If the text here compels a consideration of the validity of subversive intervention, as it seems to have for at least some of Lee's contemporaries in the wake of the Emmett Till case, it is because, as Greenblatt explains, "power ... is not perfectly monolithic and hence may encounter and record in one of its functions materials that can threaten another of its functions" ("Invisible Bullets" 50). "The simple operation of any systematic order ... will inevitably run the risk of exposing its own limi-tations" (52). Because power "defines itself in relation to threats or simply to that which is not identical to it" (50), the full awareness of its effect requires what Greenblatt terms a collective "vigilance," the kind of vigilance, I would suggest, that is practiced by Sheriff Tate and Atticus, who sanction the per-sonal subversion of an institutional power to which both men had earlier expressed and enacted allegiance. This transference contains a radical ques-tioning that insists passionately on the efficacy of action in obedience to the private commands of conscience instead of reliance on more orthodox forms of redress.[11] In the "secret courts of men's hearts" (Lee 241), tainted as they are with virulent racial prejudice, neither Tom Robinson nor Emmett Till had any chance, but Lee's novel ends with the verdict of a secret court that, though it cannot restore the status quo ante by returning Tom Robinson to his family, does destroy the complicity between racism and a legal system that had been required to serve it—negating the very arrangement that had thwarted justice in the Robinson and Till cases.

Lee's novel therefore ends where the civil rights movement begins, with a resolve born of disillusionment to improvise ways and means of jus-tice both within and outside a system that could convict Tom Robinson and acquit Emmett Till's murderers. In the presentation, discussion, containment and suppression of a court case pitting the state against Arthur Radley—a case that could have been but will not be—there is a conscious attempt to compensate for the disastrous effects of its antecedents in Tom Robinson and Emmett Till—court cases that could not have been but were. The text may be read as Lee's method of working out complex issues of conscience and subjectivity suggested by the Till case and the civil rights movement in gen-eral. Harper Lee's version of history, like the version of events agreed upon as the real story of Bob Ewell's death, is therefore not literally but symboli-cally "true," retold in a way that liberates the essential symbolic precepts from the less significant details of place, time and circumstance while remaining passionately faithful to allegorical truth.

Seeking a paradigm within the purely fictional narrative of the novel for this transformation of historical detail to conform to a thematically unified but chronologically and spatially detached "text," we need look no further than to the first-person narrator. Scout's inability to compartmentalize her own history is a good model for the way historical events or texts mesh synergistically into a kind of combination meaning which neither text comprises alone. Her most profound interpretations of the novel's events are not derived through conscious analysis, verbal instruction or logic. Instead, they seem enabled by a prelingual or prediscursive state of sleep-induced semiconsciousness in which events from different time periods come together to create a version of reality that is as individual as it is anachronistic in the sense of the word that literally means "outside of time." Here she is subject to discourses or texts that are "of" both her past and present but which operate simultaneously and across time barriers. Scout's habit of falling asleep at various times and places in the novel often leaves her midway between conscious and unconscious thought and at a point where a previous and an immediate event or text intersect, and it is in this state that Scout discovers the profound truths that constitute her "maturation" in the story. This state, in which Scout tends to think not in words but in visual images, coincides precisely with Scout's moments of deepest insight and enables her to form conclusions which are, though sparsely articulated, central to our understanding of the novel.

For example, having witnessed and experienced profound confusion over the confrontation between Atticus and the lynch mob outside Tom Robinson's jail cell in chapter 16, Scout is "drifting into sleep" (156) when the "full meaning" of the night's events materializes before her. "The memory of Atticus calmly folding his newspaper and pushing back his hat became Atticus standing in the middle of an empty street, pushing back his glasses" (156). Establishing the link between Atticus defending the town from the "mad dog" and Atticus defending Tom Robinson from the lynch mob, Scout's visual metaphorical thought process, enabled by her semiconscious state, is the nucleus of the novel's quite deep symbolic structure, a structure which continually stresses the role of Atticus as "defender" of Maycomb and southern society from its own self-destructive urges.

Scout is again wavering between conscious and semiconscious perception in Chapter 21, when she develops her previous metaphor by substituting the scene outside the Maycomb jail for that of the courtroom. She is "too tired to argue" (210) with Jem when he questions her understanding of the racial complexity of the Robinson case, but she discovers another and more profound concept. As she drifts into sleep, she describes, "an impression that was creeping into [her]" (210). Mentally transported in her dream-like state she "shivered, though the night was hot" (210). "A steaming summer night was no different from a winter morning" she understands, and in her semi-consciousness the street scene appears and the sensory impressions of the "mad dog" and courtroom dramas are merged. Accordingly, Heck Tate saying "take him, Mr. Finch" becomes Heck Tate saying "This court will come to order" (210).

Finally, as the novel comes to a close, Scout makes yet another thematically crucial connection, this time between an outside-of-text fictional narrative (and therefore an element of Lee's historical background) and the fictional events of the novel itself. Here Scout's sleep results from the soporific effect of the rain, the room's warmth and the deep voice of Atticus as he reads from "The Gray Ghost, by Seckatary Hawkins" (280). As she has throughout the novel, she awakes having internalized the sensed rather than perceived monologue, having made a text to text analogy, having responded deeply but not necessarily consciously to the hegemonic discourse surrounding her. Her interpretation of Stoner's Boy in *The Gray Ghost*, its meaning clearly shaped by the experiences she has recently had and is still in the process of retelling, illustrates an influence that is mutual, simultaneous, and only unified in the unconscious. Speaking of Stoner's Boy but using words that describe both Boo Radley and Tom Robinson, she declares, "... when they finally saw him, he hadn't done any those things ... Atticus, he was real nice" (281).

Lacan has been given credit for a restructured and reformulated "presentation of Freud's unconscious as symbolic and relational" (Ragland-Sullivan 70). Scout's semiconscious merging of texts across barriers of time and place presents a symbolic and relational translation of unconscious truth. Especially because in this novel they are so clearly rendered as the intersection of conscious and unconscious, these several examples of what I have called "text to text merging" provide a particularly apt metaphor for the relationship between historical text and imaginative literature in general as defined in the poststructuralist era. The only difference may be that while the historical mergings in the novel tend to be proleptic through their anticipation of later events and ideology from the fictionalized mid 1930s context, Scout's merging is anachronistic, reaching back in time to connect a past event to present meaning.

Lacan's description of the dream as "a way of remembering one's relationship to objects; a sign of exhaustion of regressions, and thus a threshold to the Real; a sign, therefore, of restructuring one's relationship to objects" (44) is the process Scout enacts, which is accurately "to know the *moi*" (a composite of Freud's ego), a process in which "one must read backward in spatial sense, but in the immediacy of present time" (Ragland-Sullivan 44). The dream is then "a temporal rewriting of history" (44) and the subject (in this case the narrator and authorial alter ego Scout) is "an unbridgeable gap between perceptions and alienation in relation to an external gestalt, an internal discourse, and Desire" (67). Our own "Western cultural bias—mistrust of image/object in favor of the word" (56)—may predispose a skepticism toward both viewing events as texts and trusting the unconscious text of images over conscious, time-ordered and word-ordered "reality." But Lacan's assertion that the "The *je* (the speaking or socially constructed subject) stabilizes the *moi* through naming and labeling" and "gives shape and form to the symbolic" (Ragland-Sullivan 59) also describes the interpretive enterprise with which Scout is frequently engaged. That the semiconscious intrusions by the unconscious *moi* into the conscious *je* function in *To Kill a Mockingbird* in a way which deepens and broadens textual meaning does not conflict with their essential role as "disrupters of spoken or socially structured reality" (Ragland-Sullivan 61) or the constructed symbolic order. Furthermore, Lacan has suggested that "The task of learning who one is" is "preverbal" because "language slowly cuts the subject off from its prespeech fusions and naturalness (*jouissance*) and imprints the cultural myths which adults later assume they have consciously deduced or understood through a process of education" (61). This position not only describes the relation between the verbal and prediscursive reality as it exists in Lee's imaginative narrative, but also accurately depicts the author's own relation to the external gestalt of history, the internal discourse of fictional narrative, and Desire, which in this case may be described as Lee's attempt to locate the ideology of a narrative in one historical period while existing and therefore "always already" in a subject position in another. Lacanian critics have used the term "introjection" to describe "the process of acquiring identity in reference to objects, symbols, and effects of the outside world" (Ragland-Sullivan 13), a process which takes place "prior to any awareness" (22) and involves an "ambiguity of boundary distinctions" (36) including those of time and place, of which Lacan "emphasized the crucial importance" (35). A proleptic cross-historical merging of ideology is then the operant form of "introjection" that influences the composition process of the novel. It is worthwhile to note that Scout's revelations are rendered in the language of state of being, using linking rather than action verbs—the memory "became"—as would most properly present the kind of direct "equivocation" that here takes place and is replicated in the arrangement of the novel's historical ideology, which similarly equivocates meaning from the distinct historical periods, mixing as it does clearly identifiable elements of the novel's historical past and its period of production. Aptly then, unconscious, prediscursive processes are rendered in visual images and metaphors—as in the unconscious or dream state—rather than in words, as when we are awake and conscious. Through the metaphorical language of state of being, for example, Atticus in one scene or role "becomes" Atticus in another context which is physically different but ideologically identical. The effect, like the effect created by Lee's merging of historical texts, is synergistic.

Because it merges ideology from the 1930s and 1950s, author Harper Lee's presentation of the novel's historical "texts" works in the same way. The 1930s and the 1950s are in fact the contradictory discourses bringing to bear what Catherine Belsey refers to as "intolerable pressures" which inhibit the formation of a single and coherent subject position and a single and coherent position within historical ideology. Based on the given that texts are composed within what Stanley Fish refers to as a "material reality" or what Judith Lowder Newton calls "material conditions" which "alter the representation of representation itself" (Newton 162), it follows that the historical event or "text" as it appears in fiction necessarily presents a highly subjectivized version of history, governed as that presentation unavoidably is by principles of selection and interpretation either consciously or unconsciously at work in the author, but never completely absent. From an outline of a process of historical introjection in *To Kill a Mockingbird*, we are able to make generalizations that are paradigmatic about how a merging of historical discourses can operate within a form of representation (the novel structured within history) which is never completely imaginative or completely faithful to historical fact, never completely "one or the other," never predictable in terms of its "zone of social transaction" and therefore always presenting a history that is partial, incomplete, and incapable of being accurately descriptive of any single historical period. Necessarily then, imaginative literature that is historically structured tells us as much about the relationship of ideology to material conditions and hegemony as it does about either its period of production or its historical present. I have attempted here to separate aspects of distinct discursive fields—those of the novel's historical present and its period of production—on the assumption that the clearly established discourse and material conditions of each contain revelations about both power and the relationship between historical and imaginative truth.

What requires recognition, however, is that because of its conflicting "material conditions" and the interplay of the two resultant and opposite processes of prolepsis and anachronism, the novel cannot actually be understood within or tied to any single or particular historical period. This would seem, of course, to be a "general truth" that would apply to all literature with any substantial internal historical structure, which is necessarily prejudiced in the most essential of ways by its moment of production, therefore presenting only a diluted version of its own ideology. The implied tasks for historicist readings then would seem to be to continue to work with texts in ways which acknowledge always that literary works are the product of more than one discourse or set of material conditions, and to search for concrete terms or strategies for answering the kind of historical questions that arise so frequently in literature as a result of this phenomenon.

NOTES

1. In August of 1955, fourteen-year-old Chicago native Emmett Till arrived in the Mississippi Delta to visit relatives in Tallahatchie County. On the evening of August 24, 1955, Till and his cousin Curtis Jones drove to a small grocery store run by Roy and Carolyn Bryant in the hamlet of Money. The initial incident is still the subject of debate. According to some accounts, he whistled at Carolyn Bryant. According to the testimony of Mrs. Bryant, Till grabbed her wrist and made a lewd suggestion before leaving the store. The murder trial took place in September of 1955. Though Moses Wright named in court the two white men who had taken Till from his shack, the all-white, all-male jury acquitted Milam and Bryant after deliberating 67 minutes. (For detailed accounts of the trial, see Whitfield, Halberstam, Whitaker).

2. Beyond the scope of this study but fascinating as an aspect of Lee's apparent response to Citizens Council racial theory and literature are the author's repeated allusions to Egypt and Egyptian civilization, including Jem's Chapter Seven "Egyptian phase," references to the Rosetta Stone in chapter eight and the pyramids in Chapter One, several speculative passages about the Finch family's possible origins "back in Egypt" (227), and Jem's assertion that Egyptian civilization "accomplished more than the Americans ever did" (59). In the race language around the *Brown* decision, Egypt plays a role that is conclusively established by the widely distributed Bible of Citizens Council literature, "A Manual for Southerners," which was written for schoolchildren in grades three and four and used in some southern schools in 1957 and after. The text revives earlier discredited theories of "scientific racism," including a preoccupation with Egyptian civilization as a distorted model for the effects of racial mixing or amalgamation:

> The first civilized nation in the world that we know about was Egypt. The Egyptian people of that time were pure white people. So you see that the white people built the first civilization on earth. These Egyptian people were careful to build a strong nation that they could be proud of. Even today we are surprised at some of the wonderful things they did.
>
> But about the time the Egyptians had built a wonderful country, they brought Negro slaves among them. It was not long before the Race-Mixers of those days began saying the slaves should be set free among the white

Egyptians. And finally the Egyptians set the Negro free, cleaned him up, and taught him in their schools.

Now you can already guess what happened to the Egyptian nation. Since the races were mixed, the people began marrying one another. Then the Egyptian race was no longer pure, and their nation was no longer strong. A mixed race is weak and all confused, and this makes the country weak, as we have already learned. (qtd. in Muse 174–175)

That such ideology had made its way into the everyday racial lexicon of the post-*Brown* deep South is extremely likely. In one interview from Robert Penn Warren's 1956 text, segregation seems irrefutably to establish the presence of Citizens Council doctrine in the ready vocabulary of the typical southerner. Modeling his argument almost verbatim on that contained in the Citizens Council "Manual," the Southerner states, "Negro blood destroyed the civilization of Egypt, India, Phoenicia, Carthage, Greece, and it will destroy America!" (Warren 25).

The degree of demonstrable concern in Lee's novel with questions not only of human origin but of breeding, social status and the maintenance of racial segregation is in itself a significant measure of the text's ideological orientation in the post-*Brown* decision era. But Lee's use of a strong pattern of allusion to Egypt seems a direct response to the propaganda of the Citizens Councils, and its presence in the novel again exemplifies the process of prolepsis at work in Lee's historical present.

3. Jonathan M. Wiener, "The Black Beast Rapist: White Racial Attitudes in the Postwar South," *Reviews in American History* 13 (June 1985): 224; George M. Frederickson, *The Black Image in the White Mind: The Debate on Afro-American Character and Destiny, 1817–1914* (New York: Harper & Row, 1971): 272–282.

4. Claudia Durst Johnson has investigated connections between Lee's Robinson trial and the 1932–36 Scottsboro trials, which took place in Northern Alabama and involved allegations of gang rape of two white women by nine black men. "The central parallels between the novel and Scottsboro trials," Johnson argues, "are three: the threat of lynching; the issue of a Southern jury's composition; and the intricate symbolic complications arising from the interweave of race and class when a lower-class white woman wrongfully accuses a black man or men" (5). Though the similarities Johnson notes are intriguing, they are also, I would argue, superficial in comparison to those herein noted and less compelling in terms of historical relevance. Born in 1926, Harper Lee was five years old at the time of the Scottsboro incident. As I have here suggested, the novel's most definitive historical milieu is the 1950s, and the Emmett Till case a more powerful register of the racial ideology of that period.

5. Lee enrolled at the University of Alabama School of Law in 1947. She dedicated the novel to her father, Amasa Coleman Lee, a Monroeville attorney who served in the Alabama State Legislature from 1927 to 1939, and to her sister, Alice Lee, also a practicing attorney. The novel's motto, "Lawyers, I suppose, were children once" (Charles Lamb), and the astute courtroom observations of its narrator also indicate a high level of legal knowledge and concern. Claudia Durst Johnson has noted that "the largest volume of criticism on the novel has been done by legal rather than literary scholars" (25).

6. *Jackson Clarion-Ledger*, August 25, 1985, sec. H, p. 1; *Huntsville Times*, July 19, 1987, sec. B. p. 1.

7. Whitfield notes that this statement appeared in several southern newspapers on or about Sep. 1–2, 1955 (18).

8. See Whitaker's thesis.

9. *New York Times*, September 18, 1955, p. 10; Wilkins quoted in *Memphis Commercial Appeal*, September 1, 1955, p. 1, 4; *Jackson Daily News*, September 2, 1955, p. 8.

10. That the decision may be termed subversive has also been argued by Thomas Shaffer, a legal scholar who has published the most detailed research on the codification of legal ethics in the novel. In "Christian Lawyer Stories and American Legal Ethics" (*Mercer Law Review*, Spring 1982, 877–901), Shaffer concludes that Atticus' handling of the Radley intervention is wrong because he does not have Radley arrested.

11. Claudia Carter details the development of Atticus' legal outlook into "a compassionate activism ... a model we can emulate" (13).

WORKS CITED

Belsey, Catherine. *Critical Practice*. London: Methuen, 1950.

Carter, Claudia A. "Lawyers as Heroes: The Compassionate Activism of a Fictional Attorney is a Model We Can Emulate." *Los Angeles Lawyer*, July–August 1988, 13.

Dietch, Joseph. "Harper Lee: Novelist of the South." *The Christian Science Monitor* 3 October 1961: C6.

Fish, Stanley. "Commentary: The Young and the Restless," H. Aram Veeser, ed., *The New Historicism*. New York: Routledge, 1989. 303–16.

Greenblatt, Stephen Jay. "Invisible Bullets: Renaissance Authority and its Subversion" in *Glyph* 8 (1981).

———. *Learning to Curse: Essays in Early Modern Culture*. New York and London: Routledge, Chapman and Hall, Inc., 1990.

Halberstam, David. *The Fifties*. New York: Fawcett Columbine, 1993.

Johnson, Claudia Durst. *To Kill a Mockingbird: Threatening Boundaries*. New York: Twayne Publishers, 1994.

Lee, Harper. *To Kill a Mockingbird*. Philadelphia: J. B. Lippincott Company, 1960.

Lowder Newton, Judith. "History as Usual? Feminism and the New Historicism," in H. Aram Veeser, ed., *The New Historicism*, New York: Routledge, 1989. 152–76.

Muse, Benjamin. *Ten Years of Prelude*. New York: Viking P, 1964.

Myrdal, Gunnar. *An American Dilemma: The Negro Problem and Modern Democracy*. New York: Harper & Brothers, 1947.

Newby, I. A. "Introduction: Segregationist Thought Since 1890." *The Development of Segregationist Thought*. I. A. Newby. Homewood, IL: Dorsey P, 1968.

Ragland-Sullivan, Ellie. *Jacques Lacan and the Philosophy of Psychoanalysis*. Urbana and Chicago: U of Illinois P, 1986.

Shaffer, Thomas L. "Christian Lawyer Stories and American Legal Ethics." *Mercer Law Review*, Spring 1982, 877–901.

Sullivan, Richard. "Engrossing Novel of Rare Excellence" *Chicago Tribune* 17 July 1960, 15.

To Kill a Mockingbird Then and Now: A Thirty-Fifth Anniversary Celebration. Host Charlayne Hunter-Gault. Sponsored by National Endowment for the Arts, 1995.

Waller, Ruth. "*To Kill a Mockingbird.*" *Montgomery Adviser* 14 July 1960.

Warren, Robert Penn. *Segregation: The Inner Conflict of the South.* New York: Random House, 1956.

Wexler, Sanford. *The Civil Rights Movement: An Eyewitness History.* New York: Facts on File, Inc., 1993.

Whitaker, Hugh Stephen. *A Case Study in Southern Justice: The Emmett Till Case.* Unpublished thesis, Florida State University, 1963.

Whitfield, Stephen J. *A Death in the Delta.* Baltimore: Johns Hopkins UP, 1988.

CHRISTOPHER METRESS

The Rise and Fall of Atticus Finch

In 1991, the Library of Congress and the Book-of-the-Month Club commissioned a "Survey of Lifetime Reading Habits" and discovered that *To Kill
a Mockingbird* was second only to the Bible among books "most often cited
as making a difference" in people's lives. A staple of high-school reading lists
for more than four decades, and the source for one of the nation's most
beloved films, Harper Lee's novel is bound to be on most short lists of contemporary American classics. While controversy has long surrounded the
work (it remains to this day one of the books most frequently banned from
high-school libraries), many readers would concur with the recent assessment of Lee's novel in *500 Great Books by Women*: "*To Kill a Mockingbird* only
gets better with rereading; each time the streets of Maycomb become more
real and alive, each time Scout is more insightful, Atticus more heroic, and
Boo Radley more tragically human."

Despite these recent confirmations, however, all is not well in
Maycomb. Beginning in the early 1990s, quick upon the heels of the Library
of Congress survey, a new generation of critics began to reread Lee's classic.
To Kill a Mockingbird, it appears, is not getting better with age, and each time
these new readers revisit the streets of Maycomb, those streets look less
insightful and less heroic. Hardest hit by these revisionary readings is the
novel's purported hero, Atticus Finch. For forty years the source of continu-

From *The Chattahoochee Review* 24, no. 1. © 2003 by Georgia Perimeter College.

ous accolades, Atticus has now fallen on hard times. And as goes Atticus, so goes the novel. As a result, within the short span of a decade a new critical dissensus has emerged, one which suggests that *To Kill a Mockingbird* tells two stories—or, to borrow a phrase from the novel itself—speaks two languages. That second language tells a darker tale, one that warns us that our adulation of Atticus Finch and our praise for *To Kill a Mockingbird* have less to do with the merits of the hero and the liberal vision of the novel than they have to do with our own blind spots and prejudices. *To Kill a Mockingbird* is not, as earlier readers claimed, a persuasive plea for racial justice, nor is its hero a model of moral courage. Instead, novel and hero are, at best, morally ambiguous or, at worst, morally reprehensible. Nowadays, many readers of the novel are like as not to emphasize Finch's complicity with, rather than his challenges to, the segregationist politics of his hometown, and, as a result, Lee's novel is beginning to lose its iconic status. Never in all its years has the song of the mockingbird sounded so unsweet.

It would be naïve, of course, to suggest that before the 1990s there was no negative criticism of the work. Although *To Kill a Mockingbird* won the 1961 Pulitzer Prize, sold 500,000 copies in one year, and was immediately translated into ten languages—all this before going on to sell more than 30,000,000 copies worldwide, making it the third best-selling American novel of the twentieth century—there were scattered denunciations of Lee's classic. The most famous was by fellow Southerner Flannery O'Connor, who, in a letter to Alabama writer Caroline Ivey, called the novel "a child's book." "When I was fifteen," O'Connor claimed, "I would have loved it. Take out the rape and you've got something like *Miss Minerva and William Green Hill*[.] I think for a child's book it does all right. It's interesting that all the folks that are buying it don't know they're reading a child's book. Somebody ought to say what it is."

For the most part, however, those buying the novel in 1960 and since would have agreed more with James Carville than Flannery O'Connor. In the introduction to *We're Right, They're Wrong: A Handbook for Spirited Progressives*, Carville recalls that in the wake of *Brown v. Board of Education* he still "took segregation for granted and wished the blacks just didn't push so damn hard to change it." But then he read *To Kill a Mockingbird* "and that novel changed everything."

> I got it from a lady who drove around in the overheated bookmobile in my parish—another government program, I might add. I had asked the lady for something on football, but she handed me *To Kill a Mockingbird* instead. I couldn't put it down. I stuck it

inside another book and read it under my desk during school. When I got to the last page, I closed it and said, "They're right and we're wrong." The issue was literally black and white, and we were absolutely, positively on the wrong side.

From that moment on, Carville decided to devote his life to combating racial and legal injustice. Similar testimonies run. up to the present moment. As one contemporary lawyer recently confessed, "I had lots of heroes growing up. Some were men, some were women; some were real and some were imaginary people in books I read. Only one remains very much alive for me. He is a character in Harper Lee's *To Kill a Mockingbird*.... Atticus Finch made me believe in lawyer heroes." Such testimonies have led Joseph Crespino to argue that "In the twentieth century, *To Kill a Mockingbird* is probably the most widely read book dealing with race in America, and its protagonist, Atticus Finch, the most enduring fictional image of racial heroism."

But in 1992, that all began to change. In the February 24th issue of *Legal Times*, Hofstra University Law Professor and contributing editor Monroe Freedman devoted an entire column to Lee's novel. In a provocatively entitled piece called "Atticus Finch, ESQ, R.I.P." Freedman rejected the notion that Finch was a model for lawyers. "If we don't do something fast," Freedman enjoined his readers—perhaps a few decades too late—"lawyers are going to start taking [Finch] seriously as someone to emulate. And that would be a bad mistake." Freedman's points are many, but his argument essentially boils down to this: "Atticus Finch does, indeed, act heroically in his representation of Robinson. But he does so from an elitist sense of noblesse oblige. Except under compulsion of a court appointment, Finch never attempts to change the racism and sexism that permeate life in Macomb [sic], Ala. On the contrary, he lives his own life as the passive participant in that pervasive injustice. And that is not my idea of a role model for young lawyers." "Let me put it this way," Freedman continues, "I would have more respect for Atticus Finch if he had never been compelled by the court to represent Robinson, but if, instead, he had undertaken voluntarily to establish the right of the black citizens of Macomb [sic] to sit freely in their county courthouse [and not segregated in the balcony]. That Atticus Finch would, indeed, have been a model for young lawyers to emulate."

And just how was this first witness for the prosecution against Atticus Finch received by the legal community? Total outrage, it appears. Finch was defended in the pages of *Legal Times* by none other than the president of the American Bar Association, who wrote, "Sixty years after Judge Taylor appointed Atticus Finch to defend a poor, black man in *To Kill a Mockingbird*,

these two fictional heroes still inspire us. Contrary to what Professor
Freedman asserts, Finch rose above racism and injustice to defend the principle that all men and women deserve their day in court represented by competent legal counsel, regardless of their ability to pay." Another contributor
to the *Times* was much less considered in his response. "In my book," wrote
Southern attorney R. Mason Barge, "any lawyer who takes on the establishment *pro bono publico* is a hero. I hope Mr. Freedman would agree, and if so,
I'll make a deal with him. We'll worry about racism down here, and you just
go on living in the good old days, when New York was marginally less racist
than Alabama and its habitants could arrogate moral superiority to themselves. And when you get around to cleaning up those sewers you call cities,
give me a call, and we can talk about what a bad guy Atticus Finch was."

Three months after his column appeared, Freedman informed his
readers of the following:

> During the past two years, this column has dealt with cases and
> causes involving unethical lawyers, dishonest judges, criminal
> conflicts of interest in the White House, and widespread malad-
> ministration of justice in our criminal courts. But never has there
> been such a fulsome response as to the column making the rather
> modest suggestion that a particular fictional character is not an
> appropriate model for lawyers.
>
> The mythological deification of Atticus Finch was illustrated
> by Atticans who wrote to equate my rejection of Finch, literally,
> with attacking God, Moses, Jesus, Gandhi, and Mother Teresa.

Now, if Freedman's revisionist dissent were the only controversial
rereading of *To Kill a Mockingbird*, there'd be little reason to fear for
Atticus Finch or Harper Lee's novel. But that is simply not the case. A second trial of Finch occurred not in the pages of another legal magazine, but
in Tuscaloosa, Alabama at a 1994 Symposium sponsored by the University
of Alabama School of Law. Alabama Law Professor Timothy Hoff opened
the symposium in terms that echoed the critical consensus that had
marked the novel's first thirty years: "The continued popularity of
Mockingbird," Hoff urged, "must be ascribed to its evocation of the lawyer
as hero.... There is hope in the fact that readers and movie watchers are
[still] drawn to such goodness." However, while some presenters did want
to argue for the novel's "goodness," others at the symposium urged dissent. Freedman resurrected his position of 1992 and extended its reach,
telling the Tuscaloosa audience that "[t]hroughout his relatively comfort-

able and pleasant life in Maycomb, Atticus Finch knows about the grinding, ever-present humiliation and degradation of the black people of Maycomb; he tolerates it; and sometimes he even trivializes and condones it." "Here is a man," Freedman concludes, "who does not voluntarily use his legal training and skills—not once, ever—to make the slightest change in the pervasive social injustice of his own town…. [As a state legislator] Could he not introduce one bill to mitigate the evils of segregation? Could he not work with Judge Taylor in an effort to desegregate the courthouse? Could he not take, voluntarily, a single appeal in a death penalty case? And could he not represent a Tom Robinson just once without a court order to do so?"

Strong words, but this time Freedman did not find himself alone. Teresa Godwin Phelps, a Professor of Law at Notre Dame, opened her remarks by noting the following: "For nearly a decade I have assigned *To Kill a Mockingbird* to my Law and Literature class and for the most part class discussions have followed along typical lines. We are chagrined at the intractable racism of Maycomb; we admire Atticus and discuss whether his lie to save Boo Radley from public scrutiny is justified. We come away from *To Kill a Mockingbird* feeling good about being lawyers and law students." However, she now confessed, she could no longer teach the book this way. For Phelps, the most troubling aspect of the novel is voiced by Jem late in the book. "There are four kinds of folks in the world," Jem tells Scout. "There's the ordinary kind like us and the neighbors, there's the kind like the Cunninghams out in the woods, the kind like the Ewells down at the dump, and the Negroes." According to Phelps, "*To Kill a Mockingbird* is a valiant attempt to erase some of the barriers that exist between 'kinds of folks'; however, the books fails to recognize or acknowledge the barriers it leaves erect. While the novel depicts change in one facet of law and society, it reinforces the status quo in other troubling aspects." While granting that Lee's treatment of folks like the Cunninghams represents a "true liberal vision," Phelps argues against the "Far less liberal and far more disturbing vision … put forth of the Ewells" by both Lee and Atticus. "The book teaches us to desire to be like Atticus," Phelps concludes, "courageous in the face of our community's prejudices. But it also teaches us to fear and deplore the Ewells and Lula…. We readers, like the citizens of Maycomb, see what we want to see and are blind to much else. We, like Atticus, are implicated in the town's delusions as long as we read *To Kill a Mockingbird* with uncritical acceptance."

A year later, the dissent against Atticus moved from the lawyers to the literary critics. In a 1995 anthology entitled *The South as an American Problem*—a collection of essays written mainly by professors from

Vanderbilt—Eric J. Sundquist, who is certainly one of the most influential critics of contemporary American literature, argued that, "For all its admirable moral earnestness and its inventory of the historical forces making up the white liberal consciousness of the late 1950s... [*To Kill a Mockingbird*] might well have been entitled 'Driving Miss Scout.'" Calling the novel "something of an historical relic," Sundquist argues that the work is "an icon whose emotive sway remains strangely powerful because it also remains unexamined." Sundquist's own examination takes twenty-nine pages as he reads the novel through the lens of the Scottsboro trials, *Brown vs. the Board of Education*, the lynching of Emmett Till, the rise of massive resistance, and the accomplishments of contemporary African-American literature. Here is one example, worth quoting at length, of where all this leads Sundquist:

> Atticus's moral courage forms a critical part of the novel's deceptive surface. Whether to shield his children from the pain of racism or to shield Lee's Southern readers from a confrontation with their own recalcitrance [on the race problem], Atticus, for all his devotion to the truth, sometimes lies. He employs indirection in order to teach his children about Maycomb's racial hysteria and the true meaning of courage, but he himself engages in evasion when he contends, for instance, that the Ku Klux Klan is a thing of the past ("way back about nineteen-twenty"), a burlesque show of cowards easily humiliated by the Jewish storeowner they attempt to intimidate in their sheeted costumes purchased from the merchant himself. Such moments are not distinct from the book's construction of analogies for moral courage in the face of communal racism ... but rather part of it. Indirection and displacement govern both novel's moral pedagogy and, in the end, its moral stalemate.

According to Sundquist, the novel also has a "peculiar political morality" embodied in Atticus's warning to Scout that "This time we aren't fighting the Yankees, we're fighting our friends. But remember this, no matter how bitter this gets, they're still our friends and this is still our home." Such words, for Sundquist, are an "expression of near paralysis, which at once identifies the race crisis as only a *Southern* problem," which by 1960 it no longer was. "Just as the South closed ranks against the nation at the outset of desegregation," Sundquist concludes, "*To Kill a Mockingbird* carefully narrows the terms on which changed race relations are going to be brought

about in the South" in the 1960s. Ultimately, "Atticus Finch's integrity"—
and thus the integrity of the novel itself—"is circumscribed by his admonition that moral action must respect the prejudices of 'our friends' and ultimately abide by local ethics"—a stance that, because it argues against the
need for federal intervention in the South, would have all but assured that
racial justice would have never come to the black citizens of Maycomb. Thus,
instead of Atticus being a hero who stands in opposition to his community,
Sundquist reads him as an apologist whose moral vision embodies a subtle
form of massive resistance to outside agitation.

In the few short years since Freedman, Phelps and Sundquist first
began to cross-examine Lee's lawyer hero, Atticus Finch has been called
repeatedly before the bar of judgment. One more example will suffice. In a
mammoth essay comparing Atticus Finch to Gavin Stevens, the lawyer hero
of Faulkner's *Intruder in the Dust*, Rob Atkinson, accuses Finch and Lee of
"lawyerly paternalism" and hopes that *Intruder in the Dust* will replace *To Kill
a Mockingbird* as America's most inspirational story of progressive legal
ethics. Writing in the December 1999 issue of the *Duke Law Journal*,
Atkinson argues that "the greater appeal of *To Kill a Mockingbird* may tell us
something less than wholly laudable about ourselves," for Lee's novel
expresses a "liberal-democratic vision" which suggests that lawyers are
always "above" their clients because their clients are always beholden to
them for uplifting. This is the "paternalistic" message of *To Kill a
Mockingbird*, a message that can also be seen as supporting a larger assumption in the novel: that racial progress is in the hands of good, enlightened
white people who know what is best for underprivileged, and thus always
beholden, blacks. Under this approach, Atticus's legendary defense of Tom
Robinson is radically reinterpreted. "When pressed to explain his motives for
taking the case," Atkinson writes, "Atticus's focus is distinctly on himself, not
his client. He makes clear several times that it is his own sense of personal
rectitude and his need to be seen as virtuous by others that compel him to
take Tom's case ... Atticus [may allude] to 'a number of reasons,' but he elaborates only one: 'The main one is, if I didn't, I couldn't hold up my head in
town, I couldn't represent this county in the legislature, I couldn't even tell
you or Jem not to do something again.' Each explanatory clause begins with
'I'," Atkinson concludes. "Atticus does not mention Tom Robinson at all." So
much for Atticus as an enduring fictional image of racial heroism.

Just a few years ago, the Alabama Bar Association placed a stone outside of the Monroeville County Courthouse and upon that stone a plaque
commemorating the ideals of Atticus Finch. We should not, however, mistake that long overdue gesture as representing critical consensus about this

man. No longer is the response to Lee's hero as clear-cut as when James Carville first read the work forty years ago. Ours is an age of pluralism and dissensus, and as Atticus Finch moves into a new century, some tough lawyers, and some even tougher literary critics, are beginning to build a strong case against him. The great defense lawyer is now himself on trial, and while the outcome of the proceedings are not a foregone conclusion, things are not looking good. Yes, Atticus still has his many defenders, among them most recently fellow Alabamians Claudia Durst Johnson and Wayne Flint, but with each passing year these voices of praise meet with louder and more numerous denunciations. Although it is impossible to predict what perspective on the novel future generations will hold, when this new trial is over and Atticus Finch must once again leave the courthouse, it is just possible that, on that day, no one will rise to stand.

GARY RICHARDS

Harper Lee and the Destabilization
of Heterosexuality

Unlike Lillian Smith's fiction, which, after its initial notoriety and even infamy, quickly fell out of popular circulation, Harper Lee's *To Kill a Mockingbird* (1960) met with enthusiastic critical and popular reception upon its publication and has remained one of the nation's most pervasive texts. It was, according to the *Commonweal*'s review, "the find of the year," and Robert W. Henderson raved that Lee had written both a "compassionate, deeply moving novel, and a most persuasive plea for racial justice." Almost without exception, reviewers praised her depiction of small-town southern life. Granville Hicks noted her "insight into Southern mores," and Keith Waterhouse, writing from the other side of the Atlantic, offered that "Miss Lee does well what so many American writers do appallingly: she paints a true and lively picture of life in an American small town. And she gives freshness to a stock situation." This "freshness" arises in part, suggested Frank H. Lyell, because Lee avoids the tropes and imagery of the southern gothic. "Maycomb has its share of eccentrics and evil-doers," he admits, "but Miss Lee has not tried to satisfy the current lust for morbid, grotesque tales of Southern depravity." Perhaps recalling *Other Voices, Other Rooms* and *The House of Breath*, a reviewer for *Time* agreed with Lyell, arguing that Lee's novel includes "all of the tactile brilliance and none of the preciosity generally supposed to be standard swamp-warfare issue for Southern writers."

From *Lovers and Beloveds: Sexual Otherness in Southern Fiction, 1936-1961*. © 2005 by Louisiana State University Press.

"Novelist Lee's prose has an edge that cuts through cant," this reviewer asserted, concluding, "All in all, Scout Finch is fiction's most appealing child since Carson McCullers' Frankie got left behind at the wedding."[1]

These reviewers' criticisms were few and easily dismissed. Critics seemed intent to disregard the possibility that the narrative might be Scout's adult reflections on her childhood rather than a telling of yesterday's events. Hicks thus identified Lee's central problem as "to tell the story she wants and yet to stay within the consciousness of a child," while the hostile reviewer for the *Atlantic Monthly* deemed the narration "frankly and completely impossible." The only other real concern indicted the novel's didacticism, which most reviewers were content merely to note and then dismiss as minor. The reviewer for *Booklist*, for example, concluded, "Despite a melodramatic climax and traces of sermonizing, the characters and locale are depicted with insight and a rare blend of wit and compassion," and *Time* has granted that, although "a faint catechistic flavor may have been inevitable," "it is faint indeed." The consensus was, as the *Commonweal*'s reviewer put it, that the "author unknown until this book appeared will not soon be forgotten."[2]

Lee was indeed not forgotten, for the novel won the Pulitzer Prize in 1961 and was soon adapted into a screenplay by Horton Foote. The resulting 1962 film starring Gregory Peck met with critical acclaim and simultaneously made Lee's narrative, albeit significantly altered, accessible to a wider audience. Since this time, the novel has been widely taught in American schools, in no small part, Eric Sundquist argues, because of its "admirable moral earnestness" and "comforting sentimentality." To him, as to early reviewers, the book offers "a merciless string of moral lessons" presented through "a model of conventional plot and character" that is nevertheless "an episodic story of wit and charm."[3] Because of this teachable didacticism, thousands of adolescents have been subjected to Lee's less-than-subtle symbolism and Atticus Finch's palatable liberal dicta to his children for social tolerance.

Despite—or perhaps because of—these popular circulations, *To Kill a Mockingbird* has been for the most part critically neglected, typically being dismissed simply as a popular novel or as children's literature. *The History of Southern Literature*, for instance, devotes but a solitary paragraph to the novel. Martha Cook briefly summarizes the plot and, at odds with Sundquist, tersely concludes, "*To Kill a Mockingbird* is most successful in its unsentimental portrayal of enlightened views on the rights of blacks." More substantial critical discussions of the novel remain few, with an ebbing to almost nothing of late. Only two notable exceptions emerge, essays by Sundquist and Claudia Johnson, the latter of which was expanded into the slim *To Kill a*

Mockingbird: Threatening Boundaries. And yet these works share a primary focus of contextualizing the novel's circulations of race within larger historical ones of the novel's setting and period of composition, the mid-1930s and the mid- to late-1950s respectively. Both essays approach the novel through the Scottsboro case, the Supreme Court's ruling in *Brown v. Board of Education*, Rosa Parks's bus ride, and the desegregation of the University of Alabama, and thus keep the lens of analysis primarily that of race.[4]

This evolution of critical approaches from initial fanfare at publication to general dismissal to one informed foremost by race should by now be familiar, since such an evolution parallels the shifting approaches to *Strange Fruit* and Lillian Smith's other writing, and both trajectories of critical reception reflect southern literary studies' increased awareness and interrogations of race. As the previous chapter establishes, however, the scholarship on Smith has of late expanded to incorporate other significant critical lenses and those of gender and sexuality in particular. And, as I hope to have shown, *Strange Fruit* and *Killers of the Dream* prove themselves texts subject to such approaches. This chapter argues that *To Kill a Mockingbird* not surprisingly bears comparable richness under such scrutiny.

Just as Lee's novel shares with *Strange Fruit* a narrative structure that privileges racial tensions, with Tom Robinson's trial for miscegenistic rape and his ultimate death paralleling in importance Tracy Deen and Nonnie Anderson's interracial affair and its tragic results, so too does Lee include as significant an array of sexual otherness as does Smith. But, whereas Smith overtly addresses homoerotic desire in Laura Deen, Lee explores sexual difference more obliquely through transgressions of gender, the absence and parody of heterosexual relations, and the symbolic representation of closetedness. What nevertheless emerges in *To Kill a Mockingbird* is a destabilization of heterosexuality and normative gender that seems far more radical, because of its cultural pervasiveness, than the momentary presences of overt same-sex desire in Smith's novel. That is, whereas Smith depicts struggles of isolated lesbians within southern society understood to be as homophobic as it is racist, Lee presents this society to be, without it ever being fully conscious of the fact, already distinctively queer.

Like so much southern literary production during and after World War II, *To Kill a Mockingbird* centrally preoccupies itself with gender transitivity. These violations of normative gender manifest themselves in characters as diverse as Dill Harris, Scout Finch, Miss Maudie Atkinson, and even, to a lesser degree, Atticus Finch, as well as in a number of minor figures. Lee draws attention to such transgressive performances through their alterity to normative ones, such as those of Aunt Alexandra, and by overt communal demands for gender conformity. Lee does not, however, use these transgressions as consistent cultural shorthand for homosexual or proto-homosexual identities, as Capote and Goyen do. Unlike the effeminate Joel Knox and Boy Ganchion, whose narratives culminate in struggles to negotiate and, albeit uneasily, to accept same-sex desire, Lee's gender-transitive characters do not face such moments of crisis. Their narratives end without comparable culminations and thus suggest that she is as interested in gender transitivity when it is not indicative of same-sex desire as when it is, and she seems concerned at broadest with how rarely normative gender is *ever* performed.

Of *To Kill a Mockingbird*'s central trio of young protagonists, only Jem Finch is conventionally gendered, behaving as a southern white boy his age ostensibly ought. In contrast, Scout and Dill struggle with such behaviors and seem more comfortable in gender-transitive roles. Consider first Dill. Lee not only scripts him as effeminate but also underscores his sissiness through the contrast to Jem and his crystallizing masculinity. Although the elder boy is underweight for Maycomb's football team, he nevertheless dwarfs Dill, and even Scout stands almost a head taller. Dill is in fact so small that, when the Finches first encounter him sitting in his aunt's collard patch, "he wasn't much higher than the collards." Scout and Jem are amazed when, after guessing Dill to be four-and-a-half years old based on his size, he informs them he is almost seven. "I'm little but I'm old," Dill demands when Jem offers, "You look right puny for goin' on seven."[5]

Comparisons of Dill and Jem become overt when they offer up their individual sizes and names for inspection, and, given the cultural valorizations of masculinity, Dill fares poorly when placed alongside Jem:

> Jem brushed his hair back to get a better look. "Why don't you come over, Charles Baker Harris?" he said. "Lord, what a name."
> "'s not any funnier'n yours. Aunt Rachel says your name's Jeremy Atticus Finch."
> Jem scowled. "I'm big enough to fit mine," he said. "Your name's longer'n you are. Bet it's a foot longer."
> "Folks call me Dill," said Dill, struggling under the fence. (11)

At least in his own opinion, Jem physically measures up to his full name, whereas Dill, metaphorically a foot deficient, does not and is instead forced into an appropriately truncated nickname.

If Dill's prepubescent body is less than masculine in size, his dress and actions do little to counter this effeminacy. Like Capote's delicate Joel Knox, Dill dresses in clothes perceived to be sissy, wearing "blue linen shorts that buttoned to his shirt" rather than Maycomb County boys' customary overalls. Although perhaps not necessarily feminine, his actions and desires are nevertheless likewise unconventional. He is, Scout says, "a pocket Merlin, whose head teemed with eccentric plans, strange longings, and quaint fancies" (12). Foremost among these fancies is to establish contact with Maycomb's reclusive Boo Radley. After hearing Scout and Jem rehearse communal gossip of Boo, the "Radley Place fascinated Dill" and "drew him as the moon draws water" (12–13). For all the intensity of these longings, however, he is conspicuously cowardly and will go no closer to the Radleys' than the light pole at the corner, and the resulting scenario allows Lee yet another arena to establish Dill's lack of daring in contrast to Jem's bravery. Not surprisingly, it is he rather than Dill who first enters the Radleys' yard and touches the house.

It is common knowledge that, in this characterization of Dill, Lee drew heavily upon Truman Capote's effeminate childhood identity, as he readily acknowledged. In a series of interviews with Lawrence Grobel, Capote reflects on this childhood in Monroeville, Alabama, and recalls his friendship with Nelle Harper Lee and her family: "Mr. and Mrs. Lee, Harper Lee's mother and father, ... lived very near. Harper Lee was my best friend. Did you ever read her book, *To Kill a Mockingbird?* I'm a character in that book, which takes place in the same small town in Alabama where we lived." He clearly implies Dill, whose childhood replicates Capote's so closely as sketched by biographer Gerald Clarke:

> As the years passed, the differences between him and other boys became even more pronounced: he remained small and pretty as a china doll, and his mannerisms, little things like the way he walked or held himself, started to look odd, unlike those of the other boys. Even his voice began to sound strange, peculiarly babylike and artificial, as if he had unconsciously decided that that part of him, the only part he could stop from maturing, would remain fixed in boyhood forever, reminding him of happier and less confusing times. His face and body belatedly matured, but his way of speaking never did.[6]

With Dill, Lee draws upon not only these generic effeminate mannerisms but also Capote's ubiquitous short pants, his precociousness, his string of surrogate- and stepfathers, and even his distinctive white hair that "stuck to his head like duckfluff" and formed "a cowlick in the center of his forehead" (12). Although the lascivious photo of Capote on the dust jacket of *Other Voices, Other Rooms* still haunted readers in the 1960s, when *To Kill a Mockingbird* appeared at the beginning of the decade, this image of Capote was but a few short years away from being replaced by comparably vivid others, ones that readers of Lee's novel might, if they knew Dill's biographical basis in Capote, bring with them to the text and thus to their understanding of Dill. In 1966 Capote not only published to wild acclaim *In Cold Blood* but, to celebrate the novel's completion, also hosted the Black and White Ball at Manhattan's Plaza Hotel. The publicity of each event was phenomenal, but that of the ball in particular inundated Americans with images of Capote's over-the-top campy effeminacy. As the photo spreads in *Life* and other magazines attested, the evening was, in Capote confidante Slim Keith's terms, "the biggest and best goddamned party that anybody had ever heard of" despite being "given by a funny-looking, strange little man."[7]

Having thus captured the public eye, Capote refused to leave it. In his remaining years, as his creativity and productivity waned, he shamelessly compensated by crafting an eccentric public personality for himself, which he flaunted, such as during his recurring appearances on Johnny Carson's *The Tonight Show*. As with those persons who saw the photographs of the Black and White Ball, Carson's viewers internalized images of Capote as an unabashed aging gossipy queen or, as Kenneth Reed has characterized Capote, a "madcap social butterfly and late evening television chatterbox."[8] Thus, for Lee's readers aware of Dill's basis in Capote, these images of him circulating throughout the 1960s and 1970s extratextually reinforced Dill's effeminacy.

And yet it is not Dill's gender violations but rather Scout's that command the most stringent communal surveillance and discipline. Her extended family and community—virtually one and the same—incessantly work to force her out of her tomboyish ways and into those appropriate for a young southern girl of the 1930s. As Claudia Johnson notes, however, Maycomb faces no small task. Scout abandons her feminine, given Christian name of "Jean Louise" for an adventurous and boyish nickname, invariably chooses overalls over dresses, and demands an air rifle for Christmas rather than a doll so that she can, among other things, terrorize her cousin.[9] Only rarely does she abandon such behavior to aspire to perform feminine roles, and these aspirations usually meet with scant success. Scout recalls, for instance, her "burning ambition to grow up and twirl in the Maycomb County High

School band" but notes that she develops this talent only "to where I could throw up a stick and almost catch it coming down" (105).

Just as Lee uses Jem as a foil to Dill to establish his effeminacy, so too does she present Aunt Alexandra, Atticus's sister, to force Scout's tomboyishness into sharp relief. Alexandra is the period's model of white southern femininity and casts a figure reminiscent of Alma Deen, Smith's fictionalization of the stereotypic frigid southern mother of a decade earlier. Like Alma, Alexandra subjects her body to fashion's requisite contortions so that it may be read as feminine. "She was not fat, but solid," Scout remembers of her aunt, "and she chose protective garments that drew up her bosom to giddy heights, pinched in her waist, flared out her rear, and managed to suggest that Aunt Alexandra's was once an hour-glass figure. From any angle, it was formidable" (130). Her manners and actions are comparably ladylike, and Maycomb responds to them with considerably more appreciation than Scout does: "To all parties present and participating in the life of the county, Aunt Alexandra was one of the last of her kind: she had river-boat, boarding-school manners; let any moral come along and she would uphold it; she was born in the objective case; she was an incurable gossip.... She was never bored, and given the slightest chance she would exercise her royal prerogative: she would arrange, advise, caution, and warn" (131). "Had I ever harbored the mystical notions about mountains that seem to obsess lawyers and judges," Scout offers when recalling her aunt, "Aunt Alexandra would have been analogous to Mount Everest: throughout my early life, she was cold and there" (82). Yet, because of the very aspects of this personality that Scout finds so distasteful, the town welcomes Alexandra, allowing her to fit "into the world of Maycomb like a hand into a glove" (134).

Just as Aunt Alexandra ascribes to and performs proper southern white femininity, so too does she demand the same of others—and the transgressive Scout in particular. As Johnson observes, "Aunt Alexandra brings with her a system of codification and segregation of the human family according to class, race, and in Scout's case, sex."[10] Alexandra is correspondingly adamant about enforcing normative mappings of gender onto biological sex. Lee is hardly subtle in her condemnations of such strictures, manipulating readers' sympathies through both Scout's first-person narration and its rehearsals of Alexandra's seemingly endless carping about Scout's appearance and behavior. A description of Finch's Landing, where Alexandra and her husband live, allows Scout to clarify:

> Aunt Alexandra was fanatical on the subject of my attire. I could not possibly hope to be a lady if I wore breeches; when I

said I could do nothing in a dress, she said I wasn't supposed to
be doing things that required pants. Aunt Alexandra's vision of
my deportment involved playing with small stoves, tea sets, and
wearing the Add-A-Pearl necklace she gave me when I was born;
furthermore, I should be a ray of sunshine in my father's lonely
life. I suggested I could be a ray of sunshine in pants just as well,
but Aunty said that one had to behave like a sunbeam, that I was
born good but had grown progressively worse every year. (85–86)

When Alexandra moves in with the Finches for the summer of Tom
Robinson's trial, she immediately launches a protracted assault on Scout:
"'Put my bag in the front bedroom, Calpurnia,' was the first thing Aunt
Alexandra said. 'Jean Louise, stop scratching your head,' was the second
thing she said" (129).

The women of Aunt Alexandra's missionary circle are no less relentless
in both providing suitable models for Scout and attacking her when she does
not internalize them. On the afternoon of Alexandra's tea, Miss Stephanie
Crawford pounces immediately upon Scout's entrance into the room. Cattily
observing that her presence at Tom's trial has violated traditional separations
of spheres, Miss Stephanie demands before the entire missionary circle,
"Whatcha going to be when you grow up, Jean Louise? A lawyer?" and
responds before Scout can answer, "Why shoot, I thought you wanted to be
a lawyer, you've already commenced going to court" (232). When Scout
mildly suggests that she wants to be "just a lady," a rebuffed Miss Stephanie
shifts from cajoling to outright chastising: "Miss Stephanie eyed me suspi-
ciously, decided that I meant no impertinence, and contented herself with,
'Well, you won't get very far until you start wearing dresses more often'"
(233).

Although most readers already sympathize with Scout, Lee reinforces
the dismissal of Miss Stephanie and the rest of the missionary circle's criticisms by undercutting the model of their supposedly natural southern femininity. As Scout and the women themselves realize, there is little natural
about them at all. Their painstakingly crafted bodies and carefully orches-
trated acts and gestures instead attempt to pass as natural or, at worst, artfully artless constructions. "The ladies were cool in fragile pastel prints,"
Scout remembers; "most of them were heavily powdered but unrouged; the
only lipstick in the room was Tangee Natural. Cutex Natural sparkled on
their fingernails, but some of the younger ladies wore Rose. They smelled
heavenly" (232). As Lee emphasizes with these brand names, Alexandra and
her neighbors insist on wearing only "natural" lipstick and fingernail polish

and opt for powder but no rouge, since they have communally—although, from a logical standpoint, somewhat arbitrarily—agreed that the bodily alterations of powder do not call attention to and thus expose the artifice of femininity as rouge does. And yet "Tangee Natural" lipstick and "Cutex Natural" fingernail polish are not natural. They are commercially designated, appearance-altering products named to assist women in their efforts to perpetuate the illusion of expressing an inherent femininity. Thus, in that this description makes overt the women's efforts to disguise the feminizations of their bodies, Lee exposes their attempts to conceal the genesis of gender. With the revelation, the implied logical basis of Alexandra's and others' demands for Scout's femininity—that she express the natural gender with which she is born—crumbles, since readers now see the full complicity of these women in their tacit agreements to mystify the immediate cultural origins of femininity.

As this terminology suggests, with Lee's revelation of the missionary circle's conspiracy, she anticipates in fiction precisely what Judith Butler, building upon the work of other theorists and historians of gender and sexuality, has cogently argued concerning the deployment of gender. Like Lee, Butler interrogates—to dismiss as false—gender's presumed expressivity, the enactment of an interior essential gender. In simplified terms, Butler argues that, because gender is performed rather than expressed, "there is no preexisting identity by which an act or attribute might be measured." If such is indeed the case, "there would be no true or false, real or distorted acts of gender, and the postulation of a true gender identity would be revealed as a regulatory fiction." To prevent precisely this revelation, however, gender functions to eradicate signs of its performativity: "Gender is, thus, a construction that regularly conceals its genesis; the tacit collective agreement to perform, produce, and sustain discrete and polar genders as cultural fictions is obscured by the credibility of those productions—and the punishments that attend not agreeing to believe in them; the construction 'compels' our belief in its necessity and naturalness. The historical possibilities materialized through various corporeal styles are nothing other than those punitively regulated cultural fictions alternately embodied and deflected under duress."[11] To Kill a Mockingbird reveals both these concealments, as symbolized in the accoutrements of "natural" beautification, and, through the disciplinary actions and demands exercised on Scout, the punishments for disbelief in the naturalness of the performances of polarized genders. Lee's readers thus have the potential to realize just as forcefully as Butler's that white southern femininity, like any other sort, is but "a regulatory fiction."

Such observations from Butler concerning gender's performativity are not, however, the most innovative components of her argument. Both the fame and critical usefulness of *Gender Trouble* arise primarily out of Butler's articulations of how the parody of drag has the potential to expose gender performativity's reification as expressivity: "As much as drag creates a unified picture of 'woman' (what its critics often oppose), it also reveals the distinctness of those aspects of gendered experience which are falsely naturalized as a unity through the regulatory fiction of heterosexual coherence. *In imitating gender, drag implicitly reveals the imitative structure of gender itself—as well as its contingency....* In place of the law of heterosexual coherence, we see sex and gender denaturalized by means of a performance which avows their distinctness and dramatizes the cultural mechanism of their fabricated unity." Butler does not, however, champion drag's parody as invariably subversive, as some critics have accused. "Parody by itself is not subversive," she offers, "and there must be a way to understand what makes certain kinds of parodic repetitions effectively disruptive, truly troubling, and which repetitions become domesticated and recirculated as instruments of cultural hegemony." Consistently tentative in her claims outside the hypothetical and conditional, Butler hazards only that a crucial element for the subversion of gender is the exposure of its repetitive structure. Yet this is the site where all gender transformation, whether ostensibly subversive or not, must originate: "The possibilities of gender transformation are to be found precisely in the arbitrary relation of such acts, in the possibility of a failure to repeat, a deformity, or a parodic repetition that exposes that phantasmatic effect of abiding identity as a politically tenuous construction." Nevertheless, in that any transformation calls into question "the abiding gendered self," any of the acts of Butler's catalogue—and not merely parodic repetitions such as drag recognized as such—has subversive potential.[12]

Lee's scene of the missionary circle's tea would seem to bolster Butler's suggestion that a failure to repeat stylized acts need not necessarily be parodic to expose the performativity of gender. In her description of the ladies' appearances, Scout notes that "Cutex Natural sparkled in their fingernails, but some of the younger ladies wore Rose." One could hardy say that, in having made this choice of fingernail polish, the younger women self-consciously parody femininity as Butler maintains drag performers to do. Indeed, these women cannot function in the same manner, since Butler understands much of drag queen's subversiveness to arise from their anatomically male bodies performing femininity. "If the anatomy of the performer is already distinct from the gender of the performer, and both of these are distinct from the gender of the performance," Butler clarifies, "then the performance suggests a dissonance not only between sex and performance, but sex and gender, and gender and performance."[13] Because the younger women at Alexandra's tea are, in contrast to drag queens, neither anatomically male nor knowingly parodic, no such valorizable dissonance of gender, sex, and performance can emerge from them if one retains the criteria of Butler's scenario. Nevertheless, these women's deviations from applying Cutex Natural to their nails draw attention to the false naturalness of the other women's bodies, whose nails sparkle as brilliantly as those painted Rose.

In addition to these women with the red fingernail polish, Scout herself disrupts the illusions of gender's expressivity in this scene. Until this point, she, like the novel's other gender-transitive characters, has loosely paralleled the drag queens of Butler's discussion, destabilizing gender through vaguely parodic performances of the "opposite" gender. Whereas the drag queens often satirically imitate femininity, Scout parodies— although far less self-consciously—masculinity, and one might argue that this parody operates with the subversiveness that Butler feels it capable. As is not the case with the scarlet-nailed ladies, because Scout's anatomy is distinct from the gender of her performances, they make public the same dissonances of corporeality as arise from drag performances. In the scene of Alexandra's tea, however, Lee gives Butler's theories an additional twist and suggests that a comparable disruption emerges when the drag artist attempts to perform the gender "correct" for his or, in this case, her anatomy. Scout follows her aunt's dictates and wears a "pink Sunday dress, shoes, and a petticoat" (231), casting a comic figure not unlike McCullers's Frankie when dressed for the wedding. Although this attire will supposedly correct Scout's gender trouble in the community's opinion, recollected images of Scout in her customary drag of overalls and her internalization of masculine acts and gestures so denaturalize the feminine clothes that communal representatives such as Miss Stephanie and even Miss Maudie can only focus on the absent overalls: "'You're mighty dressed up, Miss Jean Louise,' she said. 'Where are your britches today?'" (232). Scout's appearance in the pink dress thus becomes the equivalent of the drag queen abandoning her sequined gown and pumps to sport a tool belt and work boots or, as *La Cage aux Folles* and *The Birdcage* would have it, John Wayne's jeans, Stetson, and swagger. In these cases, the alterity of performances of normative gender to drag's pervading stylized repetitions establishes the former as, if anything, even more of a drag performance than the latter and thus, in Scout's case, ironically enables her enactment of *normative* gender to destabilize femininity.

Although Lee's readers may savor these destabilizations, they go largely unnoticed or ignored by characters within the novel, and the demands for
gender conformity persist, both from the missionary society and elsewhere.
Indeed, it is no one from Aunt Alexandra's circle who most dramatically
antagonizes Scout. Mrs. Henry Lafayette Dubose, another of the Finches'
neighbors, is fierce to the point of being unladylike herself in attempts to
coerce Scout into appropriate feminine behavior. Secure in her age and infir-
mity Mrs. Dubose has no qualms about public outbursts, as Scout recalls:
"Jem and I hated her. If she was on the porch when we passed, we would be
raked by her wrathful gaze, subjected to ruthless interrogation regarding our
behavior, and given a melancholy prediction on what we would amount to
when we grew up, which was always nothing. We had long ago given up the
idea of walking past her house on the opposite side of the street; that only
made her raise her voice and let the whole neighborhood in on it." In keeping with these brazen outbursts, Mrs. Dubose rejects Alexandra's tactics of
wheedling and nagging to alter Scout's behavior and instead opts for cruel
shame. The old woman repeatedly resurrects the image of Atticus's dead wife
to Jem and Scout, asserting that a "lovelier lady than our mother had never
lived" (104) and that her children are a disgrace to her memory. When the
shame of not meeting her mother's presumed expectations fails to drive
Scout out of her overalls, however, Mrs. Dubose does not hesitate to employ
fear: "'And *you*—' she pointed an arthritic finger at me—what are you doing
in those overalls? You should be in a dress and camisole, young lady! You'll
grow up waiting on tables if somebody doesn't change your ways—a Finch
waiting on tables at the O.K. Café—hah!'" (105–6).

Mrs. Dubose also allows Lee to continue yet another means of damning those persons who would enforce normative gender. Because the novel
most centrally calls for an end to southern racism through the manipulation
of a sympathetic African-American martyr and benign aristocratic paternalism, Lee's narrative invites readers to evaluate the racial attitudes of each of
the white characters and judge them racist or not. Although at times she
seeks to complicate this binarism, she marks most of the persons who
demand Scout's gender conformity—Alexandra, Mrs. Dubose, and the
majority of the missionary circle—as both lingering representatives of the
antebellum slave-owning South and undeniable racists. While Atticus and
Jack Finch abandon the Landing to pursue careers at various times in
Montgomery, Nashville, and even Boston, Alexandra chooses to remain on
the family's cotton plantation, surrounded by reminders of her ancestor's
slave-holding and his own strictures for feminine behavior. Scout recalls both
the "old cotton landing, where Finch Negroes had loaded bales and produce,

unloaded blocks of ice, flour and sugar, farm equipment, and feminine apparel," and Simon Finch's unique home: "The internal arrangements of the Finch house were indicative of Simon's guilelessness and the absolute trust with which he regarded his offspring ... [T]he daughters' rooms could be reached only by one staircase, Welcome's room and the guest room only by another. The Daughters' Staircase was in the ground-floor bedroom of their parents, so Simon always knew the hours of his daughters' nocturnal comings and goings" (84). Via these two observations, Lee suggests how strongly she holds antebellum white southern femininity to have been contingent upon the enslavement of African Americans. It is they who bear the physical burden of unloading the feminine apparel at the landing, that which can be afforded in the first place only because of slave labor's ostensible profits. Likewise, it is this labor that allows Simon Finch to construct a house specifically designed to regulate his daughters' affairs.

Just as Alexandra has retained Simon's sexist notions of gender as represented in the Daughters' Staircase, she has also seemingly retained elements of the racism implicit to this enslavement of African Americans. For instance, she stews when Atticus decides to defend an African American accused of raping a white woman, and Scout trounces her annoying cousin only when he repeats his grandmother's characterization of her brother as a "nigger-lover" (87). Moreover, Alexandra reveals Lee's stance that white southern femininity's contingency on the debasement of African Americans persists in the 1930s. Consider the scene in which Alexandra arrives at the Finches' for the summer. Her command concerning Scout's unladylike behavior follows her initial order for Calpurnia to put away Alexandra's suitcase. As the close proximity of these commands suggests, Alexandra's authority in her dictates to Scout arises primarily out of her own feminine model, and yet this model remains valid only so long as Calpurnia or another black person frees Alexandra from unfeminine physical exertion.

Mrs. Dubose, on the other hand, is a literal artifact of the antebellum South, born just before or during the Civil War. She supposedly keeps "a CSA pistol concealed among her numerous shawls and wraps," and whiffs of earlier slave-holdings permeate her employment of African-American servants, for she retains "a Negro girl in constant attendance" yet allows Jessie little of the respect that Atticus has for Calpurnia (103–4). With these links to the stereotypic Old South and its Confederate culmination, it is not surprising that Mrs. Dubose offers opinions similarly conservative to Alexandra's concerning both race and gender. In virtually the same breath that she condemns Scout's overalls, Mrs. Dubose seethes about Atticus "lawing for niggers": "'Yes indeed, what has this world come to when a Finch goes against his raising? I'll tell you!' She put her hand to her mouth. When she drew it away, it trailed a long silver thread of saliva. 'Your father's no better than the niggers and trash he works for!'" (106).

Although Mrs. Dubose's racism is overt and vociferous, Lee even more forcefully condemns that of Alexandra's missionary circle, which is all the more distasteful because of the women's hypocritical investments in so-called Christian uplift. Grace Merriweather, "the most devout lady in Maycomb," sponsors a local program after having offered her profuse support of Christianity's shouldering of the white man's burden: "I said to him, 'Mr. Everett,' I said, 'the ladies of the Maycomb Alabama Methodist Episcopal Church South are behind you one hundred per cent.' That's what I said to him. And you know, right then and there I made a pledge in my heart. I said to myself, when I go home I'm going to give a course on the Mrunas and bring J. Grimes Everett's message to Maycomb and that's just what I'm doing" (233–34). Immediately after this comment, however, she carps about the responses of Maycomb's African Americans to Tom's trial: "[T]he cooks and field hands are just dissatisfied, but they're settling down now—they grumbled all next day after that trial," Mrs. Merriweather explains to Scout. "I tell you there's nothing more distracting than a sulky darky. Their mouths go down to here. Just ruins your day to have one of 'em in the kitchen" (234). Gertrude Farrow, "the second most devout lady in Maycomb," responds with her own complaints, maintaining, "We can educate 'em till we're blue in the face, we can try till we drop to make Christians out of 'em, but there's no lady safe in her bed these nights" (235). With this smug paternalism, fear of black male sexuality, and hypocritical racial enlightenment, Lee underscores that she, unlike Smith, does not consider southern white women less racist than their male counterparts because of an inherent female morality, and tempts readers to dismiss all that these women value and represent, including traditional white southern femininity.

With the exception of the women of the missionary circle, Lee does not, however, allow readers wholly to dismiss these racist characters and instead elicits some sympathy for Mrs. Dubose and Alexandra in particular. Part 1 closes with Atticus's articulation of Mrs. Dubose's heroism in defeating her addiction to morphine: "I wanted you to see what real courage is, instead of getting the idea that courage is a man with a gun in his hand. It's when you know you're licked before you begin but you begin anyway and you see it through no matter what. You rarely win, but sometimes you do. Mrs. Dubose won, all ninety-eight pounds of her." As Atticus suggests to Jem, despite her racism, Mrs. Dubose is "a great lady" and "the bravest person I ever knew" (116). Alexandra garners comparable sympathy in the novel's final pages. Even if she does not necessarily counter her previous racism, she is nevertheless shaken at news of Tom's death and concedes that Atticus has done the right thing, albeit to little avail in the community's eyes: "I mean this town. They're perfectly willing to let him do what they're too afraid to do themselves—it might lose 'em a nickel. They're perfectly willing to let him wreck his health doing what they're afraid to do" (239).

With this confession, Alexandra hints at the complexity of her character. She by no means replicates her brother's saintly attitudes and actions, and, even in the emotional aftermath of hearing of Tom's death, Alexandra tersely says of Atticus, "I can't say I approve of everything he does" (239). Nevertheless, she distinguishes herself from her catty guests who, rather than recognize the significance of Atticus's actions, hold them to be misguided. Yet this ambiguous relation to race has been anticipated by Alexandra's capricious relation to gender. As Scout knows all too well, Alexandra is "fanatical" that her niece appear and behave femininely. However, Alexandra allows and even fosters significant transgressions from normative masculinity in her grandson Francis. Exasperated that her husband's shiftlessness excludes the chivalry necessary to secure her position on the figurative pedestal of white southern femininity as delineated by Smith, Scott, and Jones, Alexandra inculcates in Francis behavior that is strikingly different from his grandfather's and, as a result, hardly masculine. "Grandma's a wonderful cook," Francis boasts to Scout. "She's gonna teach me how" When Scout giggles at this image, Francis counters, "Grandma says all men should learn to cook, that men oughta be careful with their wives and wait on 'em when they don't feel good" (86–87). Alexandra thus reveals her investment in white southern femininity to be so strong that she is willing to sacrifice corresponding southern masculinity so that the former's delicacy not be impinged upon. The result is that Francis Hancock, grandson of one of the novel's most outspoken gender conformists, is a gossiping sissy who slicks back his hair and, as his Christmas wish list reveals, craves the clothes of a fashionable young dandy: "a pair of knee-pants, a red leather booksack, five shirts and an untied bow tie" (85). As his sexually ambivalent name suggests, he does not have a strong masculine identity but instead, at his grandmother's urging, a Wildean penchant for foppery, one often culturally understood to designate effeminacy and, as Capote suggests, homosexuality.

Despite this active promotion of gender transitivity in Francis and hints of racial enlightenment at the novel's conclusion, Alexandra nevertheless remains too exclusively invested in traditional white southern femininity to emerge as a viable alternative to Mrs. Dubose and the women of the missionary society. Lee instead posits Miss Maudie Atkinson, arguably the novel's most sympathetic white adult female character, as the preferable model of southern womanhood for both Scout and readers. Unlike Alexandra, Miss Maudie is not overtly distraught about the transgressive performances of gender and indeed has constructed a public identity contingent upon adroit manipulations of such performances. This is not to suggest, however, that she jettisons social conventions. When she chooses, she can rival her neighbors in her successful enactment of white southern femininity. Just as she appears on her front porch each evening freshly bathed to "reign over the street in magisterial beauty" (47), Miss Maudie can also smoothly integrate herself into that larger world "where on its surface fragrant ladies rocked slowly, fanned gently, and drank cool water" (236). She in fact maintains this role when others falter, as when she coolly orchestrates the remainder of the tea after Alexandra crumbles at news of Tom Robinson's death.

Although not conveyed in the film adaptation, Miss Maudie is, however, "a chameleon lady," and these polished feminine performances are checked by others as transgressive as any of Scout's: working "in her flower beds in an old straw hat and men's coveralls" (46), thrusting out her bridgework with a click of her tongue as a sign of friendship, nursing charred azaleas at the sacrifice of her hands, and even meditating arson. Indeed, some of the most striking imagery associated with Miss Maudie is blatantly martial, casting her in the role of biblical warrior:

> If she found a blade of nut grass in her yard it was like the Second Battle of the Marne: she swooped down upon it with a tin tub and subjected it to blasts from beneath with a poisonous substance she said was so powerful it'd kill us all if we didn't stand out of the way.
>
> "Why can't you just pull it up?" I asked, after witnessing a prolonged campaign against a blade not three inches high.
>
> "Pull it up, child, pull it up?" She picked up the limp sprout and squeezed her thumb up its tiny stalk. Microscopic grains oozed out. "Why, one sprig of nut grass can ruin a whole yard. Look here. When it comes fall this dries up and the wind blows it all over Maycomb County!" Miss Maudie's face likened such an occurrence unto an Old Testament pestilence. (47)

Minor though this battle may seem, Lee's martial imagery and Miss Maudie's transformation into a prophet of the Old Testament stand in marked contrast

to her graceful offerings of dewberry tarts at Alexandra's tea. With her public image thus in constant flux between these two gender norms, the
"chameleon" Miss Maudie offers the most appropriate identity for Scout and
Jem's "absolute morphodite" (72) snowman to assume. Throughout its construction, the snowman evinces an uneasy coexistence of femininity and masculinity, resembling first Miss Stephanie Crawford and then Mr. Avery. This
irresolution is rendered understandable only when Jem sticks Miss Maudie's
sun hat on the snowman's head and thrusts her hedge clippers in the crook
of its arm. Insofar as the feminine and masculine already commingle in the
culturally readable Miss Maudie, the ambiguously sexed and gendered
Absolute Morphodite can also be made coherently legible by giving it her
personality.

Lee suggests several things with Miss Maudie's "chameleon" self-fash-
ioning, not least of which is that she may function comparably to Scout to
disrupt reified southern white femininity. With her constant alternating performances of masculinity and femininity, clad one hour in the work clothes
of a manual laborer and the next in Mrs. Dubose's requisite dress and
camisole, Miss Maudie undercuts the constancy with which the rest of the
missionary circle express their femininity. That is, her public performances,
deliberately staged for the entire neighborhood's viewing, make overt the
comparable manipulations of gender that the other women wish not to be
exposed as so easily mutable. Yet, because these alternations have grown predictable, Miss Maudie's performances do not disrupt with the force that, say,
Scout's unexpectedly feminine presence at the tea does. As Butler acknowledges, any stylized repetition of acts—even initially transgressive and/or subversive ones—can be domesticated through their very repetition, since such
predictable recurrences promote reification. Miss Maudie's presence nevertheless suggests how token a normatively gendered performance may be and
still appease such cultural strictures as Lee understands them. Because Miss
Maudie periodically participates in such ostensibly gender-reifying rituals as
the missionary tea, even while she understands such participation to be simple performances, her neighbors are content to allow her otherwise inexcus-
able transgressions of gender. Thus, whereas Butler emphasizes almost
exclusively the punishments associated with a rejection of gender's necessity
and naturalness, Lee not only identifies such punishments in Scout but also
counters in Miss Maudie ways in which such discipline might be negotiated
and avoided. One does not have to agree to believe in gender's expressivity
Lee offers, so long as one condescends to perform as if one does at strategically appropriate times. Indeed, as the women of the missionary circle prove,
such belief is the exception rather than the rule.

Lee further promotes readers' investments in Miss Maudie and her alternatives to southern white femininity by having her harbor little of the overt racism of Alexandra, Mrs. Dubose, and the missionary circle. With the exception of Atticus, Miss Maudie emerges—even if problematically— as the novel's most racially enlightened white character, one of the "handful of people in this town who say that fair play is not marked White Only; the handful of people who say a fair trial is for everybody, not just us; the handful of people with enough humility to think, when they look at a Negro, there but for the Lord's kindness am I" (239).[14] She realizes how pervasively racism permeates Maycomb and therefore both supports and is grateful for Atticus's stirring defense of Tom Robinson: "I was sittin' there on the porch last night, waiting. I waited and waited to see you all come down the sidewalk, and as I waited I thought, Atticus Finch won't win, he can't win, but he's the only man in these parts who can keep a jury out so long in a case like that. And I thought to myself, well, we're making a step—it's just a baby-step, but it's a step" (218–19). And yet, for all her interest in the trial's outcome, Miss Maudie nevertheless refuses to participate in the spectacle. In its aftermath, however, she abandons what may be perceived of until this point as a passive role and deftly squelches the missionary circle's attack on Atticus. Lee has Miss Maudie willing to condescend to participate in the women's charade of femininity but unwilling to tolerate their racism when they attack the sole figure to assume a public—and, in Miss Maudie's opinion, truly Christian—stance for legal equality.

Just as Miss Maudie nurses little racism in comparison with her neighbors, she also holds none of Maycomb's morbid curiosity about the Radleys. When Scout rehearses the lurid tales of Boo to Miss Maudie, she tersely dismisses the gossip as "three-fourths colored folks and one-fourth Stephanie Crawford" (50) and counters by emphasizing tolerance toward Arthur's right to do as he pleases. In a tactic similar to Atticus's suggestion that, to understand a communal outsider or misfit, one must "climb into his skin and walk around in it" (34), Miss Maudie urges Scout to consider Arthur's perspective: "'Arthur Radley just stays in the house, that's all,' said Miss Maudie. 'Wouldn't you stay in the house if you didn't want to come out?'" (48). And yet Miss Maudie sympathizes with Arthur having to function within a family and community intent on controlling and demonizing him. When Scout asks if Arthur is crazy, "Miss Maudie shook her head. 'If he's not he should be by now. The things that happen to people we never really know'" (50). Miss Maudie thus proves as exemplary in her tolerance of Arthur Radley's communal otherness as she does with differences of gender and race and emerges to readers precisely as Scout has characterized: "the best lady I know" (49).

Miss Maudie's male counterpart is, of course, Atticus Finch, the novel's almost sainted hero. He not only displays the same ostensibly enlightened attitudes as Miss Maudie but also, via privilege conferred on him by masculine spheres, works publicly for social equality and tolerance. His defense of Tom Robinson is the most significant of these efforts, but Atticus also proves himself equally determined to accord Arthur Radley some degree of communal respect. When he catches Scout, Jem, and Dill "busily playing Chapter XXV, Book II of One Man's Family" (44), their improvised production of the Radleys' fabled saga, Atticus immediately halts the performance, just as he later interrupts the children's attempt to leave a note for Boo. "Son," Atticus says to Jem in perhaps the harshest tones Lee ever allows her hero, "I'm going to tell you something and tell you one time: stop tormenting that man" (53).

Given that Atticus shares these attitudes with Miss Maudie, it is not surprising that he also is both tolerant of gender nonconformity and, in the opinion of his family and community, something less than masculine himself. His heroism, like that of Mrs. Dubose, is not contingent upon being "a man with a gun in his hand." Quite the contrary, Atticus avoids stereotypically male violence to resolve conflict and uses a gun only when forced, as in the case of the rabid dog. Thus, just as Miss Maudie adroitly deploys her femininity, so too does Atticus strategically choose when a masculine performance is in order, content in the meantime to forego such behavior. "He did not do the things our schoolmates' fathers did," Scout recalls; "he never went hunting, he did not play poker or fish or drink or smoke. He sat in the living room and read" (94). Indeed, Atticus's failure to engage in such activities causes considerable anxiety in his children. "[T]here was nothing Jem or I could say about him when our classmates said, 'My father—,'" Scout confesses. Instead, having internalized the community's rigidly binaristic understandings of gender, she and Jem feel this failure "reflected upon his abilities and manliness" (93).

No matter how reassuringly different from the rest of Maycomb in either their ethics or performances of gender, Atticus and Miss Maudie are nevertheless problematic characters. With the capacity for manifold tolerances located within solitary figures such as these, Lee seems to posit an identity inherently resistant to any oppression of any cultural difference. That is, she suggests that all tolerances are congruent, that is, if one is tolerant of racial otherness, one will of course be equally tolerant of gendered otherness and even that difference that can only be speculated about, as in the case of Boo Radley. In contrast to this understanding, tolerance might more appropriately be considered similar to oppression as Sedgwick has theorized it. As cited earlier, she reminds that "it was the long, painful realization, *not* that all oppressions are congruent, but that they are *differently* structured and so must intersect in complex embodiments." Just as each oppression is thus "likely to be in a uniquely indicative relation to certain distinctive nodes of cultural organization," so too is each tolerance likely to reflect a potentially singular organization.[15] Therefore, despite certain similarities, tolerance of racial otherness is not the same as tolerance of gendered otherness, yet Lee's characters tend to obfuscate these differences and thus leave readers with an oversimplified representation of social mechanisms and interactions.

Regardless of this oversimplification, what emerges from Lee's novel is a portrait of a southern community in which performances of normative gender are surprisingly the exceptions rather than the rule. Not only is the narrator in whom readers so heavily invest a tomboy, but the two most sympathetic adult white characters are figures who defy normative gender roles and instead perform "appropriately" only to strategic ends. Those characters who do subscribe to these roles are hardly sympathetic and racist almost without exception. Moreover, in Lee's handling of them, these same characters unwittingly reveal the constructedness of gender that they seek to conceal and, in the case of Alexandra, even foster overt transgressions. Maycomb is thus, for all its demands for gender conformity, an arena of dizzyingly varied gender performances.

Although perhaps not at first apparent, just as *To Kill a Mockingbird* is a novel permeated with valorized gender transitivity, it is also remarkably deplete of heterosexuality as conventionally represented through traditional marriage. As Claudia Johnson reminds, unmarried people—widows and widowers, spinsters and bachelors—fill the Finches' neighborhood: Atticus, Miss Maudie, Miss Stephanie, Miss Rachel, Miss Caroline, Mrs. Dubose, Mr. Avery, and both of the Radley sons, Nathan and Arthur. One is, in fact, hard-pressed to name a character besides Tom Robinson who both figures centrally in the novel and is within a stable marriage. And yet Tom's marriage seems readable as primarily part of Lee's heavy-handed characterization of him as "a quiet, respectable, humble Negro" (207) who heads a harmonious nuclear family of "clean-living folks" (80) and thus contrasts to the incestuous widowed Bob Ewell. If anything, to shore up how differently Tom and Helen live from the Ewells in their dump, Lee succumbs to stereotypes of African Americans when she sketches crowds of black children playing marbles in the Robinsons' front yard and the little girl standing picturesquely in the cabin's door: "Dill said her hair was a wad of tiny stiff pigtails, each ending in a bright bow. She grinned from ear to ear and walked toward our father, but she was too small to navigate the steps. Dill said Atticus went to her, took off his hat, and offered her his finger. She grabbed it and he eased her down the steps" (242). Indeed, such images are only slightly removed from those of happy plantation darkies that permeate earlier southern literature.

Neither the immediate Finch household nor its larger familial connections offer such a warm portrait of connubial life. Scout explains that Atticus is a widower, his wife having died only a few years into the marriage: "She was a Graham from Montgomery; Atticus met her when he was first elected to the state legislature. He was middle-aged then, she was fifteen years his junior. Jem was the product of their first year of marriage; four years later I was born, and two years later our mother died from a sudden heart attack" (10). That Atticus, already late to marry by Maycomb's standards, allows so many years to elapse without remarrying is something of a travesty in communal opinion. Amid her demands that Scout begin wearing dresses and that Atticus stop defending "niggers," Mrs. Dubose repeatedly offers that "it was quite a pity that our father had not remarried after our mother's death" (104). Despite these communal injunctions, however, Atticus shows no signs of taking another wife and instead seems content to function as the sole parent to his children.

Unlike Atticus, his younger brother, John Hale Finch, never marries and, although somewhat casually, evinces a phobia of reproduction. "I shall never marry," Jack wearily confesses to his brother after mishandling Scout's conflict with Francis. "I might have children" (91). Indeed, Lee offers in Jack a character readable as gay by persons understanding sexuality within a rigid binarism of heterosexuality and homosexuality and thus assuming an absence of the former to designate the presence of the latter. Moreover, Jack's life parallels those of Goyen's gay Folner and Smith's lesbian Laura, and all three characters seem fictional counterparts to queer persons discussed by historians such as George Chauncey, John D'Emilio, and Allan Bérubé. Like so many of these persons at mid-century, Jack is an aspiring professional who leaves familial constraints to study and live in a large urban area and thereby minimize small-town life. After finishing medical studies in Boston, Jack returns not to Maycomb but rather to Nashville and visits his family in Alabama only once a year at Christmas. He remains a bachelor at almost forty and has as his only acknowledged companion a much-doted-upon cat. When, during one of his visits, Jack offers to show snapshots of

Rose Aylmer, Scout explains that the cat is "a beautiful yellow female Uncle Jack said was one of the few women he could stand permanently" (83). But even if Lee does not intend Jack to be read as gay, and readers do not understand him as such, he nevertheless stands as yet another character whom Lee chooses to have uninvolved in heterosexual marriage during the course of the novel.

Jack further disrupts communal heteronormativity with his parody of its courtship. Scout recalls the performance he gives with the help of Miss Maudie:

> We saw Uncle Jack every Christmas, and every Christmas he yelled across the street for Miss Maudie to come marry him. Miss Maudie would yell back, "Call a little louder, Jack Finch, and they'll hear you at the post office, I haven't heard you yet!" Jem and I thought this a strange way to ask for a lady's hand in marriage, but then Uncle Jack was rather strange. He said he was trying to get Miss Maudie's goat, that he had been trying unsuccessfully for forty years, that he was the last person in the world Miss Maudie would think about marrying but the first person she thought about teasing, and the best defense to her was spirited offense, all of which we understood clearly. (48)

Regardless of Jack's asserted reasons for instigating these exchanges, they ultimately function to spoof heterosexuality by wrenching its rites of courtship from their usual contexts. Much like Scout during her performance of femininity at Alexandra's tea, Jack and Maudie are ostensibly behaving as their community expects, enacting through appropriately gendered roles the rituals to culminate in heterosexual marriage. Jack plays the role of the aggressive male suitor, while Maudie that of his coy mistress. Yet, just as Scout's customarily transgressive behavior renders her normative performances disruptive, Jack and Maudie's usual silences in expressing heterosexual desire denaturalize their displays of heterosexuality and reveal them to be artificial. Unlike Scout, however, Jack and Maudie are fully conscious of this revelation and artfully stage it in the public arena to create even more of a spectacle.

Such a performance would not be nearly so significant if Lee tempered it with normative enactments of heterosexual desire, ones that reveal such rituals to unfold as they supposedly ought in set cultural scripts. Instead of doing this, however, Lee offers a series of parodies, ones that, although not self-consciously satiric, nevertheless function to establish heterosexuality as existing in the novel primarily in comic deviations from its fictional norm. The first of these parodic heterosexual pairings appears in Miss Caroline's traumatic discovery of Burris Ewell's head lice. When her scream arrests the attention of the entire class of children, the chivalric Little Chuck Little emerges to rescue and console her:

> Little Chuck grinned broadly. "There ain't no need to fear a cootie, ma'am. Ain't you ever seen one? Now don't you be afraid, you just go back to your desk and teach us some more."
> Little Chuck Little was another member of the population who didn't know where his next meal was coming from, but he was a born gentleman. He put his hand under her elbow and led Miss Caroline to the front of the room. "Now don't you fret, ma'am," he said. "There ain't no need to fear a cootie. I'll just fetch you some cool water." (30)

Lee strengthens Little Chuck's chivalry when Burris defies Miss Caroline's questions about his hygiene, family, and school attendance. "Little Chuck Little got to his feet," Scout recalls. "'Let him go, ma'am,' he said. 'He's a mean one, a hard-down mean one. He's liable to start somethin', and there's some little folks here.'" Unlike the questionably masculine Atticus, Little Chuck is quite willing to opt for violence, doing so despite his diminutive size: "[W]hen Burris Ewell turned toward him, Little Chuck's right hand went to his pocket. 'Watch your step, Burris,' he said. 'I'd soon's kill you as look at you. Now go home'" (32). The hero ultimately triumphs, and the damsel, although emotionally shaken, as is befitting her more delicate sex, is saved.

Like Jack and Maudie, Little Chuck and Miss Caroline thus enact sex-appropriate roles. Lee undercuts these performances, however, with the situational irony that arises between the ideal of heterosexual chivalry and the reality of the classroom's scenario. The foes from whom Lee's hero must protect the damsel are neither a dragon nor a rival knight bur rather a nomadic head louse and a surly prepubescent first grader. For that matter, the hero is no aristocratically virile Lancelot. Little Chuck Little is only a step above common white trash, far from adult, and, as Lee emphasizes with his name, ridiculously small. As a result, she presents readers not with a reifying performance of heterosexual chivalry but rather with a quasi-sexualized relationship comically deviant in its transgressions of differences in class and age and thus unable to be sexually enacted.

Lee comparably undercuts chivalric courtship in Jem's ritualized visits to Mrs. Dubose. Although these afternoons of reading to her are supposedly penance for the destruction of her camellias, the visits replicate the mythic suitor's persistent wooing of his beloved with stirring pronouncements of affection. Jem composes no sonnets for his partner, but Lee nevertheless keeps him firmly within romantic expression, having him read to Mrs. Dubose from *Ivanhoe*, a novel emblematic of the romanticization of heterosexual courtship. Just as Jem is no Petrarch or Sidney, however, Mrs. Dubose is neither Laura nor Stella: "She was horrible. Her face was the color of a dirty pillowcase, and the corners of her mouth glistened with wet, which inched like a glacier down the deep grooves enclosing her chin. Old-age liver spots dotted her cheeks, and her pale eyes had black pinpoint pupils. Her hands were knobby, and the cuticles were grown up over her fingernails. Her bottom plate was not in, and her upper lip protruded; from time to time she would draw her nether lip to her upper plate and carry her chin with it. This made the wet move faster" (111). Lee thus reverses the asymmetries of the relationship between Little Chuck and Miss Caroline. Although hovering at puberty, Jem is a male suitor of a socially appropriate age to enter into such a ritual, but Mrs. Dubose is, in contrast, a grotesquely old female beloved. The end result, however, is much the same, in that readers encounter yet another image of implied transgressive heterosexuality.

Although with Dill's proposal of marriage and Scout's acceptance, this pair enacts heterosexual rituals further than any of the three couples discussed so far, much the same destabilizing humor emerges from the two. As Scout recalls, Dill "asked me earlier in the summer to marry him, then he promptly forgot about it. He staked me out, marked as his property, said I was the only girl he would ever love, then he neglected me" (46). Like Little Chuck Little, Scout and Dill are too young by societal standards to engage in the heterosexual acts that usually accompany marriage. Their woeful ignorance of these acts' intricacies and results emerges in a discussion of babies' origins, where neither child is too clear on the process. Moreover, in that Scout and Dill are both gender transitive, they present a pairing as superficially disconcerting as Capote's Joel Knox and Idabel Thompkins. In each case, the genders are ostensibly transposed, and the woman rather than the man disciplines wandering affections through violence. When Dill chooses homosocial interactions with Jem rather than pseudoheterosexual ones with Scout, she foregoes feminine tears and coaxing and instead "beat him up twice but it did no good, he only grew closer to Jem" (46).

Lee concludes the novel with a final non-normative heterosexual pairing, that of Scout and Boo Radley. After he saves Scout and Jem from the

malevolent Bob Ewell, the shy Boo is in the awkward situation of himself
needing to be seen safely home, and Scout kindly assists him:

> "Will you take me home?"
> He almost whispered it, in the voice of a child afraid of the
> dark.
> I put my foot on the top step and stopped. I would lead him
> through our house, but I would never lead him home.
> "Mr. Arthur, bend your arm down here, like that. That's right,
> sir." I slipped my hand into the crook of his arm.
> He had to stoop a little to accommodate me, but if Miss
> Stephanie Crawford was watching from her upstairs window, she
> would see Arthur Radley escorting me down the sidewalk, as any
> gentleman would do. (281)

As with the other parodic images of heterosexual courtship, this one is
marked by socially disruptive elements such as an incongruity of ages, an
inverted incongruity in levels of maturity, and, at least with Scout, transgressions of gender norms. This image, however, crucially differs from those that
precede it. Whereas the pairings of Little Chuck and Miss Caroline, Jem and
Mrs. Dubose, and Dill and Scout are each unself-conscious in its parody of
heterosexuality, and the performances of Uncle Jack and Miss Maudie are
deliberately satiric so as to expose those characters' distance from heterosexuality Scout intentionally orchestrates her interactions with Boo to replicate
the contours of a heterosexual relationship. She has, in essence, learned the
lessons taught by Miss Maudie. Just as she purchases a certain amount of
freedom by periodically appeasing the neighborhood through her performances of femininity at the missionary teas, Scout potentially negotiates a
comparable freedom for Boo when she crafts the illusion of his normative
heterosexuality. That is, although Boo may continue to transgress communal
norms by eschewing a public existence, that community is more apt to accord
him this transgression because he performs "correctly" during his brief foray
into the public arena. Although this image includes disruptive elements, it
nevertheless comes closer to fulfilling communal expectations of Boo's
appropriate sexual behavior than the rumors of macabre voyeurism circulating in the absence of observed sexual performances.

As these delineated differences suggest, Lee's parodies of heterosexuality are not identically structured, nor do they work to exactly the same ends.
These pairings nevertheless remain parallel in that they fill the text's relative
void of normative heterosexuality. Moreover, despite the lack of sexual desire

and the often comic or horrific elements in these parodies, they frequently provide far more gratification than the novel's actual marriages. Scout recalls, for instance, her closeness with Dill and the sadness she feels in his absence. "[S]ummer was the swiftness with which Dill would reach up and kiss me when Jem was not looking, the longings we sometimes felt each other feel," Scout remembers. "With him, life was routine; without him, life was unbearable. I stayed miserable for two days" (118). In the novel's final pages she comparably notes the gratification provided by the relationship with Boo Radley and her anxiety about her lack of reciprocation: "We never put back into the tree what we took out of it: we had given him nothing, and it made me sad" (281). Even Jem's horrendous interactions with Mrs. Dubose prove extraordinarily meaningful to him, and part 1 significantly closes with him, having heard Atticus's explanations of Mrs. Dubose's situation, symbolically recanting his hatred. Readers' final image is of Jem meditatively fingering the perfect snow-on-the-mountain camellia she sends him so as to die "beholden to nothing and nobody" (116).

In contrast to the meaningful bonds arising within these relationships scripted as parodies of heterosexual courtships, when Lee does on rare occasion depict marriage, the union seems unenviable. Consider that of Alexandra. One of the novel's least sympathetic characters, she is also married to a virtual nonentity. Scout recalls Uncle Jimmy as "a taciturn man who spent most of his time lying in a hammock by the river wondering if his trotlines were full" (9) and only reluctantly amends her recollections of Christmases at Finch's Landing to mention him: "I should include Uncle Jimmy, Aunt Alexandra's husband, but as he never spoke a word to me in my life except to say, 'Get off that fence,' once, I never saw any reason to take notice of him" (81). His relationship with Alexandra seems so strained that her protracted visit to the Finches seems a welcomed respite from a less-than-pleasant marriage, a respite not unlike that sketched by Kate Chopin for Clarisse Laballière at the conclusion of "The Storm." Of Alexandra's own childbearing within marriage, Scout explains, "Long ago, in a burst of friendliness, Aunty and Uncle Jimmy produced a son named Henry, who left home as soon as was humanly possible, married, and produced Francis" (81–82). The elder Hancocks' marriage thus seems emotionally and sexually unfulfilling, and, unlike Tom Robinson's children, Henry regards his parents' household as something to escape and then avoid, only a convenient place to deposit his son while he and his wife "pursued their own pleasures" (82).

Although generations of Finches before Atticus and his siblings have married with greater frequency and presumably more gratification, they nevertheless often transgress the boundaries of normative heterosexuality. As

Atticus gently reminds his sister, the Finches have something of a penchant for mild incest: "Once, when Aunty assured us that Miss Stephanie Crawford's tendency to mind other people's business was hereditary, Atticus said, 'Sister, when you stop to think about it, our generation's practically the first in the Finch family not to marry its cousins. Would you say the Finches have an Incestuous Streak?'" Alexandra's reply is a cryptic affirmation and denial: "[N]o, that's where we got our small hands and feet" (132). She claims her ancestors' transgressive acts so long as they result in bodies culturally understood as refined, but she implicitly denies that such acts are truly incestuous, presumably because they are not confined within the nuclear family and are therefore socially valid and even welcomed by most nineteenth-century standards. Alexandra's dismissal notwithstanding, Atticus's accusations seem, in hindsight, to designate all the more transgressive acts when readers encounter the novel's only other suggestion of incest, that between Bob Ewell and his daughter Mayella. Although the relationships between sexual participants are markedly different, Lee nevertheless prompts readers to map back onto Alexandra's ancestors the very acts that Atticus publicly condemns.

Just as Lee offers heterosexuality represented through marriage as either absent, unfulfilling, or culturally transgressive in each of these scenarios, so too does she characterize the sexual interactions that come under scrutiny at Tom Robinson's trial in a similar manner. As Atticus proves to no avail, Tom's rape of Mayella Ewell, arguably the novel's central heterosexual act, is a fiction. The sexual interactions that occur between the two are, nevertheless, simultaneously unfulfilling and culturally transgressive insofar as they are miscegenistic. Indeed, this manifestation of heterosexuality is far more transgressive within a southern context than Tracy Deen and Nonnie Anderson's interracial affair in *Strange Fruit*. Rather than have a white man instigate a sexual relationship with a black woman, as Smith does, Lee chooses to have a white woman seduce a black man. As Atticus explains to the jury, Mayella thus violates one of the mid-twentieth-century South's strongest taboos: "She was white, and she tempted a Negro. She did something that in our society is unspeakable: she kissed a black man. Not an old Uncle, but a strong young Negro man" (206). Because of these social strictures, the interaction is hardly fulfilling. Mayella's sexual gratification ceases immediately upon her father's murderous presence, and the hesitant Tom Robinson meets with an end as gruesome as that of Richard Wright's comparably tempted Chris Sims.

Sexuality thus emerges in *To Kill a Mockingbird* in much the same way that gender does: normative expressions are rare, whereas transgressive ones abound, often manifesting in the novel's most sympathetic characters.

Although Lee's community sets up enduring heterosexual marriages as the norm, they are almost nonexistent and, with the one exception of Tom and Helen Robinson, never gratifying. Images of transgressive heterosexuality fare somewhat better in Lee's handling but are usually contingent upon the relative presence or absences of sexual desire. In its presence arise, on the one hand, incestuous relationships that either beget elitist whites or accompany the domestic violence of white trash and, on the other hand, interracial relationships that invariably lead to humiliation and death for African Americans. In contrast, the absence of sexual desire in heterosexual relationships often promotes liaisons that are simultaneously disruptive parodies of heterosexuality and mutually gratifying. Moreover, each of the sympathetic white characters engages in neither heterosexual marriage nor transgressive heterosexuality during the novel. And, although this absence of marriage does not necessarily designate a character such as Atticus, Jack, or Miss Maudie to be nonheterosexual or even homosexual, Lee nevertheless offers in Jack a character easily understandable as such to readers who have internalized the absoluteness of a heterosexual/homosexual binarism. Scout and Jem are therefore coming into adulthood not within an utterly conventional "tired old town" (9), as emphasized in Horton Foote's screenplay, but rather within a community whose instabilities of gender and sexuality mark it as, in the broadest sense, queer.

Although southern community as Lee imagines it is thus, as a whole, pervasively queer in its circulations of gender and sexuality, she nevertheless conspicuously creates individuals who emerge as outsiders within this social matrix. Indeed, as the title indicates, the novel's most pervasive and unsubtle symbolism concerns itself with communal negotiations of these outsiders and their alterity to others. The valorized mockingbird becomes the all-too-readable symbol of the innocent Tom Robinson, shot seventeen times by a white guard while attempting to escape imprisonment. In fact, with heavy-handedness justifying Sundquist's critique of the novel, Lee has Braxton Underwood's editorial overtly expose and then explain the symbol: "Mr. Underwood simply figured that it was a sin to kill cripples, be they standing, sitting, or escaping. He likened Tom's death to the senseless slaughter of songbirds by hunters and children, and Maycomb thought he was trying to write an editorial poetical enough to be reprinted in *The Montgomery Advertiser*" (243). Unlike Underwood's editorial, however, Lee's novel more broadly identifies Tom's crucial otherness as his race rather than his physical handicap. Thus, when readers map the defining attributes of the mockingbird onto Tom, who seems to represent all African Americans in Lee's figurations, he emerges as the harmless victim of empowered whites' destructive racial discrimination.

Tom Robinson is not, however, the only figure that the mockingbird symbolizes. With somewhat greater subtlety, Lee uses the bird to represent the equally innocent Boo Radley, who, like the mockingbirds that Atticus saves from Scout's and Jem's rifles, ultimately escapes meaningless slaughter. To expose Boo's heroism and thus bring him to public attention, Scout realizes, would "be sort of like shootin' a mockingbird, wouldn't it?" (279). Despite sharing this symbol with Tom, however, Boo crucially differs in that it is not the color of his skin that dictates his status of cultural outsider. But rather than grounding Boo's communal alienation in an identifiable alternative to race, Lee instead offers only damning speculative rumors about him and his identity, and he remains with few exceptions within the confines of his dilapidated house until the novel's closing chapters. With this figure and his unique relationship to the community, Lee thus shifts her focus away from white southern responses to racial otherness and instead presents a scenario that obliquely—if not always coherently—parallels ones crucially informed by sexual otherness. That is, because Lee surrounds Boo with so many of the silences and absences that structure the frequent closetedness of same-sex desire, she invites readers to speculate that Boo's reclusiveness is comparable to closeted sexuality and thus explore what bearing this literal representation of closetedness might have on an understanding of the figurative. Such a consideration of this parallel in turn invites a reading of the mockingbird to represent persons negotiating same-sex desire as well as social recluses and African Americans.[16]

To assert that Lee's representation invites such a reading is not, however, to argue that Boo is gay. Although the structure of reclusiveness as Lee presents it may strongly resemble that of the closet, they are not the same. Indeed, fissures almost immediately begin to surface if one approaches Boo as directly representative of a closeted gay or lesbian individual. Perhaps foremost, Lee never establishes the transgressive elements of Boo's identity to be anything other than reclusiveness. Although this may at first seem closely akin to closetedness, reclusiveness can be a social deviancy in and of itself rather than a silencing or secreting of deviancy, as closetedness is. The more appropriate comparison of reclusiveness to actual homosexuality, however, reveals how differently these two components of identity are structured and thus how Lee's potential metaphor for a closeted gay individual is somewhat tenuous. Homosexual acts can usually be kept hidden while an individual circulates with relative freedom within a community, whereas a recluse is most forcefully marked by the very desire *to be* hidden, to avoid *any* communal circulations. In short, a homosexual's closet is figurative; a recluse's is literal. By giving Boo a reclusive rather than an identifiably homosexual identity, Lee creates a situation in which he, in effect, cannot come out of the closet, for coming out would erase the transgressive element of his identity.

Although this fissure between Lee's representation of reclusiveness and the actualities of closeted gayness suggests the uniqueness of the gay closet, her depiction's employability as a symbol or parallel to closetedness nevertheless should not be invalidated. In other ways, Boo's reclusiveness does remind readers of closetedness, insofar as it can be essentialized, and the trajectory of his life loosely replicates one of the most pervasive and cherished narratives of coming out. Consider first the parallels between a closeted gay person whose sexuality is not an open secret and Boo as he initially appears— or, more correctly, does not appear—in the novel. Absence is a—if not *the*— crucially defining factor for each. Just as Boo is physically absent within his community, definitive knowledge of a gay person's sexual identity is comparably absent in some or all others' understandings of him or her. As a result, these identities are constituted largely by rumor, conjecture, or otherwise indirect knowledge. A closeted person's hidden sexuality provides his or her community little basis for a more accurate understanding of his or her particular queerness, and he or she is thus usually left to exist within a communal space permeated with, at best, homophilia confirmed through knowledge of others' gay identities or, at worst, homophobia bolstered by derogatory images of homosexuality.

Although sequestered within his house, Boo nevertheless exists within similar currents imposing upon him an identity in his absence. There are those townspeople, such as Atticus and Miss Maudie, who base their opinions of Boo on his youth and, although they have not seen him in years, studiously attempt to squelch gossip. "I remember Arthur Radley when he was a boy," Miss Maudie reflects. "He always spoke nicely to me, no matter what folks said he did. Spoke as nicely as he knew how" (50). On the other hand, the majority of Maycomb thrives on rumors, elaborating on them to create a horrific monster. Jem's thorough internalization of these images, gleaned from "bits and scraps of gossip and neighborhood legend" (44), for instance, allows him to give a full response to Dill's request for a description of Boo: "Boo was about six-and-a-half feet tall, judging from his tracks; he dined on raw squirrels and any cats he could catch, that's why his hands were bloodstained—if you ate an animal raw, you could never wash the blood off. There was a long jagged scar that ran across his face; what teeth he had were yellow and rotten; his eyes popped, and he drooled most of the time" (17).

Maycomb's gossip thus demonizes Boo in his absence as savagely as homophobic discourse can.

Jem's description of the imagined Boo also reveals Lee's understanding that popular imagination has a pronounced need to script a transgressive individual as knowable through his or her very body. As a result, Jem conspicuously includes Boo's bloodstained hands as indelible markers of his lack of civility and other deviant behavior. Such presumptions about a transgressive body have also long existed in popular imaginings of homosexuals. The most recurring presumption, of course, is of gender transitivity, but others involve the ostensible effects of same-sex acts on the gay or lesbian body. During World War II, for instance, military physicians reasoned for the detection of gay men during clinical examinations, since sexual activity would have invariably and permanently distended their rectums and made their throats capable of accepting tongue depressors without display of gag reflexes.[17]

These popular images of Boo further parallel homophobic understandings of gays and lesbians in that both script transgressive individuals as disrupting familial unity and ensuring parental fear, anxiety, and embarrassment. Jem, Scout, and Dill revise their "melancholy little drama" of the Radleys' lives to include precisely this. Scout recalls Mrs. Radley's characterization in particular: "Mrs. Radley had been beautiful until she married Mr. Radley and lost all her money. She also lost most of her teeth, her hair, and her right forefinger (Dill's contribution. Boo bit it off one night when he couldn't find any cats and squirrels to eat.); she sat in the living room and cried most of the time, while Boo slowly whittled away all the furniture" (44). In the children's imaginations, Boo's deviancy is so devastating to his family that its members become unfit to function within greater society. Boo's mother can only mourn that which she had lost in her son, even as he continues to destroy the actual house.

Such sentiments parallel those sometimes shown by parents when they learn of their children's gayness. Sedgwick reflects on precisely this when she writes, "I've heard of many people who claim they'd as soon their children were dead as gay. What it took me a long time to believe is that these people are saying no more than the truth."[18] These feelings have historically arisen in no small part because the prevailing and often overlapping ideologies of most twentieth-century social institutions—military, legal, religious, and medical—have labeled homosexuality deviant. A gay or lesbian person was—and sometimes still is—thus often simultaneously treasonous, criminal, sinful, and psychologically disturbed, left without legitimate space in any of these institutions. Not insignificantly, these simultaneous stigmatizations are precisely what Lee rehearses in the communal gossip of Boo. At various moments, he emerges within these narratives as criminal, sinful, mentally ill, or all three. If neighborhood legend is to be believed, Boo's first transgressions are indeed vaguely criminal. As a teenager, he becomes involved with "the wrong crowd," "the nearest thing to a gang ever seen in Maycomb" (14). Mr. Radley's response to his son's transgressions is swift and exacting, and, even if the specifics remain unknown, there is the suggestion that Mr. Radley's punishments are so extreme that Boo is permanently traumatized. After these events, "[t]he doors of the Radley house were closed on weekdays as well as Sundays, and Mr. Radley's boy was not seen again for fifteen years" (15). Despite there being no proof of further illegal behavior, Boo nevertheless becomes within popular imagination "a malevolent phantom" responsible for a range of criminal activities. "Any stealthy small crimes committed in Maycomb were his work," Scout recalls. "Once the town was terrorized by a series of morbid nocturnal events: people's chickens and household pets were found mutilated; although the culprit was Crazy Addie, who eventually drowned himself in Barker's Eddy, people still looked at the Radley Place, unwilling to discard their initial suspicions" (13).

Just as Boo breaks the law but neither to the extent nor with the malevolence that his community wishes, so too does he presumably sin, if only according to the strictures of his father's conservative religion. Miss Maudie explains to Scout that Mr. Radley's religious preferences are not those of Maycomb's stolid Baptists and Methodists but rather the biblical fundamentalism of "a foot-washing Baptist" who believes "anything that's pleasure is a sin" and "take[s] the Bible literally" (49). Indeed, because of these sectarian differences, the Radleys hardly deign to interact with their fellow townspeople. "They did not go to church, Maycomb's principal recreation, but worshiped at home," Scout offers. "Mrs. Radley seldom if ever crossed the street for a mid-morning coffee break with her neighbors, and certainly never joined a missionary circle" (13). Nevertheless, no one presumes the family—and Mr. Radley in particular—to lack either religious conviction or devotion: "Miss Stephanie Crawford said he was so upright he took the word of God as his only law, and we believed her, because Mr. Radley's posture was ramrod straight" (16).

Lee leaves little doubt, however, as to how readers are to accept this figure. Scout's memories reveal that Lee's biblical patriarch displays all the warmth and friendliness of Faulkner's Simon McEachern: "He was a thin leathery man with colorless eyes, so colorless they did not reflect light. His cheekbones were sharp and his mouth was wide, with a thin upper lip and a full lower lip.... He never spoke to us. When he passed we would look at the ground and say, 'Good morning, sir,' and he would cough in reply" (16). Moreover, Lee has characters that readers presume to be trustworthy damn Mr. Radley and, by extension, his coercive fundamentalist Christianity. Calpurnia, for example, offers one of her rare comments on "the ways of white people" to curse Mr. Radley's corpse as "the meanest men ever God blew breath into" (16–17). Miss Maudie is somewhat more temperate in her explanations of the Radleys, but she too implicitly critiques the effects of Mr. Radley's religious fanaticism: "'You are too young to understand it,' she said, 'but sometimes the Bible in the hand of one man is worse than a whiskey bottle in the hand of—oh, of your father.'" "There are just some kind of men who—who're so busy worrying about the next world they've never learned to live in this one," Miss Maudie concludes, "and you can look down the street and see the results" (49–50).

As with so much of Boo's story, Miss Maudie leaves unsaid the specifics of these results; however, Miss Stephanie Crawford elaborates on the facts of Boo's narrative to suggest a logical series of causes and effects. Angered by his son's minor infractions of the law, Mr. Radley ensures "that Arthur gave no further trouble" (15), and Boo disappears. The community hypothesizes that Mr. Radley exerts the patriarchal authority invested in him by Scripture to discipline Boo's rebelliousness so excessively that Jem, amplifying communal gossip, judges "that Mr. Radley kept him chained to the bed most of the time" (16). Even Miss Maudie mournfully replies to Scout's inquiry if Boo is crazy, "If he's not he should be by now. The things that happen to people we never really know. What happens in houses behind closed doors, what secrets—" (50). Given the effectiveness and perhaps even excessiveness of this unspecified discipline suggested by Boo's physical absence, a rebellion against this patriarchal authority seems not only understandable but also expected.

Yet, within both familial and communal responses, Boo's reaction to his father's oppression is figured as proof of mental instability. The very placidity and methodicalness with which Boo supposedly interrupts work on his scrapbook to stab his father in the leg with a pair of scissors bespeak his insanity as well as hint at Lee's appropriation of an unresolved Freudian Oedipal conflict. According to Miss Stephanie's polished version of the tale, "As Mr. Radley passed by, Boo drove the scissors into his parent's leg, pulled them out, wiped them on his pants, and resumed his activities" (15). His mother immediately presumes utter insanity in her son and runs "screaming into the street that Arthur was killing them all," and Maycomb as a whole "suggested that a season in Tuscaloosa might be helpful to Boo." Even Mr.

Radley concedes that, although "Boo wasn't crazy, he was high-strung at times" (15). If Lee suggests with this identity, triply damned by crime, sin, and insanity, that Boo's family and community play a significant role in the imposition and, after Mr. Radley's death, self-imposition of the closet, she also depicts the community as equally, if perhaps somewhat paradoxically, preoccupied with making Boo come out of that space. Even as Jem, Scout, and Dill participate in the elaborations on the closet-bolstering rumors, the children are also fascinated with Boo and plot scheme after scheme to lure him into communal interactions and thus supposedly to learn his true identity. "Wonder what he does in there," Dill murmurs before suggesting, "Let's try to make him come out ... I'd like to see what he looks like" (17). Such a paradoxical response to deviant identity was and, according to Sedgwick, continues to be a staple reaction to homosexuality: "'To the fine antennae of public attention the freshness of every drama of (especially involuntary) gay uncovering seems in anything heightened in surprise and delectability, rather than staled, by the increasingly intense atmosphere of public articulations of and about the love that is famous for daring not speak its name.'"[19] That is, as discourses proliferate around homosexuality, whether homophobic or homophilic, there persists and even increases a fascination with deviant sexuality being made knowable in public arenas.

To Kill a Mockingbird culminates with this knowability of the deviant when Boo literally comes out to rescue Scout and Jem from Bob Ewell, and the final chapters of the novel explore personal and anticipated communal responses to this knowability. Lee's narrative dictates these responses, however, by less than subtly establishing Boo as thoroughly sympathetic despite his cultural otherness. Just as she scripts Tom Robinson as quiet and respectable, she creates in Boo a figure epitomizing self-sacrifice and heroism. Each of his previous interactions with the children has been a gesture of friendliness and consideration: leaving intriguing trinkets in an oak tree as tokens of affection, providing a quilt for the shivering Scout as she watches Miss Maudie's house burn, and mending Jem's ripped pants. Boo's ultimate gifts, however, are Scout and Jem's very lives, as Atticus recognizes. Thus, whereas Tom eventually proves as innocent as Harriet Beecher Stowe's martyr with the same name, Boo, a protector of children as innocent as Little Eva, proves as heroic as the Christian knight to whom his name Arthur alludes.

If Boo's actions are thus antithetical to those attributed to him by gossip, so too is his body at variance with images circulating in popular imagination. Instead of a drooling, bloodstained oaf, Scout encounters a man easily mistakable for an unknown ordinary townsperson. As she surveys Jem's bedroom in the aftermath of the encounter with Bob Ewell, but before she knows Boo's identity, Scout notes the presence of the children's rescuer and finds him immediately readable as benign: "The man who brought Jem in was standing in a corner, learning against the wall. He was some countryman I did not know. He had probably been at the pageant, and was in the vicinity when it happened. He must have heard our screams and come running" (268). He wears the most ordinary of clothes for Maycomb—khaki pants and a denim shirt—and, despite a paleness unsettling in a community of sunburned farmers, verges on being thoroughly generic in Scout's initial notice of him.

Even after Scout learns who this figure is, however, she finds Boo to be anything but the monster of communal gossip. She no longer fears his house and even pauses to savor the view from its porch when she escorts him home. The walk comes close to fulfilling the visions made possible by the maturity she gains during the summer of Tom's trial: "I imagined how it would be: when it happened, he'd just be sitting in the swing when I came along. 'Hidy do, Mr. Arthur,' I would say, as if I had said it every afternoon of my life. 'Evening, Jean Louise,' he would say, as if he had said it every afternoon of my life, 'right pretty spell we're having, isn't it?' 'Yes, sir, right pretty,' I would say, and go on" (245). The novel's final didactic lines underscore this sympathetic character even further. Although Scout drowsily refers to the events of *The Gray Ghost* as Atticus puts her to bed, she might as well be discussing Boo:

> He guided me to the bed and sat me down. He lifted my legs and put me under the cover.
>
> An' they chased him 'n' never could catch him 'cause they didn't know what he looked like, an' Atticus, when they finally saw him, why he hadn't done any of those things ... Atticus, he was real nice...."
>
> His hands were under my chin, pulling up the cover, tucking it around me. "Most people are, Scout, when you finally see them." (283–84)

Like the wronged Stoner's Boy whom Scout recalls in *The Gray Ghost*, Boo is an innocent victim of social accusations. When Scout finally meets him and can judge his identity for herself rather than rely on malicious rumors, he strikes her not as a freakish demon but instead as simply "real nice."

In its generic form, this narrative is one often championed as the ideal for the advancement of social tolerance. The cultural outsider is known only in the abstract and accordingly demonized for his or her rumored differences until prolonged or heroic interactions establish reassuring commonalties for the cultural insider and ultimately ensure acceptance. Within gay communities this narrative is particularly familiar, since one of the most consistently promoted courses of action is coming out. Gay persons, the valorized narrative goes, must confront society to demythify homosexuality and thus allow others to understand same-sex desire more accurately, with the ultimate goal being acceptance or at least tolerance of homosexuals. In fact, the narrative usually figures the closet as a site of fear, cowardice, and self-loathing, and persons who remain within this space often stand accused of retarding and even jeopardizing the tolerance fostered by persons who have already come out.

The terms of this acceptance and/or tolerance, however, mark one of the most divisive splits within these communities. At one end of the conventional spectrum are those persons who hold gayness to be radically different from a usually—and inaccurately—homogenized straightness and urge acceptance of this alterity. At the other end of this spectrum are those who emphasize perceived commonalties between heterosexual and homosexual persons, downplaying differences between the two and within each to stress gays and lesbians' "normalcy" when compared to, again, homogenized straight persons. Despite minor differences, this rhetoric implies all persons are first and foremost human and deserve to be treated as such.

Like most persons with culturally minoritized identities, gays and lesbians struggle with these negotiations of difference and sameness, debating the personal and political efficacy of not only these extremes but also the more complex and more common intervening stances. But, as historian John D'Emilio has suggested, such debates did not emerge only when the Stonewall riots electrified gay and lesbian communities in 1969. At precisely the moment when Lee was completing *To Kill a Mockingbird*, a crucial handful of American homosexuals were engaged in one of the most significant rounds of these debates. Nascent homosexual communities such as those considered in George Chauncey's work experienced tremendous growth that frequently solidified a group identity during and immediately after World War II. With this emergent identity, D'Emilio argues, came the struggle for its public acknowledgment. Early advocates for this recognition, such as those persons organizing the Mattachine Society in 1951, tended toward political radicalness, often bringing with them Communist affiliations and usually characterizing their efforts as working toward militant "homosexual emancipation." It is perhaps not surprising, however, that in this era of Joseph McCarthy's Communist paranoia, the probings of the House's Un-American Activities Committee, Dwight Eisenhower's seemingly benign presidency, and the return to prewar cultural and familial normalcy with a vengeance, comparable conservatism also crucially affected emerging gay activism. Indeed, by the mid-1950s the leadership of these organizations dramatically shifted from its radical instigators, such as Harry Hay and Charles Rowland, to persons such as Marilyn Rieger and Kenneth Burns and constituted what D'Emilio terms a retreat into respectability.

The political strategy advocated by Rieger, Burns, and others like them, that which eventually came to characterize much of gay activism until Stonewall, directly countered the strategy of the Mattachine's original and early organizers. Whereas Hay and Rowland considered gays and lesbians a minority with its own unique culture, Rieger and Burns denied such a status. "We know we are the same," Rieger argued at the 1953 Mattachine convention, "no different from anyone else. Our only difference is an unimportant one to the heterosexual society, *unless we make it important.*" According to this logic, homosexuals should therefore come out and prove their utter normalcy to gain equality. "[B]y declaring ourselves, by integrating," Rieger continued, "not as homosexuals, but as people, as men and women whose homosexuality is irrelevant to our ideals, our principles, our hopes and aspirations," would activists "rid the world of its misconceptions of homosexuality and homosexuals." By mid-century, Rowland and Hay had been forced to cede their positions of leadership, and Rieger's rhetoric was the standard. The *Mattachine Review* and the *Ladder*, respective mouthpieces for the Mattachine Society and the exclusively female but comparably conservative Daughters of Bilitis, urged readers to prove through their dress and activity that they were "average people in all other respects outside of our private sexual inclinations." The Daughters of Bilitis in particular cautioned lesbians against wearing pants, keeping their hair short, and frequenting bars, plaintively suggesting that they do "a little 'policing' on their own."[20]

Although this strategy faced significant challenges before Stonewall, especially in the 1960s, presented through contrasting models for political action offered by the civil rights movement,[21] this conservatism nevertheless remained pervasive in gay communities and their activism throughout the 1950s, when Lee was writing *To Kill a Mockingbird*. Indeed, she ultimately resolves the novel's negotiations of closetedness in a manner comparable to this political strategy. Like gay activists of the day, Lee condemns the closet as a site of darkness, death, and decay. "The house was low," Scout recalls of the Radleys' home, and "was once white with a deep front porch and green shutters, but had long ago darkened to the color of the slate-gray yard around it. Rain-rotted shingles drooped over the eaves of the veranda; oak trees kept the sun away. The remains of a picket drunkenly guarded the front yard—a 'swept' yard that was never swept—where johnson grass and rabbit-tobacco grew in abundance" (13). Yet, when the cultural outsider who has been forced into this space decides to come out, he reveals himself to be no flamboyant Randolph or Folner but instead precisely what Marilyn Rieger expected of gays and lesbians: practically "no different from anyone else" and warmly embraced by an accepting community.

Like Rieger, however, Lee does not completely eradicate all differences in Boo. Although Scout may at first take his body to be that of an ordinary farmer, it nevertheless reveals subtle differences, most noticeably in its pale-ness. "His face was as white as his hands, but for a shadow on his jutting chin," Scout recalls from her one interaction with Boo. "His cheeks were thin to hollowness; his mouth was wide; there were shallow, almost delicate indentations at his temples, and his gray eyes were so colorless I thought he was blind. His hair was dead and thin, almost feathery on top of his head" (273). Moreover, Boo is painfully inept in navigating unfamiliar spaces. "Every move he made was uncertain, as if he were not sure his hands and feet could make proper contact with the things he touched" (279–80), Scout remembers.

As Lee figures these differences, though, they do not alienate Boo from others but rather endear him to them. Upon seeing Boo's understandable dif-ficulties in negotiating crowds and strange environs, Scout derives satisfac-tion in both helping Boo and living out her imagination interactions: "'Won't you have a seat, Mr. Arthur? This rocking-chair's nice and comfort-able.' My small fantasy about him was alive again: he would be sitting on the porch ... right pretty spell we're having, isn't it, Mr. Arthur? Yes, a right pret-ty spell. Feeling slightly unreal, I led him to the chair farthest from Atticus and Mr. Tate. It was in deep shadow. Boo would feel more comfortable in the dark" (274–75). As in the imaginations of Rieger and other conservative gay activists of the 1950s, where mainstream culture would willingly help gays and lesbians function in society once they proved their normalcy was not for-feited by differing sexual desires, when Scout can ascribe to Boo a sympathet-ic identity, she is more than generous in assisting him during his foray into public space.

Heart-tugging though Lee's final pages may be, they nevertheless pres-ent potentially disturbing images when Scout offers this assistance to Boo. He is cast almost as helpless, unable to negotiate even the simplest of actions, such as stroking Jem's hair or climbing steps. When one reads this help potentially to symbolize heterosexual society's response to uncloseted gays and lesbians, it suggests a disconcerting balance of power. Just as Boo is wholly reliant on Scout, in this reading, homosexuals are exclusively dependent on heterosexuals' acceptance to function outside the closet. Lee's plot even imagines this acceptance as so overwhelming that the closet may have to be reinstated as a haven from heterosexuals' attention. Heck Tate is adamant that Bob Ewell dies by accidentally falling on his knife so that Boo Radley can escape not so much being brought to trial but the communal adoration of him as a hero. Attuned to the fickleness of popular response, Tate realizes that the very people who have disseminated the rumors about Boo will, upon hearing of his exploits, disregard his heretofore emphasized differences and virtually smother him with acceptance. As a result, Tate thus effectively erases all traces of Boo's coming out, leaving them to exist only in Scout's memories.

With these final images Lee once again reveals how radically her novel differs from those of Capote and Smith if one entertains this specific reading of Boo's closetedness. Unlike *Other Voices, Other Rooms* and *Strange Fruit*, in which homosexuality is markedly at variance with cultural norms and gay or lesbian individuals face overwhelming forces of homophobia, *To Kill a Mockingbird* ultimately imagines southern community to be already queer and permeated with transgressions of gender and sexuality. The implications are that, within this community, so long as a transgressive person is not too excessively or multiply different from those around him or her, and thus in harmony with the general cultural queerness, an acknowledgment of sexual otherness brings exaggerated acceptance rather than communal disfavor. This acceptance is so pervasive that it threatens to eradicate the very elements of identity necessitating the closet in the first place and therefore indirectly bolsters this space as a site of refuge. Thus, like the gay activists organizing across the United States at precisely the moment that Lee was composing her novel, she presents a community in which, once difference has been dismissed as minor and similarity acknowledged as already existing, no more innocent mockingbirds need ever be killed, no more African Americans need ever face racism, and, if only figuratively, no more gays and lesbians need ever face homophobia.

NOTES

1. Review of *To Kill a Mockingbird*, by Harper Lee, *Commonweal* 9 (December 1960): 289; Robert W. Henderson, review of *To Kill a Mockingbird*, by Harper Lee, *Library Journal* (15 May 1960): 1937; Granville Hicks, "Three at the Outset," review of *To Kill a Mockingbird*, by Harper Lee, *Saturday Review* 23 (July 1960): 15; Keith Waterhouse, review of *To Kill a Mockingbird*, by Harper Lee, *New Statesman* (15 October 1960): 580; Frank H.

Lyell, "One-Taxi Town," review of *To Kill a Mockingbird*, by Harper Lee, *New York Times Book Review* (10 July 1960): 5; and About Life and Little Girls," review of *To Kill a Mockingbird*, by Harper Lee, *Time* (1 August 1960): 70–71.

2. Hicks, "Three at the Outset," 15; "Summer Reading," review of *To Kill a Mockingbird*, by Harper Lee, *Atlantic Monthly* 206 (August 1960): 98; review of *To Kill a Mockingbird*, by Harper Lee, *Booklist* 57 (1 September 1960): 23; and "About Life and Little Girls," 70; review of *To Kill a Mockingbird*, *Commonweal*, 289.

3. Eric J. Sundquist, "Blues for Atticus Finch: Scottsboro, *Brown*, and Harper Lee," in *The South as an American Problem*, 182, 183, 186, 187.

4. Cook, "Old Ways," 529. See Sundquist, "Blues for Atticus Finch," 181–209; Claudia Durst Johnson, "The Secret Courts of Men's Hearts: Code and Law in Harper Lee's *To Kill a Mockingbird*," *Studies in American Fiction* 19 (Autumn 1991): 129–39; and Claudia Durst Johnson, *To Kill a Mockingbird: Threatening Boundaries* (New York: Twayne, 1994)

5. Harper Lee, *To Kill a Mockingbird* (1960; reprint, New York: Fawcett, 1962), 11, hereafter cited in the text by page number.

6. Grobel, *Conversations with Capote*, 53; and Clarke, *Capote: A Biography*, 42.

7. Clarke, *Capote: A Biography*, 389. See also Amy Fine Collins, "A Night to Remember," *Vanity Fair* 431 (July 1996): 120–39.

8. Kenneth T. Reed, *Truman Capote* (Boston: Twayne, 1981), 15–16. See also Clarke, *Capote: A Biography*, 410–15.

9. See Johnson, "The Secret Courts of Men's Hearts," 131, 134–38.

10. Ibid., 136.

11. Judith Butler, *Gender Trouble: Feminism and the Subversion of Identity* (New York: Routledge, 1990), 140–41.

12. Ibid., 137–38, 139, 141.

13. Ibid., 137.

14. For a discussion of Lee's conservative representations of racial equality, see Sundquist, "Blues for Atticus Finch," 181–209.

15. Sedgwick, *Epistemology of the Closet*, 33.

16. For a brief discussion of closetedness not specific to gayness, see Sedgwick, *Epistemology of the Closet*, 72.

17. See Allan Bérubé, *Coming Out under Fire: The History of Gay Men and Women in World War Two* (1990; reprint, New York: Penguin, 1991), 8–33, 149–74.

18. Eve Kosofsky Sedgwick, *Tendencies* (Durham, N.C.: Duke Univ. Press, 1993), 2.

19. Sedgwick, *Epistemology of the Closet*, 67.

20. John D'Emilio, *Sexual Politics, Sexual Communities: The Making of a Homosexual Minority in the United States, 1940–1970* (Chicago: Univ. of Chicago Press, 1983), 79, 113. See also Martin Duberman, *Stonewall* (New York: Plume, 1983), 174.

21. See D'Emilio, *Sexual Politics, Sexual Communities*, 129–149; and Duberman, *Stonewall*, 73–166.

Chronology

1926	Nell Harper Lee is born on April 28 in Monroeville, Alabama, the youngest of three daughters, to Amasa Coleman Lee and Frances Fincher Lee. Her father worked as a lawyer, was publisher of the *Monroe Journal*, and served as a state senator.
1931–42	Attends public schools in Monroeville. Truman Capote lives next door during the summer and the two remain friends until his death in 1984. The character of Dill in *To Kill A Mockingbird* is modeled after Capote.
1944–45	Attends Huntington College, Montgomery, Alabama.
1945–50	Studies law at the University of Alabama, as her father did, but does not complete degree.
1949–50	Studies for one year at Oxford University, then moves to New York City.
1951	Frances Fincher Lee, mother, dies.
1950s	Works as a reservation clerk with Eastern Air Lines and British Overseas Airways in New York.
1957	Approaches literary agent with two essays and three short stories, one of which will be expanded to become her only novel, *To Kill a Mockingbird*. Encouraged by Lippincott editor Tay Hohoff, Lee quits the airline business to devote her full time to writing.
1959	Accompanies Truman Capote to Holcomb, Kansas, to help research his book *In Cold Blood*.

1960	Eight years in preparation, *To Kill a Mockingbird* is published. The book will remain on the best-seller list for eighty weeks and will be translated into ten languages; becomes Literary Guild and Book-of-the-Month-Club selections, Reader's Digest Condensed Book; and is published in paperback by Popular Library.
1961	Lee is awarded the Pulitzer Prize for Fiction—the first woman to do so since 1942. Receives Alabama Library Association Award, and Brotherhood Award of National Conference of Christians and Jews. "Christmas Me" is published in the December issue of *McCalls*. "Love—In Other Words" is published in the April issue of *Vogue*. Father, Amasa, dies.
1962	Horton Foote writes the screenplay of *To Kill A Mockingbird*, which is produced as film by Universal Studios. Novel receives Best Sellers' Paperback of the Year Award.
1966–72	Becomes member of the National Council on the Arts.
1972	*To Kill A Mockingbird* is adapted in London as a stage play by Christopher Sergel.
1987–	Harper Lee lives in New York City, returning each winter to Monroeville, Alabama, to stay with her older sister, Alice Lee. She famously continues to live as a recluse, refusing all interviews and awards.
1995	Thirty-fifth anniversary edition of *To Kill a Mockingbird* is published.
1999	*To Kill a Mockingbird: The 40th Anniversary Edition of the Pulitzer Prize-Winning Novel* is published by HarperCollins.
2001	Is elected into the Alabama Academy of Honor. To celebrate Lee's induction, an essay contest on *To Kill a Mockingbird* is held. Lee attends the awards ceremony for the contest, which becomes an annual event.
2005	Lee makes a rare appearance at the invitation of Veronique Peck, widow of Gregory Peck, to be honored by the Los Angeles Public Library at a benefit dinner to raise funds for computers and literacy programs. The movie *Capote*, directed by Bennett Miller, opens to much success; Catherine Keener plays the role of Harper Lee.

Contributors

HAROLD BLOOM is Sterling Professor of the Humanities at Yale University. He is the author of 30 books, including *Shelley's Mythmaking* (1959), *The Visionary Company* (1961), *Blake's Apocalypse* (1963), *Yeats* (1970), *A Map of Misreading* (1975), *Kabbalah and Criticism* (1975), *Agon: Toward a Theory of Revisionism* (1982), *The American Religion* (1992), *The Western Canon* (1994), and *Omens of Millennium: The Gnosis of Angels, Dreams, and Resurrection* (1996). *The Anxiety of Influence* (1973) sets forth Professor Bloom's provocative theory of the literary relationships between the great writers and their predecessors. His most recent books include *Shakespeare: The Invention of the Human* (1998), a 1998 National Book Award finalist, *How to Read and Why* (2000), *Genius: A Mosaic of One Hundred Exemplary Creative Minds* (2002), *Hamlet: Poem Unlimited* (2003), *Where Shall Wisdom Be Found?* (2004), and *Jesus and Yahweh: The Names Divine* (2005). In 1999, Professor Bloom received the prestigious American Academy of Arts and Letters Gold Medal for Criticism. He has also received the International Prize of Catalonia, the Alfonso Reyes Prize of Mexico, and the Hans Christian Andersen Bicentennial Prize of Denmark.

CLAUDIA DURST JOHNSON is professor emerita of English, University of Alabama. Her many books include *To Kill a Mockingbird: Threatening Boundaries* and *Understanding To Kill a Mockingbird: A Student Casebook to Issues, Sources, and Historic Documents*.

FRED ERISMAN, the author of numerous scholarly articles, is Lorraine Sherley Emeritus Professor of Literature at Texas Christian University.

R. A. DAVE is professor of English and head of the department at Sardar Patel University.

WILLIAM T. GOING is emeritus professor of English at Southern Illinois University Edwardsville. He is the author of many scholarly articles and the book *Essays on Alabama Literature*.

COLIN NICHOLSON is senior lecturer in English literature at Edinburgh University. He has published widely on Scottish, American, Canadian, and English Writing.

ERIC J. SUNDQUIST, professor of English at UCLA, has written numerous books and articles on southern literature, including *Faulkner: The House Divided, To Wake the Nations: Race in American Literature, The Hammers of Creation: Folk Culture in Modern African-American Fiction*, and *Strangers in the Land: Blacks, Jews, Post-Holocaust America*.

DEAN SHACKELFORD, who died in September 2003, was an associate professor in the English Department at Southeast Missouri State University. He had also taught at the University of South Carolina and Benedict College in Columbia, and Concord College in Princeton, West Virginia. He published on Flannery O'Connor, Jean Toomer, William Faulkner, and Harper Lee, among others, in such journals as *Mississippi Quarterly, Southern Quarterly*, and *The Tennessee Williams Annual Review*.

PATRICK CHURA is assistant professor of English at the University of Akron. His book *Vital Contact: Downclassing Journeys in American Literature from Herman Melville to Richard Wright* was published by Routledge in 2005. He has published articles on Eugene O'Neill, Harper Lee, and Shakespeare.

CHRISTOPHER METRESS is associate professor of English at Samford University in Birmingham, Alabama. He has written numerous articles and reviews and is the editor of *The Lynching of Emmett Till: A Documentary Narrative* and *The Critical Response to Dashiell Hammett*.

GARY RICHARDS is an associate professor of English at the University of New Orleans and also teaches in the Africana studies and women's studies programs. He is the author of *Lovers and Beloveds: Sexual Otherness in Southern Fiction, 1936–1961*.

Bibliography

Adams, Phoebe. "Summer Reading." *Atlantic* (August 26 1960): 98–99.

Asimov, Michael. "When Lawyers Were Heroes." *University of San Francisco Law Review* 30 (1996 Summer):1131–1138.

Cauthen, Cramer R. and Donald G. Alpin. "The Gift Refused: The Southern Lawyer in *TKM, The Client* and *Cape Fear.*" *Studies in Popular Culture* 19, no. 2 (Oct. 1996): 257–275.

Childress, Mark. "Looking for Harper Lee." *Southern Living* 32, no. 5 (May 1997):148–150.

Chura, Patrick. "Prolepsis and Anachronism: Emmett Till and the Historicity of *To Kill a Mockingbird.*" *Southern Literary Journal* 32, no. 2 (Spring 2000): 1–26.

Dave, R. A. "*To Kill a Mockingbird*: Harper Lee's Tragic Vision." In *Indian Studies in American Fiction*, edited by M. K. Naik, S. K. Desai, S. Mokashi-Punekar, 311–324. Dharwar: Macmillan Co. of India, 1974.

Erisman, Fred. "The Romantic Regionalism of Harper Lee." *The Alabama Review* 26, no. 2 (April 1973): 122–136.

Freedman, Monroe H. "Atticus Finch, Esq., R.I.P." *Legal Times* (February 24 1992).

Griffin, Pauline "Her South is Authentic." *Southern Observer* (October 1960): 149.

Going, William T. "*Store* and *Mockingbird*: Two Pulitzer Novels about Alabama." In *Essays on Alabama Literature*, 9–31. Tuscaloosa: The University of Alabama Press, 1975.

————. "Truman Capote: Harper Lee's Fictional Portrait of the Artist as an Alabama Child." *Alabama Review* 42, no. 2 (1989): 136–149.

Hicks, Granville. "Three at the OutSet." *Saturday Review* (July 23 1960) XLIII (30): 15–16.

Johnson, Claudia Durst. *To Kill a Mockingbird: Threatening Boundaries.* New York: Twayne, 1994.

————. *Understanding To Kill a Mockingbird: A Student Casebook to Issues, Sources, and Historic Documents.* Westport, CT: Greenwood, 1994.

Jones, Carolyn. "Atticus Finch and the Mad Dog: Harper Lee's *To Kill a Mockingbird.*" *Southern Quarterly* 34, no. 4 (Summer 1996): 53–63.

Le May, Harding. "Children Play; Adults Betray." *NY Herald Tribune Book Review* (July 10 1960): 5.

Lyell, Frank H "One Taxi Town." *New York Times Book Review* (July 10 1960) 5, 18.

Metress, Christopher. "The Rise and Fall of Atticus Finch." *The Chattahoochee Review* 24, no. 1 (Fall 2003): 95–102.

Mitgang, Herbert "*To Kill a Mockingbird.*" *New York Times Book Review* (July 13 1960) 33.

Moates, Marianne M. *A Bridge of Childhood: Truman Capote's Southern Years.* New York: Holt, 1989.

Nicholson, Colin. "Hollywood and Race: *To Kill a Mockingbird.*" In *Cinema and Fiction: New Modes of Adapting,* edited by John Orr and Colin Nicholson, 151–159. Edinburgh: Edinburgh University Press, 1992.

Richards, Gary. "Harper Lee and the Destabilization of Heterosexuality." In *Lovers and Beloveds: Sexual Otherness in Southern Fiction, 1936-1961,* 117–157. Baton Rouge: Louisiana State University Press, 2005.

Shackelford, Dean. "The Female Voice in *To Kill a Mockingbird:* Narrative Strategies in Film and Novel." *Mississippi Quarterly* 50, no. 1 (Winter 1996-97): 101–113.

Shields, Charles J. *Mockingbird: A Portrait of Harper Lee.* New York: Holt, 2006.

Sullivan, Richard "Engrossing First Novel of Rare Excellence." *Chicago Tribune* (July 17 1960) 15.

Sundquist, Eric J. "Blues for Atticus Finch: Scottsboro, *Brown,* and Harper Lee." In *The South as an American Problem,* edited by Larry J. Griffin and Don H. Doyle, 181–209. Athens, GA: The University of Georgia Press, 1995.

Acknowledgments

"The Issue of Censorship" by Claudia Durst Johnson. From *Understanding To Kill a Mockingbird: A Student Casebook to Issues, Sources, and Historic Documents*, pp. 197–216. © 1994 by Claudia Durst Johnson. Reproduced with permission of Greenwood Publishing Group, Inc., Westport, CT.

"The Romantic Regionalism of Harper Lee" by Fred Erisman. From *The Alabama Review* 26, no. 2., pp. 122–136. © 1973 by The University of Alabama Press. Reprinted by permission.

"*To Kill a Mockingbird*: Harper Lee's Tragic Vision" by R. A. Dave. From *Indian Studies in American Fiction*, pp. 311–323. © 1974 by Karnatak University, Dharwar and the Macmillan Company of India. Reprinted by permission.

"Store and Mockingbird: Two Pulitzer Novels about Alabama" by William T. Going. From *Essays on Alabama Literature*, pp. 9–31. © 1975 by William T. Going. Reprinted by permission.

"Hollywood and Race: *To Kill a Mockingbird*" by Colin Nicholson. From *Cinema and Fiction: New Modes of Adapting 1950–1990*, pp. 151–159 © 1992 by Edinburgh University Press. Reprinted by permission.

"Blues for Atticus Finch: Scottsboro, *Brown*, and Harper Lee" by Eric J. Sundquist. From *The South as an American Problem*, pp. 181–209. © 1995 by the University of Georgia Press. Reprinted by permission.

"The Female Voice in *To Kill a Mockingbird:* Narrative Strategies in Film and Novel" by Dean Shackelford. From *Mississippi Quarterly* 50, no. 1, pp. 101–113. ©1996 by Mississippi State University. Reprinted by permission.

"Prolepsis and Anachronism: Emmett Till and the Historicity of *To Kill a Mockingbird*" by Patrick Chura. From *Southern Literary Journal* 32, no. 2 (Spring 2000), pp. 1–26. © 2000 by the Department of English at the University of North Carolina at Chapel Hill. Used by permission of the Univeristy of North Carolina Press.

"The Rise and Fall of Atticus Finch" by Christopher Metress. From *The Chattahoochee Review* 24, no. 1 (Fall 2003), pp. 95–102. © 2003 by Georgia Perimeter College. Reprinted by permission.

Reprinted by permission of the Louisiana State University Press from *Lovers and Beloveds: Sexual Otherness in Southern Fiction, 1936–1961* by Gary Richards. Copyright © 2005 by Louisiana State University Press.

Every effort has been made to contact the owners of copyrighted material and secure copyright permission. Articles appearing in this volume generally appear much as they did in their original publication with few or no editorial changes. Those interested in locating the original source will find bibliographic information in the bibliography and acknowledgments sections of this volume.

Index

To Kill a Mockingbird abbreviated as *TKAM*. Characters in literary works are indexed by first name (if any), followed by the name of the work in parentheses.

197